Secret-Judaism and the Spanish

Also by Michael Alpert

EL EJÉRCITO REPUBLICO EN LA GUERRA CIVIL (1936–1939)

LA GUERRA CIVIL EN EL MAR

A NEW INTERNATIONAL HISTORY OF THE SPANISH CIVIL WAR

LAS REFORMAS MILITARES DE AZAÑA (1931–1933)

TWO SPANISH PICARESQUE NOVELS

Secret-Judaism and the Spanish Inquisition

Michael Alpert
Emeritus Professor of Modern and Contemporary History of Spain
University of Westminster
London

Five Leaves Publications
www.fiveleaves.co.uk

Secret Judaism and
the Spanish Inquisition
by Michael Alpert

Published in 2008 by Five Leaves Publications,
PO Box 8786, Nottingham NG1 9AW
info@fiveleaves.co.uk
www.fiveleaves.co.uk

An earlier edition of *Secret Judaism and the Spanish Inquisition*
was published in hardback by Palgrave in 2001
under the title *Crypto-Judaism and the Spanish Inquisition*

ISBN 978 1 905512 29 4

Five Leaves acknowledges financial support
from Arts Council England

Five Leaves is a member of Inpress Books
(www.inpressbooks.co.uk),
representing independent publishers

Typesetting and design by Four Sheets Design and Print
Printed in Great Britain

Contents

List of Illustrations

List of Abbreviations

ADC   Archivo Diocesano de Cuenca
AHN, Inq.   Archivo Histórico Nacional (Madrid), Inquisition Section
L., C.   Legajo, Carpeta (Box, File)

1 Map of Spain and Portugal (Inquisition Courts are underlined)

Introduction

It was early 1722. In the draughty hall of the Court of the Spanish Inquisition in Toledo, high on the central plateau of New Castile, a trial for a crime against the Catholic Faith – committing acts of Judaizing – was reaching its end. The accused was a 27-year-old unmarried woman, Isabel de Paz, who lived with her parents in the town of Almagro, a few miles to the south of Toledo. The charge, now proven by Isabel's confession, was read to her in the medieval language of the Inquisition court, which, like the court's procedure, had been unchanged since its establishment in 1478:

> a native and inhabitant of the town of Almagro, aged twenty-seven years, unmarried and here present. Whereas the said Prosecutor through the accusation that he presents to this Court, has listed her offences, namely that, given that the said Isabel de Paz is a baptized and confirmed Christian, enjoying the privileges and prerogatives of that state, yet, unappreciative of such great benefit, she has abandoned the fear of Our Lord, the salvation of her soul, and, despising the justice of this holy Court, has gone back to the old and superseded Law of Moses, performing its rites and ceremonies, believing that she can be saved in that Law, committing the crimes of an Infidel, Heretic and Apostate from our Holy religion, creator and concealer of heresy, an obstinate, perjured and insufficient confessant, of all of which I accuse her in general, and in particular of the following.[1]

The Prosecutor went on to read, following the closely regulated procedure of canon law, the testimonies given against Isabel de Paz. The witnesses were always anonymous – 'a certain person whose name has been given' in 'a town which is named' – though Isabel could hardly have failed to realize that 'the very close older relative of the accused' was her father, who had confessed to the inquisitors the Judaizing practices of his family.

According to the inquisitors' charges, Isabel had, among other offences, fasted (that was, as will be seen, the way in which the Spanish Judaizers kept the Jewish holy days), 'in observance of the said Law of Moses'. She had obeyed, as best she could, the dietary laws of the Old Testament, eating no fish unless they had scales and fins, and no pork. She had refrained from carrying out her usual domestic duties on the holy days and on Saturday, the Jewish Sabbath. She had done this, declaimed the Prosecutor, 'in hatred of this our Catholic religion and true Apostolic Faith'.

At the beginning of her trial, Isabel had denied everything and insisted that she was a devout and sincere Christian. Only after many months spent in the loneliness of her cell, and after hearing the prosecutor read out testimony after testimony – which she knew must have come from other prisoners accused of the same Judaizing offences and who were forced by fear, despair or torture to reveal every detail of their religious lives, implicating their friends and closest relatives – did Isabel, on the advice of the lawyer appointed by the Inquisition court to defend her, request to make a complete confession of her sin.

Isabel had not merely *Judaized* – that is, taught by her parents, practised what she knew and could of the Judaism of her ancestors, baptised Catholics since 1497 at the latest. She had also perjured herself before the Inquisition by concealing her sin and that of her family and acquaintances. Even when she had confessed, there was an aggravating factor: she was *diminuto impenitente*, that is she had kept things back, and so the prosecutor demanded the heaviest sentence. This was not only the confiscation of all Isabel's property, her appearance at the terrifying public *auto de fe* where she would stand clad in the penitent's yellow robe, the sanbenito, hear her 'crimes' read out, and make a solemn abjuration of her sins, but also the end to her life on this earth, for the prosecutor wanted her to be 'relaxed to civil justice and the secular arm to be punished as an example to others'.

In their decision, the court of inquisitors stated that they wished to act 'with justice and mercy', and sentenced Isabel to the more usual punishments. At an *auto de fe*, an 'act of faith' or public ceremony – though by the eighteenth century it was usually held inside a church – Isabel would appear dressed in the sanbenito, on which was painted a St Andrew's Cross with two crosspieces. She would wear a paper mitre on her head and would clasp a large candle of yellow wax between her hands. She would hear her sentence and be reconciled with the Church at an impressive and awe-inspiring ceremony. Compared with other victims, her punishment was not too severe. She would be imprisoned in the Inquisition's penitential prison – the *cárcel de la penitencia* – for a year, though this was an open prison very different from the secret cells in which she had been held during her trial. She would have to wear the sanbenito over her clothes, so that everybody would know her crime as she begged in the streets of Toledo, given that all her property was forfeit. She would have to hear Mass and sermons, visit holy shrines and be catechized by experienced men, while all the time her religious conduct would be under close scrutiny. After her year's imprisonment, Isabel, as a convicted though penitent heretic, would be forbidden to wear gold, silver, pearls, silk or any fine cloth, but at least she would be able to escape from the public shame she had suffered in Toledo, because for six further years she would be exiled from that city, from Almagro, where she had lived with her parents, and from the capital of Spain, Madrid. Furthermore, in order that she should not escape and go and Judaize abroad, she was forbidden to approach within twenty leagues of the coast or the frontiers of Spain.

On 15 March 1722, together with thirty one other convicted Judaizers, Isabel appeared at the *auto de fe* in the church of St Peter the Martyr at Toledo. The first ten names on the list had already died, through age, shock of imprisonment or disease. Effigies of them were taken to the stake and burnt. The remains of those that had died long enough before for their bodies to have decomposed had been dug up; their bones were carried in procession by convicted common criminals, and consigned to the flames. Number eleven on the list, the aged María de Ribera, was tied to the stake and her shrivelled body burnt. Sebastian Antonio de Paz, Isabel's father, who ran the government's tobacco monopoly in Almagro, was sentenced to life imprisonment and, the following day, mounted on an ass like a common criminal, was drawn around the city and received two hundred lashes from the public executioner. This sentence was also imposed on Ana María, his wife. Isabel was treated somewhat less harshly, perhaps because the inquisitors thought she was under her parents' thumb or because she had at last confessed voluntarily. Most of the other victims – all known as 'penitents' because the impenitent were burned at the stake – received harsh sentences of life imprisonment, while many were also flogged. All as a matter of course lost their property, which in any case had been sequestered on their arrests and auctioned to pay for their upkeep.[2]

After the long day in the church came the moment of solemn abjuration. As the daylight faded or perhaps in the ghostly light of candles, Isabel had to repeat the following legal formula:

> I, Isabel de Paz, born and resident at Almagro, present here today before Your Lordships as Apostolic Inquisitors against heretical depravity and apostasy in this city and judicial district of Toledo, by apostolic and ordinary authority, standing before this Cross and the Holy Sacraments, abjure, detest and reject all kinds of heresy and apostasy which stand against the Holy Catholic Faith and the Apostolic Law of Jesus Christ, our Redeemer ... especially that of which I am accused and into which I as an evil person have fallen and have confessed ... and I swear and promise to keep and guard for ever that Holy Faith which Holy Mother Church holds, guards and teaches ... humbly and patiently to receive any penances which have been or may be imposed on me ... and I desire and consent and it pleases me that if at any time (may God forbid it) I should go or act against what I have said or any part of it, that I should be considered and treated as relapsed and impenitent ... and I should submit myself to correction and severity ... so that all appropriate penalties and punishments be carried out on my person ...

Isabel, daughter of a middle-class businessman in a small town, uttered her abjuration in the presence of a grandee of Spain, the Duke of Medina Sidonia, for whom attending penitents at an *auto de fe* was an act of great religious merit. One may assume that Isabel was convinced that she had been wrong to practise Judaism. She must have felt great relief as she listened to the solemn pronouncement of absolution that reconciled her to the Church. Her parents were not to go to the stake. Her incommunicado imprisonment was over; she was not to suffer the disgrace and pain of public exposure and flogging.

Three days later, on 18 March 1722, her abjuration was reread to her, and she was enjoined to say nothing to anybody about her imprisonment or interrogation, under pain of excommunication. The Inquisition ruled through absolute secrecy.

Isabel de Paz's file includes a report dated one year after the *auto de fe*, in which two priests praised her Catholic conduct. She had complied with all the requirements demanded and was now living an exemplary life. One may fairly assume that she was released.

Isabel de Paz was one of the at least 1400 Judaizers – apart from the fornicators, bigamists and others who came under the jurisdiction of the Holy Office, as the Inquisition was also known, – who were victims of the Spanish Inquisition during the first fifty years of the eighteenth century. The formulaic language of the Inquisition court of Toledo reveals little of what she had done to be accused of heresy. What sort of Judaism she had practised, why she did so and where she had learnt it can be discovered only by close reading of the trial evidence. While some people in Spain thought that the tendency to Judaize was inherent, biologically taken in with one's mother's milk – a view which would be called racist today – for the Inquisition Judaizing was a religious crime like others, though more serious. What mattered most was that heretics should confess fully and implicate their accomplices so that they also might be persuaded to confess and save their souls. One who made a voluntary confession received the lightest of penances, while those who concealed details and refused to admit what the Inquisition knew for certain they had done – the *negativos* – might even be abandoned by the Church, released to the secular arm and burnt to death, though always with the possibility of a repentance at the last moment, which would demonstrate the absolute power of faith. Only if the accused died unrepentant could the whole procedure of the Inquisition and the *auto de fe* be considered to have failed, but even then the smoking pile of ashes, the stink of burnt flesh and the half-consumed corpse would serve to demonstrate the horrible fate of an obstinate heretic.

The origin of the phenomenon of Spanish crypto-Judaism – the secret practice of Judaism by people who were, as their ancestors before them, baptised Catholics – is the purpose of the early part of this book. What did crypto-Jews mean for the Spanish Church and the Spaniard in the street, and what did they mean for Jews who lived full Jewish lives in other countries? Others have studied secret Judaism in the early years of the Inquisition in the late fifteenth and early sixteenth centuries. This book examines, through individual case-histories of the seventeenth and eighteenth centuries, the vicissitudes of secret Jews in their eighth or later generation after baptism, as they were arrested and imprisoned, interrogated and tortured, and finally reduced to making full confessions of their beliefs and actions, before in most cases repenting and being reconciled with the Church at the *auto de fe*.[3]

What was the nature of the secret Judaism of these people, known to Jewish historians as Marranos,[4] as it appears in the evidence presented in hundreds of cases preserved in the archives of the Inquisition courts of Toledo and Cuenca? There are important series of correspondence between the Supreme Inquisition Council – 'La Suprema' – and the local courts, as well as summaries of cases sent up regularly from the district courts to La Suprema, but only in the records of the interrogations of witnesses – usually themselves accused of Judaizing – and of the accused can one find the immediacy of the words of the people involved.

Despite the figures, which indicate that 60 per cent of the victims of the Holy Office were persons tried for making heretical statements, priests accused of the seduction of women while hearing their confession, and others charged with bigamy, fornication and the group of crimes coming under the heading of superstition, and that only 40 per cent were accused of Judaizing,[5] it was the secret Jews who suffered the greatest severity, for hardly ever did the other offences attract the supreme punishment. The Judaizer, man or woman, was regularly punished with flogging and prison, and about 10 per cent of Judaizers went to the stake. The attack on the Judaizer as a person was even more cruel, at least in modern eyes, because, guilty as he or she might be of an offence against religion, the Judaizer was not criminal in any other sense yet was punished like a thief or prostitute.

The task of describing the secret Judaism of the Spanish Jews is challenging. In the words of David Willemse:

Few people have really immersed themselves in the dusty bundles of often voluminous papers. It is not at all easy to read them because the handwriting is difficult and the composition of the bundles themselves often leads to confusion about the procedure of the trial.[6]

It is difficult, besides, to use the inquisitorial trial documents to lay bare the structures of crypto-Jewish life in seventeenth- and eighteenth-century Spain, as is the intention of this study. This is not because they are untrue. The trial documents are for the most part the statements of accused Judaizers, which are then used as evidence at the trials of the people whom the witness mentioned as having been involved in Judaizing acts. While it is true that the testimony was given at subsequent trials in written form, and that the witness was not called in person, and while defence counsel was not given the chance to question witnesses nor even to challenge the veracity of the statements they had made perhaps many years earlier, it must be stressed that the courts were meticulous about their interrogation of witnesses. They did not want to be put on false tracks. Nor was one statement enough to put a person in the dock. The accused could name their enemies and the court was obliged to discount the latters' testimony, but more often than not it was the close family of the accused, also in prison, who gave the really incriminating evidence. There was no reason for the Inquisition to falsify testimony since the Holy Office was not obliged to defend its procedure, nor was it subject to appeal. If, however, the local court was not scrupulous in its methods of obtaining evidence, the Supreme Inquisition Council, which in the latter epoch that this book describes read the trial documents with painstaking care, would administer a fierce rebuke. Certainly, though, it is very likely that more is hidden than is revealed, despite the 'complete' confessions made by the Judaizers, psychologically destroyed as they were. Nevertheless, scrutiny of the statements of the accused and the witnesses, who were nearly always themselves Judaizers under trial, allows a picture to be put together of the most intimate aspects of the religious life of a society which had set itself aside in one single though vitally important aspect of its existence.

In order to begin to approach a comprehensive view of the crypto-Jewish phenomenon, the historical context must be fully traced. How and why did crypto-Judaism begin in Spain?

1
The Extent of *Convivencia*

From the earliest years of Christianity in Spain, the ruling Visigoth monarchy instituted measures to force the Jews to accept Christian baptism.[1] Although early Moslem rule in Spain, from the eighth to the mid-twelfth centuries, is justifiably seen as a golden age of cooperation and mutual respect (*convivencia*) it is also true that Jews were no more than tolerated by the Moorish rulers. They were '*Dhimma*', tolerated but inferior to Moslems and subject to discriminatory legislation. The occasional Jewish political notable was an exception to the rule.[2]

In the twelfth century the fundamentalist Almohades destroyed Jewish communities, whose inhabitants fled to the relatively tolerant society of Christian Spain, where Jewish administrative capacities were valued.[3]

To the font!

In Christian Spain the baptisms of large numbers of Jews had multiple causes, and it is difficult to characterize them as voluntary or as forced. Social and economic tensions within the communities, the weakening of faith through the effects of rationalist philosophy, the wealth of opportunities available to converts for advancement in politics and in the Church itself, together sometimes with conviction of the truth of Christianity – all these factors must be added to the mass baptisms imposed when the Jewish districts of so many towns were sacked in the summer of 1391. Nevertheless, the fundamental motive for a Jew to go to the font must have been the discrimination to which he was increasingly subjected with the aim of separating Jews from Christians in a country which had earlier been remarkable for its tolerant relations between different religious cultures.

The Fourth Lateran Council, meeting in November 1215, required Jews to wear a badge. The point was to keep Jews identifiable and separate from Christians, perhaps for fear of conversion of the latter to Judaism, perhaps in order to prevent sexual relations taking place and perhaps to establish in Christian minds the special status of Jews. Christians were forbidden to consult Jewish doctors; Jews were not allowed to employ Christian women. Regulations attempted to prevent the appointment of Jews to any position where they would have authority over Christians, though in the particular circumstances of Spain where huge stretches of land were being reconquered from the Moors and colonized, the monarchs resisted pressure from their parliaments, the nobility and the Dominican order, in order to retain the Jews' valuable administrative services.[4]

By the middle of the thirteenth century, it was increasingly believed that if the Jews were not baptized, the second coming of Jesus would not occur. The more Jews were baptized, the greater the febrile urge to convert those who hesitated. The mendicant orders learned to argue with the Jews on the basis not only of the biblical text itself but also through the legislative, homiletic and mystical *Talmud* and other works. Armed with these texts, the missionary priests knew that Judaism was a religion which offered Jews a complete framework for a vibrant life and culture, and thus was not likely to disappear without an effort to convert the Jews.

An arm of the missionaries was the disputation about the meaning of biblical passages. The most famous one was held in Barcelona in 1263.[5] Yet Jews and Christians read the same texts in different ways. The Jews were still seen as contumacious and negative, an expression which would appear in the texts of the Inquisition for centuries. There was no alternative to force, if they were to be made Christian.

In Aragon, King Pere III (1276–1285) had to dismiss the powerful Jews of Saragossa from his service in order to obtain the support of the Aragonese nobles. During his reign, in 1280, one of the most influential works in converting Jews was written: the *Pugio Fidei adversus Mauros et Judaeos* (The Dagger of Faith against Moors and Jews), by the Dominican Raimundo Martini, who had taken part in the disputation of Barcelona in 1263.

In southern Spain, Islamic territories were steadily being occupied throughout the thirteenth and fourteenth centuries by Christian armies. Córdoba fell to the Christians in 1236, Murcia in 1241, Jaén in 1246 and Seville in 1248. The lands had to be colonized and administered. Alfonso X of Castile (1252–1284), despite his famous legislative text, the *Siete Partidas*, which set limits to the official employment of Jews, used the Jewish bourgeoisie in his financial administration and in his diplomacy because he could control the Jews more easily than the nobles or the clergy.[6] By the end of his reign, the Reconquest of Moslem Spain by the Christians was complete except for the kingdom of Granada, which would remain under Moslem rule until 1492. Pressed by the nobility, Alfonso turned against the Jews, and was followed by his son Sancho IV, who in 1288 forbade the Jews of Castile to buy land.

It is hardly surprising that several decades of economic, political, social and particularly religious attacks on the integrity of Jewish life led to the appearance, beginning in 1294 in Saragossa, of accusations of sacrilege and ritual murder. The common people dealt daily with Jews, yet came to accept that they were outside the normal rules. Inevitably, at moments of stress, it became easy to provoke riots and attacks on the Jews, who were seen not only as different and to be shunned socially, but also evil. They were said to commit foul sacrilege on consecrated wafers which they stole because they knew that these were the body of Christ. The Jew, therefore, was not merely separated from society but demonized. The Jews existed only to be baptized, according to the Synod of Zamora, meeting in 1312, which repeated and strengthened absolute social separation between Christians and Jews. The Black Death of 1348 appeared to justify the common suspicion that the Jews, enemies of humankind, poisoned the wells.

Thousands of Jews were baptized, but many of the baptisms were opportunistic or simply false. Even in the case of a Jew baptised sincerely, it should have been evident that the formal act of accepting a new religion should be undergone after and not before the neophyte became convinced of the truth of his new faith. The great majority of the converts possessed neither the education to read books such as the *Pugio Fidei*, nor to follow the theological arguments based on Christian interpretations of the Hebrew Bible and rabbinical literature. Jews were baptized with the minimum of Christian instruction or none at all. Whether a Jewish tailor, baker, vintner, bailiff or the wife of one of these became convinced of the divine nature of Jesus of Nazareth would depend on many factors. He or she was required only to comply with the commands of the Church. To speak, therefore, of false converts, is an oversimplification. Indeed, the falsification was to be found in those who forced Jews to the baptismal font without assuring themselves that the converts believed or even understood what the sacrament of baptism meant.

Destruction of the Jewish communities

After 1369, under King Henry II of Castile, the Jewish communities were physically persecuted, fined and, if unable to pay, their members were sold into slavery. During his reign, like his predecessors, Henry used Jews as high functionaries and administrators, but the Jews as always depended precariously on the goodwill of the king, himself subject to contrary pressure from the nobles and the rising Christian bourgeoisie. The only rights that the Jews might enjoy were those the king gave them when it suited him. Thus even the apparently powerful Jewish magnates lived in constant insecurity, which increased on Henry's death. When his successor John I died in 1390, leaving the baby Henry III on the throne, the weakness of the monarchy permitted open physical attack on the Jews.

The fourth wave of the Black Death laid Europe waste between 1388 and 1390, creating social chaos which discharged itself on the Jews, aliens in the social body.[7] Many more Jews were baptized during the missionary campaign led by the demagogic priest of Ecija, Fernán Martínez. Beginning in Seville on Ash Wednesday 1391, a series of physical attacks, murders and destructions of Jewish quarters spread to Córdoba, Toledo, Valencia, Játiva, Barcelona, Lérida and Logroño, that is all over southern and eastern Spain, Catalonia and into Castile. Almost all the Jewish communities were torn apart. Large numbers accepted baptism in exchange for their lives and those of their families.[8]

Religious confusion

The mass baptisms which followed the attacks of summer 1391 on the Jewish communities of Spain continued until the second decade of the fifteenth century.[9] In some cases it was the prosperous families, well assimilated into Christian society and very influenced by the rationalist currents of the age, which accepted baptism, but the motives and indeed the statistics of baptism cannot be stated with certainty. Certainly some embraced Christianity but continued to practise Judaism, while others accepted their new religion with enthusiasm and practised it with sincerity and fervour. Yet some who were baptized unwillingly must have gone on to accept Christianity fully while others, willingly baptized, remained secretly Jews. The impossibility of making clear distinctions is well expressed by a renowned Spanish historian:

> The complicated religious mosaic of Medieval Spain has to be understood: the opportunities and interests which affected people's

decisions, the fluctuations of royal policy, the disagreements within Jewish families themselves, all has to be balanced against the variety of natural temperaments, to try to explain such surprising reactions.[10]

Jews were ill-prepared for the second great disputation, at Tortosa in 1413 and 1414.[11] The conversionist sermons of the Dominicans, added to the depression of the Jewish communities, and the examples of converts to Christianity such as the highly respected Yehoshua Ha-Lorqui of Alcañiz and Rabbi Solomon Ha-Levi of Burgos, who became respectively Jerónimo de Santa Fe and Pablo de Santa María, archbishop of Burgos, were powerful factors in persuading Jews to become Christians.[12] The disasters and destructions of ancient communities in Spain, where the Jews had arrived, according to tradition, as aristocrats of the House of King David deported from Jerusalem by the Roman emperor Titus in the year 72, seemed to prove that God had abandoned His people.

False converts?

However, by now the behaviour of the tens of thousands of converts was giving rise to concern. In 1393, John I had promulgated legislation with the aim of forcing the new converts to cease to eat, dress and behave like Jews. Thirteen years earlier the same king had forbidden Old Christians to speak scornfully to the converts, calling them 'pigs' – *marranos* – or 'renegades' – *tornadizos* –.[13] The proper term was *conversos* or *cristianos nuevos*, that is 'converts' or 'New Christians'.

Nevertheless, practical conditions meant that the converts continued to live in the Jewish districts. The same family might include both converts and those who had not accepted baptism. For many converts it was simply easier to go back to live among Jews when the immediate danger had passed. Thus it was widely suspected that the converts were continuing to live as Jews. Around the year 1488 a volume was published anonymously, called *El Libro llamado el Alborayque* (The Book of Al-Buraq – the horse of the Prophet Mohammed), which portrayed that creature as having had a wolf's mouth, human eyes, the ears of a greyhound, the body of an ox, the tail of a snake and legs with the hooves of different animals. Converts, claimed the author, had the negative characteristics of these animals: cruelty, cunning and laziness. They were neither one thing nor the other: no longer Jews, but not genuine Christians either.[14]

In 1449, political and social crisis led to riots in Toledo, when Pedro Sarmiento, commander of the town fortress, the Alcázar, led a protest against a new tax. The rebels attacked the convert tax-collectors, tortured

them until they confessed to Judaizing, and then burnt them alive.
In June 1449 Sarmiento published an edict, known as the *Sentencia-
Estatuto*, which reapplied much earlier laws forbidding Christians of
Jewish ancestry – New Christians – to occupy positions of authority over
people of uninterrupted Christian descent, known as Old Christians.
This issue of purity of descent, or, as it became known, *limpieza de sangre*
(literally, cleanness of blood), grew to be of major importance and
remained so until the mid-nineteenth century when an end was put to
the genealogical investigations of candidates for certain posts or honours
to see if they had a Moslem or Jewish forebear.[15]

Enmity towards the *conversos* was inextricably linked with the political
and social crisis, but was nonetheless religious in its origin. It was
precisely because the converts were thought to be false that they were
considered to be enemies and linked in the public mind with hated
rulers.

Even a genuine convert to Christianity ought not, according to some
views, have authority over Christians from birth, but the assumption
that the convert was false in any case spread rapidly in the latter decades
of the fifteenth century. Popular anger was discharged on the converts of
Carmona, an important town near Seville, in 1462, and on those of
Toledo in 1467. Periods of food shortage and plague seemed to coincide
with rumours, often true, of corruption in high places. In the 1460s poets
and moralists alleged that the Court was riddled with corruption and
heresy, and called for a general reform by an Inquisition with the power
of the State behind it.[16]

Inflation and poor harvests between 1471 and 1473 increased the
bitterness and the insecurity of both converts and Jews, trapped between
the ambitions of the Christian nobility and the town mobs, as in this
example in Córdoba:

One day, while a religious procession was passing through the streets
of the city, a young *converso* girl poured out some water from her
house into the street. The blacksmith bellowed that the girl had
poured urine on to the procession and declared war upon the heretics
and detractors of religion. The homes of the *conversos* were set on
fire . . . The conflict spread to all parts of the city . . . The *conversos*
armed themselves and fortified their quarters. The blacksmith's men
spread inflammatory rumours. Labourers and peasants streamed in
from the villages ready for rioting and pillage . . . Now all took a hand
in burning, looting and killing, sparing neither age nor sex. The
disturbances reached their peak in the middle of March 1473, after

sixteen successive days. The *conversos* who succeeded in escaping from the city wandered about in the fields without finding a safe shelter, as the peasants assaulted and robbed them wherever they gathered... The municipal council of Córdoba passed an ordinance to exclude *conversos* from posts in the municipality.[17]

Why and how was the Inquisition established?

Ferdinand of Aragon and Isabella of Castile, who married in 1469 and became joint rulers of Spain in 1479, known as the *Reyes Católicos* – the Catholic Monarchs – conducted a campaign against rebellious nobles in Andalusia, a region well populated by both Jews and *conversos*. They came to realise that the *conversos* were widely suspected of Judaizing and that a large-scale, State-supported investigation was needed if suspicion and hatred of the *conversos* was to cease to be a pretext for rebellion and riot.

The Catholic Monarchs asked Pope Sixtus IV for a bull to allow them to set up a State Inquisition, which he did on 1 November 1478. In 1480 they appointed the first inquisitors, the Dominican friars Miguel Morillo and Juan de San Martín. In their statement appointing the inquisitors, the monarchs deemed themselves entitled to appoint

worthy men who may investigate in any part of our said kingdoms... and proceed against those accused and blemished by infidelity and heresy, as well as against those who protect and favour them.[18]

The first *auto de fe,* a public statement of loyalty to Christianity by the civil power, proclaiming the heresy of the accused, their formal admission of guilt, their abjuration and reconciliation with the Church accompanied by the imposition of suitable penances, or, in the case of obstinately negative heretics, execution by burning at the stake, took place in Seville on 6 February 1481. On 17 October 1483, Friar Tomás de Torquemada, a descendant of converts, became Inquisitor-General. By the end of the 1480's, Inquisition courts and their panoply of gaols and agents, known as *familiares*, had been instituted everywhere. Courts sat in Valencia and Saragossa, Teruel, Barcelona, and in Palma de Mallorca. The Holy Office covered Logroño in the wine-producing area of La Rioja, Córdoba in the heavily populated Guadalquivir valley of Andalusia, Cuenca, the mountain city halfway between Madrid and the Mediterranean coast, whose bishopric still preserves hundreds of its cases, Granada after its fall in 1492, high up in the Sierra Nevada of Southern Andalusia, whose court heard cases from Málaga and its coast, Murcia in the arid south-east, Llerena close to the Portuguese frontier, Santiago de Compostela, far away in Spain's rainy north-west, Toledo, seat of the Primate of Spain, almost in the centre, and Valladolid, the principal city of Old Castile. After the discovery and first settlements of America, the Inquisition would sit in Cartagena de Indias, on Colombia's Caribbean coast, in Mexico City and in Lima.[19]

Both political and religious considerations governed the royal decision to establish the Inquisition. It was without doubt a royal body, run by the Supreme Inquisition Council – the *Consejo de la Suprema Inquisición* or simply *La Suprema*.

It was not easy to distinguish between the political and the religious motives of the attack on the *conversos* and their descendants. According to Alfonso X's famous code, the *Siete Partidas*, it was the king's responsibility to see that the death sentence was carried out on heretics and that their property was forfeited. The Inquisition merely 'relaxed' the culprit to the secular arm. It was the latter which inflicted the punishment which came before the period of penitence in the Inquisition's gaol or burned the heretic at the stake. Besides, heresy was thought of as a crime of social subversion. Religious dissidence was an offence against society.

The Inquisition did not persecute Jews. Though there were Jews living in Spain in the Inquisition's first 14 years of life, before all remaining Jews were expelled in 1492, the Holy Office concerned itself only with Christians and specifically with recently converted Jews or their descendants. Like previous rulers, the Catholic Monarchs continued to surround themselves with Jewish advisers and administrators, including Abraham Seneor, who ran the royal finances, his son-in-law Meir Melamed, principal tax farmer of the royal income, David Alfacar, principal tax collector for Murcia and Cartagena, and Isaac Abarbanel, a major financial agent for Queen Isabella of Castile. Isabella also employed converts such as Hernando del Pulgar, her chronicler, while in Aragon Ferdinand's finances were run by the converts descended from famous Jewish families of Saragossa, Alfonso de la Caballería, Luis de Santángel and his son-in-law Gabriel Sánchez.

How Jewish were the converts? Race or religion?

One of the major questions asked in Jewish historiography of the Inquisition is whether the weight of rabbinical opinion in the fourteenth and fifteenth centuries held that most of the converts were to be classified, in terms of Jewish law, as *Anussim*, that is as having been forced to accept Christian baptism and thus to be treated as full Jews living in error against their will, or whether, on the contrary, they were *Meshummadim* or apostates because they had voluntarily accepted Christianity, without even trying to maintain a Jewish way of life.[20] Traditionally the former point of view was the one adopted by Jewish historians. A recent revisionist historiography, however, denies that any meaningful number of the converts practised Judaism secretly. In this view, the Inquisition persecuted converts and their descendants because this easily identifiable group had seized hold of the levers of power in the cities of Castile against the interests of the Old Christian nobles and bourgeoisie. Previously, when they were Jews, the paths to secular power had to a considerable extent been barred to them. This thesis holds that the wave of hostility towards the converts arose from racial enmity against a social class characterized by its ancestry and its success, and not because the converts and their descendants secretly practised Judaism.

As critics of the revisionist thesis have shown, its argument is based on the assumption that the hatred shown towards the converts was racial rather than religious. Indeed, Benzion Netanyahu, the leading exponent of this view, draws parallels between the Spain of the Inquisition and the Nazi regime in Germany.[21]

It must be true that many of the converts and their descendants were loyal Christians and did not Judaize. Probably the majority of them had by 1480 been assimilated to the Old Christian population. Possibly the early Inquisition occasionally abused its power and failed to verify the real conduct of the accused. But this in itself does not disprove the truth of most of the Inquisition accusations. One cannot simply deny the *religious* evidence of Judaizing so carefully collected by a scholar of the eminence of Haim Beinart, for instance, in his volumes reproducing the Inquisition trials of Ciudad Real and his work on other cities.[22]

Scrutiny of the seventeenth- and eighteenth-century records of the Inquisition's trials suggest that the accused were indeed guilty of Judaizing. Since the records were kept in absolute secrecy, there was no motive for falsifying them. To deny their truth, one would have to suggest that the Inquisition was comparable to the witch-hunts from which Spain, happily, was largely free. However, to accuse a woman of being a witch and flying on a broomstick was irrational. To say that people were cutting a fowl's throat rather than throttling it, or washing all the blood out of a joint of meat, is to describe what Jews did and still do, as moreover the Inquisitors themselves could have seen with their own eyes until the Jews were expelled from Spain in 1492. In any case, no witch in history ever escaped to join a community of witches in another country, while thousands of Spanish and Portuguese Jews fled the Iberian peninsula from the fifteenth until the eighteenth century to do precisely that.

If, as some historians assert, the Inquisition was created to attack the converts falsely and accuse them for reasons other than their ostensible crime of practising Judaism, it is strange that the total number of victims, at its highest estimates, is only a fraction of the number of converts. A reasonable estimate assumes a total of 25,000 converts punished by the Inquisition between its foundation and 1520, from a total of converts which is estimated at 250,000.[23] So, while this agrees with the view of the revisionist historians in that the figure is minimal, it also disproves the theory that *all conversos* were attacked because they were descended from Jews rather than because they were Judaizing.

The revisionist thesis insists that converts were hated because they were Jews by ancestry, but the argument fails to explain the great success of genuine converts such as Pablo de Santa María, bishop of Cartagena and then archbishop of Burgos, or Jerónimo de Santa Fe. The comparison between the Inquisition and twentieth-century racism does not hold water, even though there were, it is true, Spanish writers who asserted that Judaism was transmitted biologically. If the motive of the Catholic Monarchs and the Inquisition had really been racial antagonism, the obvious solution would have been to expel all converts whose loyalty to Christianity was doubtful. On the contrary, however, the converts were not allowed to leave Spain because it was feared, with justification, that they would join a Jewish community abroad.

The entire history of the Spanish Jews indicates that, despite the restrictive legislation that they suffered from the age of the Visigoths until Expulsion, the laws were applied so inconsistently that they had to be frequently reiterated, whatever the Dominicans, the rival Christian bourgeoisie and the mob wanted, since the kings, and very often the Church and the nobles, needed the Jews. It is hard, then, to accept the revisionist picture of a Spanish Church rabid with racial hatred, cruelly torturing, handing over to the secular arm to be burnt at the stake, or imposing humiliating penances on people whom the Inquisitors, learned experts in canon law, knew were loyal and faithful Christians whatever their ancestry.

The hostility and suspicion shown towards the converts arose precisely because they were suspected, often with justification, of Judaizing. Inquisition trial records demonstrate that crypto-Jewish practices were taught from one generation to the next. The crypto-Jews did not need the Church's list of Jewish practices, announced in public to encourage denunciations, in order to learn them. Even assuming that the descriptions of

Jewish practices published by the Inquisition did help to teach the crypto-Jewish family groups how to practise their Judaism, it would still signify that the latter wanted to know more than they could learn from their own resources and that their Jewish consciousness was strong though their knowledge was weak.

The views of contemporary Jewish authorities

Some Jewish historians have used rabbinical sources to discover how the Jewish authorities themselves saw the Marranos. What was the view taken by Jewish communities who lived outside the Iberian peninsula towards those converts who managed to escape, as they did from the beginning of the sixteenth century and continued to do right into the eighteenth? The sources for this are the opinions given in responses sent by rabbis to communities which asked for their advice on the application of Jewish law to difficult problems.

At the beginning of the fifteenth century, when the rabbis had to consider how to apply the law to the first generation of forced converts – the *Anussim* – they took a very tolerant attitude towards them. As the century advanced, however, according to some historians rabbinical attitudes became more critical because later generations of converts seemed to be committing the sins of idolatry, worshipping false gods and images, profaning the Sabbath and the festivals of the Jewish calendar, eating forbidden food and so on, when such offences were no longer necessary in order to preserve their lives, the one consideration which most Jewish authorities had seen as valid. Other authors, however, point out that other responsa are particularly tolerant to the converts.[24]

The major point that emerges, and one which is crucial to the question of whether other Jews considered the Marranos as proper Jews, is that even the most severe rabbis insisted that Jewish law was still applicable to the converts in the case of marriage, divorce and levirate marriage (where a childless widow must reject the offer of marriage which must nevertheless be made to her by her dead husband's brother, before she may remarry). The reason for rabbinical insistence was that, however removed from Judaism the daily behaviour of the converts might be, it was still the custom among them to marry endogamously, and since a Jew is defined in Jewish law as one who has a Jewish mother, not even a rabbi who felt very hostile to the converts could say that the laws of marriage, divorce and levirate marriage no longer applied.[25] The rabbis insisted that a woman who fled Spain and reached a Jewish community to 'shelter under the wings of the Divine Presence', as the phrase is put in the responsa, had to obtain a divorce from her husband who had stayed in Spain, before she could marry again. This is an important point. The rabbis of the ex-Spanish communities, now scattered around the Mediterranean, knew that, by refusing to allow women to marry without obtaining divorces from their convert husbands, or forbidding childless widows to remarry because they were unable to obtain release from their convert brothers-in-law, they were condemning the women to difficult lives. Yet the alternative was to declare the converts who refused to leave Spain to be no longer Jews. This the rabbis did not do.

A solution was found to the marriage problem after the Expulsion, when the rabbis of Salonika, the principal centre of ex-Spanish Jews, decided that marriages performed in the Iberian peninsula after the Expulsion were no longer valid Jewish marriages because of doubts about the validity of the witnesses.[26] In this way the rabbis automatically freed any married woman – or indeed man – who arrived in their communities. Such couples had to be remarried according to Jewish law and the records of such marriages and the circumcisions of the men provide useful data in calculating the numbers of Marranos arriving in a community such as the Spanish and Portuguese synagogue founded in London in 1656.[27]

The fact that the converts married among themselves is very important, because it demonstrated that, despite their Christian lives, they wanted to maintain their Jewish status and that of their children, as well as to preserve something of Jewish life in their homes. Frequently the Rabbis used the Talmudic expression 'Children captive among Gentiles' to describe the position of the converts. Even after the Expulsion, the rabbis continued to take this view of Jewish converts in Spain. When any Marrano escaping from the Inquisition arrived in a free community outside Spain such as Salonika, Venice, Leghorn, Bayonne, Bordeaux, Amsterdam or London, until well into the eighteenth century, he or she was accepted as a Jew and not required to submit to a rite of conversion.

To summarize this part of the question, the revisionist historians insist that the number of converts who continued to practise Judaism was minimal and that Judaizing was merely a pretext and not the real reason for the activities of the Inquisition, which were largely social, political and racist in intent. It seems, however, highly unlikely that an institution so powerful and so aware of its own role, jealous of its prerogatives and proud of its mission as the Inquisition was, should have allowed itself to be manipulated to the point of imprisoning, torturing, extracting false confessions and false abjurations from genuine Christians – that is, acting out a mockery of its own procedures. It seems certain that

Judaizing among the converts of the fifteenth, sixteenth, seventeenth and the first half of the eighteenth centuries was indeed a serious problem for the Holy Office, even though the majority of descendants of converts probably did in the end assimilate with the general population. Furthermore, the work of the Inquisition must have increased greatly after 1492, both because of the large number of Jews who must have accepted baptism that summer rather than be expelled, and because the latest converts were the descendants of those who had resisted conversionist pressure for a century at least.

Was the Inquisition a weapon in the class war?

The riots, economic and social in origin, which occurred between 1449 and 1471 in Toledo, Burgos, Medina del Campo – the great market of Castile – Valladolid, Sepúlveda and Seville, reaching their apogee with the massacres which took place in eastern Andalusia in 1473–1474, discharged people's rage and frustration on the Jews and on the *conversos*, both of whom constituted the class of administrators, public officials and tax collectors.[28]

For the *conversos* and their descendants, baptism opened the doors of lay and ecclesiastical professions which were barred to Jews. Within a generation after the mass baptisms of 1391, family networks of converted Jews were ensconced in important positions in the principal cities of Castile and Andalusia: Seville, Toledo, Córdoba, Burgos and Segovia. The senior treasurers – the *contadores* – and chief secretaries of the monarchs were converts, while others enjoyed distinguished careers in the Church. The absorption of Jewish converts into Christian society made it difficult to know who actually had Jewish ancestry, and thus led in later years to the falsification of genealogies together with ample possibilities of blackmail once Jewish ancestry became a cause of family disgrace. If, in strict terms of canon law, baptism had wiped away the impediments which Jews had suffered, in reality hatred of the converts and their success was clearly expressed in Pedro Sarmiento's *Sentencia-Estatuto* of 1449, which stated that Jews and their baptized descendants remained Jews, without the right to accede to posts to which their abilities entitled them, a view diametrically opposed to the Christian one, according to which baptism did in fact create a new person. The important question is, therefore, to what point did the accusations of false conversion and Judaizing hurled against the converts constitute a pretext for attacks whose real cause was social and economic? The converts, or some of them, may or may not have been false, but was this merely an excuse for an attack on a social class brought about by a social and economic crisis?

The following frequently quoted text, written by Andrés Bernáldez, the parish priest of the Sevillian village of Los Palacios, epitomizes the opinions and prejudices of the age:

> [The Jews] were merchants, salesmen, tax farmers and collectors, shop-keepers, bailiffs of estates, barbers, tailors, shoemakers, tanners, weavers, dealers in spices, pedlars, silk merchants, blacksmiths, silver-smiths and the like; none worked on the land or was a farmer or carpenter or stonemason, but all sought easy occupations and ways of earning a living with little effort. [29]

These New Christians were thus not all prosperous high functionaries, tax farmers, court doctors and the like. The *conversos* interrogated by the Inquisition between 1495 and 1500 tend, true enough, not to have been directly connected with the cultivation of the land. Most of them were middling artisans, often in textiles, such as tailors, weavers, dyers and old-clothes dealers. Another clearly defined group were the tanners and other leather-workers. There were blacksmiths and shoemakers also. [30] Then came the more prosperous people, the jewellers and the silver-smiths, who sometimes acted as moneylenders. These occupations, together with a great variety of others including candlemakers, spice dealers and confectioners, and the associated retailing, added to the professions of physician, surgeon and pharmacist, were those of the converts.

The only conclusion to be reached from all these lists of occupations is that they required skill and training. The Jews and *conversos* belonged usually to the class of skilled urban workers, artisans, traders and admin-istrators of one kind or another. Of course, these occupations were not pursued only by Jews and converts, but the documents show that these were the major roles that they played in society.

Yet to insist on explaining the Inquisition as a weapon in the class war seems to be to apply the Marxist model to a pre-capitalist epoch, one where it was religion that constituted the fundamental form of self-identification and the unifying force of any group. [31]

To sum up, the vast majority of the descendants of the *conversos* became genuine Catholics. A minority, reinforced at the end of the fifteenth century by the large number baptized in 1492 and then in Portugal a few years later, practised secret Judaism. In addition, there were those who Judaized a little, sometimes or who possessed a more or less syncretic version of Catholicism and Judaism. It may also be likely that the Inquisition's more energetic moments, often interspersed with long periods when there were no *autos de fe*, reflected factors other than the extent of crypto-Judaism. Yet this does not mean that the accusations, as described in the trial documents, were false. It may be true that behind the attacks on the Toledo converts in 1449 lay hatred of a social group of middle-class professions. Yet old-clothes sellers, pedlars and other such humble *conversos* also suffered at the *auto de fe*.[32] The social hatred displayed does not necessarily mean that significant numbers of the *conversos* did not Judaize.

The need for an efficient inquisitorial system which would discriminate between genuine converts and those who continued to Judaize became more and more evident as important works were published which insisted, against the general view, that a convert or New Christian was a Christian for all purposes and should not be considered in any way inferior to an Old Christian. On 24 September 1449 and through the convert Cardinal Juan de Torquemada, uncle of the future inquisitor-general, Pope Nicholas V issued the bull *Humani Generis Inimicus*, forbidding all discrimination between Christians and converts on the basis of racial origin. This papal statement was reinforced in Spain by books such as *Defensorium Unitatis Christianae* by Alonso de Cartagena, bishop of Burgos, the son of Pablo de Santa María (the convert Solomon Ha-Levi). If in the Christian world there were no longer to be Jews or Greeks, according to St Paul, then the converts and their descendants were Christians with all the rights and duties of such.

2
The Inquisition Begins Work

The Inquisition set to work with ferocious rigour. Thousands of potential victims fled to Portugal, to Moslem Granada or, if they had the necessary resources, to Rome, where they were allowed to live unmolested.

The figures for the number of victims of the Inquisition in the early years, from its foundation until the death of Ferdinand of Aragon in 1516, are speculative, given the absence of reliable internal statistics from the Holy Office itself, but in the diocese of Seville the figure of six hundred burnt at the stake has been given for the period 1483 to 1515. Andrés Bernáldez, an acute observer who was in a position to give figures without exaggeration, claims that seven hundred were burnt and five thousand reconciled with the Church.[1] As would be expected at this most energetic stage of the Inquisition's existence, this figure is slightly higher than the usual proportion in later years between those reconciled and those released to the secular arm. It does not seem improbable. In another Andalusian city in an area with a large Jewish and convert population, Córdoba, between 1483 and 1516, 263 Judaizers were burnt in person and 24 more in effigy, having died or fled.

There is no reason to suppose that the Inquisition forged evidence against the converts whose religious conduct it investigated. Nevertheless, given that 31,312,768 maravedis were calculated to have been confiscated by the Inquisition from penitents in Andalusia between 1488 and 1497, one might well conclude that the severity of the persecution was due more to financial concerns than to the desire to suppress the Judaizing heresy.[2] In the first part of the sixteenth century the Inquisition took enormous sums from its victims. Almost 87 million maravedis were confiscated by eight courts between 1536 and 1543 alone. More than half of this sum came from the confiscations of property arising from two *autos de fe* in Cuenca, most of the rest from Granada and from the *auto de fe* held in Córdoba on 24 January 1540, where the confiscations produced 10,501,126 maravedis.[3]

In some cases, the sequestrations of movable goods and money which took place when the suspect was arrested, and the confiscation of all property which was almost always part of the sentence imposed on the repentant Judaizer, must have produced huge profits for the coffers of the Holy Office. Yet these spectacular figures do not mean that the confiscations covered the constant expenses of the courts, the salaries of the inquisitors, the notaries, doctors, gaolers, porters and others, the costs of maintaining the physical fabric of the Inquisition building and gaol, not to speak of the food of the prisoners while under interrogation, besides what the courts were required to hand over to the *Suprema* and the Royal Treasury. It was financial stringency which in 1501 put an end to the energetic activity of the first two decades of the Holy Office. The Pope was obliged to earmark several Church sources of income in order to maintain the Inquisition. Why this was so becomes clear when the details of individual prisoners are scrutinized. Most of them were people of humble position. Their property, seized by the officers of the Holy Office on their arrest, was not enough to feed them in prison, pay the wages of the gaoler and others and cover medical costs, particularly because the gaol was secret. There was no public announcement that the prisoners were in prison. Their relatives were probably also in gaol or hiding. They were not going to bring food and clothes to the prison as was the case with ordinary inmates. One example out of many of an annual balance is that of the Inquisition court in Murcia, which in 1675 had a an income from sequestrations of 6,003,924 maravedis but expenses of 6,883,505 maravedis.[4] In all, the Inquisition, despite occasional prizes, did not gain financially from its sequestrations of property.[5]

The activity of the Inquisition in its first forty or so years has been well documented by Beinart's detailed study and publication of the trials in the third city where an Inquisition court was set up: Ciudad Real in New Castile. This court existed for two years only, between 1483 and 1485, when it was merged with the court of Toledo.

There was admittedly a political motive in the assault on the converts of this city, because Ciudad Real had been the centre of the rebellion against the monarchy led by the master of the Military Order of Calatrava, Rodrigo Téllez de Girón.[6] The political motive, nevertheless, does not negate the Judaizing of the converts. As Beinart writes, '[W]hen stripped of its outer mantle of Christianity, the Converso community of Ciudad Real emerges as an essentially Jewish community.'[7]

In 1483 there were fifty *converso* families. In the seventeen *autos de fe* which took place between 16 November 1483 and 6 May 1485, ten of which included sentences of burning at the stake, no family was left untouched. At least two hundred people were tried, and 52 of them were executed.[8]

In Toledo the first *auto de fe* took place on 12 February 1486. From then until 1501 2,791 people were tried, of whom 1,096 were burnt at the stake, together with the effigies of another five hundred who had died or managed to flee. The bones of the dead were disinterred and burnt and their ashes crushed and scattered. According to the most detailed study of the Toledo Inquisition court, from 1505 onwards the number of trials fell rapidly. In a few decades, crypto-Judaism had disappeared from New Castile.[9]

Hernando del Pulgar, a *converso* himself and the chronicler of the Catholic Monarchs, calculated the number of *conversos* burnt at the stake in their reign as 12,000 for Old and New Castile. In Aragon, the murder of the Inquisitor Pedro de Arbués led to a violent assault on the *conversos*. In 1486 and 1487 the city of Lérida, one hundred miles west of Barcelona, saw 123 effigies of secret Jews burnt; presumably Lérida was within reach of safety in the Pyrenees for those Judaizers who were warned in time.[10] The figures for Valencia up till 1530 reveal over two thousand trials for Judaizing, leading to 909 relaxations to the secular arm.[11]

The total number of victims condemned and punished between 1481 and 1512 has been estimated at roughly fifty thousand, though it is an approximate calculation because the documents for some courts are missing and the dates *ad quem* vary greatly.[12] Nevertheless, the most complete calculation shows a total of 15,791 trials in the first twenty years of the Holy Office (1480–1500). Then the figure falls rapidly. In 1500 there were 1,500 trials, but by 1540 the number had fallen to 240 and, though there are certainly ups and downs, the figure does not begin to reach five hundred a year again until well into the following century.[13] It would seem very likely, therefore, that the figure of fifty thousand victims in the first thirty-one years of the Holy Office includes people who confessed voluntarily, were not tried and did not appear at an *auto de fe*.

Expulsion of the Jews: 1492

The prime reason for expelling Jews who refused to be baptized was to put an end to the existence of models of Jewish life which the converts

saw daily among their acquaintances and even within their own families. According to the edict of Expulsion:

> [g]reat harm [is] caused to Christians [that is, Jewish converts to
> Christianity and their descendants] by the common life, dealings
> and communication that they have had and do have with Jews, who
> always try by whatever stratagems and means they can, to subvert
> and turn faithful Christians away from our Holy Catholic Faith,
> separate them from it and incline them and pervert them towards
> their own wrongful belief and opinion.[14]

Without neighbours or relatives who still lived Jewish lives, deprived of
rabbis who could teach Hebrew, Jewish doctrine and practice, without
butchers skilled in the techniques of Jewish animal slaughter, deprived
of Hebrew texts of the Scriptures and their exegesis, of rabbinic and
prayer texts, there could be no more Jewish community. In that way the
conversos, lacking all points of Jewish reference, would be more easily
absorbed into the Christian majority.

At the end of the fifteenth century the unification of nations under
strong monarchs was brought about through religion. This was true not
only in Spain; in Elizabethan England, Englishness was taken to mean
fidelity to the national Church of England. In Islamic countries Jews and
Christians were tolerated as 'Peoples of the Book', but only Moslems were
considered to be real citizens with the rights of such at law. It was in religious terms that the Catholic Monarchs Ferdinand of Aragon and Isabella
of Castile saw the unification and expansion of their country, in the same
year that Columbus discovered America and the last Moslem kingdom in
the peninsula, Granada, fell to Christian armies. There was, therefore, no
place for the Jews in Spain. Previously Jews had lived in the difficult
position of *servi regis* – that is, they were personal servants of the king,
occupying a special situation in the social structure. When the Catholic
Monarchs decided that religious maximalism was the road to power, to
national discipline, unity and greatness, Catholicism became the political
instrument and the link between monarchs, land and people. In this
structure the *conversos* had a place, provided that they were genuine Catholics. But the presence of Jews, *the others*, compromised the unity of the
nation. There is a very clear exposition of this idea in the writing of the
distinguished seventeenth-century diplomat Diego de Saavedra Fajardo:

> While religion is the unifying force in the Republic, it can also
> become the force which most shatters it and reduces it to several

forms of government when it is not one religion, for there cannot be concord and peace among those who see God in different ways. This is because, if diversity in customs and dress opposes people to each other, how much more conflict will be caused by people's natural inclination and fidelity to the Author of Creation and their anger and zeal in understanding that which is so important? Freedom of conscience leads to the ruin of the State.[15]

Robbery of Jewish property was unlikely to have been the principal motive for the expulsion of the Jews, although many people probably did profit from their departure. Jews were unable to realize the full value of their property and did not have the right to take gold and silver with them. Nevertheless, in Spain it seems to have often been the wealthier Jews who accepted last-minute baptism, and they of course retained their property. The Catholic Monarchs were perfectly aware of the risks they took in expelling the Jews, who channeled tax income towards the royal treasuries of Aragon and Castile. It must have been expected that the great administrators and tax farmers, the Seneor, Caballería and Santángel families, would not leave Spain but would continue after baptism to act with as much benefit to the country as previously, as they indeed did.

The Edict of Expulsion was issued on 31 March 1492, giving the Jews four months' notice to accept baptism or leave. By 1 August, all the Spanish Jews would have to be baptized or gone. So much did the Catholic Monarchs want to encourage conversion rather than lose the Jews, that they allowed even Jews who left Spain to return, have themselves baptized and be accepted into Christian society. Indeed, many did so, since they found the difficulties of leaving with their families, obtaining a price for their property, travelling to the frontier or the sea, getting passage on a ship, together with the uncertainty for their safety on board and wherever the ship took them, too great to overcome. Even much later, in the seventeenth and eighteenth centuries, the Inquisition documents provide evidence of descendants of Jews from the Iberian Peninsula who were returning to Spain and presenting themselves for baptism.

Statistics of the expulsion

The evidence for the numbers of Jews who left Spain is so contradictory and based on such uncertain figures for the existing Jewish population that it is very difficult to draw a reliable picture. Most older authors made assumptions, unsupported by statistics. The Jewish authors may fairly be assumed to have exaggerated the number of the exiles, because to do so magnified the catastrophe and lessened what was seen as betrayal by the weaker members of the community who accepted baptism. This makes it difficult to accept the frequently quoted figure of 300,000, given by the distinguished counsellor of Isabella and Ferdinand and well-known Bible exegete, Don Isaac Abarbanel.[16] Spanish authors, also, probably wishing to underscore the enormity of the Jewish 'problem' in Spain and the cosmic significance of the achievement of the Catholic Monarchs, also exaggerated the figures.

Julio Caro Baroja suggests that Abarbanel possessed an old census of Jews, based on family tax records, which gave his figure of 300,000. He calculates the Jewish population of Spain in 1492 as 400,000, of whom he asserts, without explaining why, that 240,000 accepted baptism and 160,000 went into exile.[17] This figure for Jews – 400,000 – still living in Spain in 1492 does not, presumably, include the accumulation of the descendants of converts over a century at least.

The figure of 160,000 exiles helps to explain the survival and powerful influence of the Spanish Jews in Greece, Turkey and many cities around the Mediterranean, even though most of the exiled Jews are thought to have gone to neighbouring Portugal.[18]

Nevertheless, given the total population of Spain of between 7 and 8 million, and the existence of a sizeable number of converts and descendants of converts, if there really were as many as 400,000 Jews at the time of the Expulsion then it would suggest that the Jewish population a century earlier, before the wave of attacks and the consequent mass baptisms began in 1391, was colossal. After a century of baptisms of Jews, it seems unlikely that there could still be 400,000 in 1492. A more likely figure is 80,000 to 90,000, living mostly in Castile.[19] Another figure is from Andrés Bernáldez, the parish priest of Los Palacios who was such an acute observer of the events of his time. He repeats what he was told by one of the rabbis who returned from the uncertainties of life in exile and asked Bernáldez to baptise him.[20] This figure is 35,000 or 36,000 families, which would be about 170,000 individuals. Bernáldez also quotes Meir Melamed, the son-in-law of Abraham Seneor, who had given these figures to his father-in-law, though Bernáldez does not say where he obtained this information. Henry Kamen finds these figures unacceptable against the background of a total population which he gives as 5,265,000; 170,000 Jews would be about 3 per cent, in a Spain where a century of pressure had decimated the Jewish communities. Kamen prefers a figure of 80,000 to 90,000 Jews, which he bases on taxation statistics founded on the number of households with actual incomes high enough to pay taxes. However, this does not include families whose poverty left them out of the taxpaying net, so such a form of calculating population may well indicate only minimum figures. Besides, Kamen thinks that the multiple of 6 used to calculate the number of individuals per family is too high. It is not clear, however, why this should be so when, up to very modern times, it was usual for the parents of at least one of the spouses to live with them, together with unmarried siblings and other single women or widows. It is also quite likely that the servants or some of them may have been Jewish.[21]

Of this, say, minimum number of 85,000 Jews, faced with expulsion or baptism, how many opted for one and how many for the other? The general view is that most Castilian Jews went to Portugal, the nearest country. Of those who set sail from Mediterranean ports or ventured across the Straits of Gibraltar, many must have died in shipwrecks, at the hands of callous shipmasters or on the inhospitable coasts of North Africa. The old, the sick and the frail would have died in considerable numbers, given that the journey from the interior of Spain, in the heat of the summer, must have been more than they could bear. Yet there were sufficient Jewish exiles to create important and long-lasting communities in Italy and in the Ottoman empire. All this tends to support the view that the number of Jews still in Spain at the Expulsion must have been larger than 85,000.

Kamen also insists that only a minority of the 85,000 left Spain, but, if only a minority left, and if the majority of this minority went to Portugal, where did the new Spanish communities all over the Mediterranean come from, and how did they manage to take over existing communities? Kamen's view is that there is little documentation about the emigrants and that the new communities must have been built up later, as converts steadily left the peninsula over the following decades. Kamen's conclusion is that of 70,000 Castilian Jews a little over half emigrated, though a substantial number returned quickly. Adding the emigrants from Aragon, where the Jewish communities had been decimated over the previous century, Kamen fixes the number of exiles as 40,000 or 50,000.

This figure suggests that about the same number remained in Spain and accepted baptism. Kamen leaves the argument here, and does not challenge the figures for those punished by the Inquisition over the following decades. If this latter figure is accurately assessed at the 50,000 which has been given, it would suggest that virtually all the Jews who opted for baptism in 1492 were punished or at least had to confess as false converts and Judaizers.

These low figures give food for thought and redress the balance after the exaggerations of previous statistics. Their defect, however, is that they are based on taxation returns, which refer to households and not individuals, that they minimize the figures for emigrants to Portugal and the Ottoman empire, and that they do not take into account Inquisition statistics, which historians may tend to underestimate because so much documentation has been lost.

Those who remained

Of the new converts of 1492 and the descendants of previous ones, the figure of 50,000 punished by the Inquisition in its early years was given by the authorities of the cathedral of Toledo. However, did those authorities really investigate all the Inquisition courts? Or was the purpose of the statement to defend the statute of *limpieza de sangre* by stressing how dangerous it was to appoint people of Jewish descent to positions of ecclesiastical importance? And how widespread was such descent? Without answers to these questions, the figure of 50,000 cannot be verified.

Nevertheless, a high figure cannot be ruled out. The ferocity of the Inquisition in its first forty or fifty years against converts suspected of Judaizing wiped out Spanish secret Judaism almost completely. However, the converts of 1492 were people who – both they and their ancestors – had rejected all the pressures and blandishments of the missionaries for a whole century, including the mass attacks of 1391, the conversionist campaign of 1413–1414 and the intellectual and spiritual pressure of Christian and anti-Jewish written works. They had seen the destruction of the Jewish community of Toledo in 1449 and those of Ciudad Real, Córdoba, Jaén, Segovia and Valladolid between 1465 and 1475. The converts of 1492 were, thus, Jews who had survived, but could not withstand the alternative of exile. It is, consequently, possible that the proportion of false converts among the last 45,000 or so Jews baptized in Spain may have been quite high, so the figure of 50,000 victims of the Inquisition is not an unfeasible order of magnitude.

By 1550, it can be assumed, most descendants of *conversos* were well on the way to complete assimilation with the Christian population. Indeed, two famous books – *El tizón de la nobleza* (Stain on the Nobility) for Castile, and *El libro verde* or (Green Book) for Aragon – proved that marriage into *converso* families had been widespread among the nobility and other classes of society.

Portugal

Events such as the attacks on the Spanish communities in 1391 had not happened in Portugal, save for one, motivated more by robbery than by religious hatred, on the Jewish quarter of Lisbon in 1449. Indeed, the number of surviving manuscripts and of incunabula published in the decade before the forced conversion of 1497 demonstrates a high level of prosperity and tranquillity for Portugal's Jews.[22]

The impression of care conveyed by the precise figures given by Andrés Bernáldez, the observant parish priest of Los Palacios, is underlined when he gives a detailed statistical list of the numbers of emigrants and the routes taken by Jews who crossed into Portugal in the summer of 1492:

From Benavente to Braganza	3,000
From Zamora to Miranda	30,000
From Ciudad Rodrigo to Vilar Formoso	35,000
From Alcántara to Marvão	15,000
From Badajoz to Elvas	10,000

According to Bernáldez, the figures had been rounded down, so that at least 93,000 Jews left Spain for Portugal, from Castile alone.[23] These migrants were added to the converts who had been fleeing Spain for Portugal ever since the Spanish Inquisition had begun its work in 1480.[24] Given a Portuguese population of about 1 million, this figure seems somewhat high.

It was not for humanitarian motives that the Portuguese authorities received the mass of fleeing Spanish Jews. On the contrary, except for a few Jews who had skills which Portugal badly needed and who paid only four cruzados in entry tax, the Jews had to pay eight cruzados per head in instalments. Those who had not paid after eight months were sold as slaves. In 1493, several hundred children aged between two and ten were forcibly taken from their parents and abandoned in the archipelago of Santo Tomé on the coast of Africa. Most died.[25]

The Portuguese King João II died in 1495 and was succeeded by Manoel I (1495–1521). Following negotiations for the new king to marry Isabel, daughter of the Spanish monarchs, on 5 December 1496, Manoel gave all Jews, whether Portuguese or recent Spanish immigrants, ten months to leave or accept baptism. Yet it was evident that Portugal needed its Jews even more than Spain did hers, given that it was deeply involved in long voyages of exploration in which the Jews played an important role as experts in cartography and navigation, not to speak of the necessary finance. What was wanted was not the disappearance of the Jews but their conversion to Christianity.

Therefore, on 19 March 1497, seven months before the final date previously set for the Jews to decide whether to accept baptism or to leave the country, all Jews were ordered by the authorities to gather along the quays of Lisbon to embark for exile. Fearing perhaps that he might lose so many useful citizens, Manoel issued a decree which prohibited their departure and ordered the Jews to be baptized. Even though he was advised that forcible baptism was against canon law, Manoel insisted that his devotion to the Faith allowed him to proceed in this way for the greater good.[26]

This was the origin of the phenomenon of Portuguese crypto-Judaism, and would be reflected in the Inquisition trials and *autos de fe* of seventeenth- and eighteenth-century Portugal as well as in Spain. The Portuguese Jews, together with the Spanish Jews who had entered Portugal in 1492, were forcibly baptized. Unlike the earlier Spanish *conversos*, they did not submit as a result of decades of pressure and persuasion. These forced baptisms in Portugal in 1497 could not have been religiously meaningful to the Jews. Yet, though by canon law baptism should be voluntary, once carried out it was a valid sacrament, and this was the legal justification for accusing the Judaizers of heresy.

However, the king of Portugal seems to have recognized the unsatisfactory nature of this mass baptism, together with Portugal's urgent need of the New Christians, whom the Dominicans were already harassing, so on 30 May 1497 he issued a decree of protection. Over the next twenty years all investigations into the religious conduct of the New Christians were banned, while the Church was to complete the task of convincing the converts of the truth of their new faith.

After the compulsory baptisms, some New Christians tried to leave Portugal and go to places where other Jews, often members of the same families, lived in relative freedom in communities originating from the Iberian peninsula, such as Antwerp, some Italian cities, North Africa and the Middle East. The result was the decrees of 20 and 24 April 1499, which aimed to make it hard for the Jews to leave by forbidding Old Christians to negotiate with New Christians for the sale of their property.

The Portuguese New Christians, or at least a proportion of them, were commonly thought to be continuing to live as complete Jews.[27] The mob was well aware of the suspicion in which they were held, and needed little excuse to attack them and sack their property, as they did in Lisbon in 1504 and April 1506. On the latter date, during public supplications against the plague, a convert was unwise enough to shout out that what the crowd thought was a miracle was no more than an optical illusion. The man was murdered and the mobs, inflamed by the Dominicans, gave themselves up to three days of murder and pillage. Such behaviour was intolerable for the authorities, who needed the New Christians; Sixty of the rioters were hanged and two Dominican friars garrotted. In order to try to reassure the New Christians, on 1 March 1507 the Portuguese authorities reinstituted the law of 30 May 1497, which guaranteed freedom from investigation of their religious practices for twenty years, and annulled the decrees of 1499 which had sought to impede the selling of property by New Christians who wanted to leave. Clearly alarmed at the danger of losing valuable subjects, on 21 April 1512 the king extended the period during which the New Christians were to be free of investigation until 30 May 1534, thirty-eight years after the compulsory baptisms.

Nevertheless, during the next twenty years the New Christians would be treated with favour one minute and with prejudice the next. Despite the decrees which extended the period for the New Christians to be properly taught to live as Christians, in 1515 the king asked for a bull, which the Pope refused, to allow an Inquisitorial tribunal to be established.

The Portuguese Inquisition

At the end of 1521, King Manoel died, and was succeeded by João III. At this time the New Christians were the victims of hatred for social and economic reasons because, just as in Spain, they were often tax farmers or tax collectors, though the hatred was expressed through accusations against the genuineness of their Christian behaviour. A secret investigation did indeed reveal that Judaizing was widely practised among them. Unlike his father, who was influenced by varying pressures for and against the New Christians, João III was hostile to them. In 1531 he, also, asked the Pope for a bull to establish a State Inquisition. The bull was granted, but much delay hindered the setting up of the Inquisition in Portugal. Nevertheless, on 14 June 1532 the New Christians were forbidden to leave the country, which set a limit to the liberties they had previously been granted. Duarte de Paz, a member of one of the most important New Christian families, travelled to Rome and negotiated the suspension of the bull. On 7 April 1534 he extracted another bull from the Vatican, the first of a long series of what were known as pardons or *perdão,* which recognized the injustice of labelling the New Christians as heretics. Since they had been baptized by force, they had never really been part of the body of the Church. The word *perdão* would appear frequently in the political discussions about the New Christians in the following century. It meant not that Judaizing would be pardoned but that the New Christians could not be punished for that crime while they had not had the chance to be properly taught Christianity, and that their past behaviour could not be used in evidence against them.

After much diplomatic negotiation, on 23 May 1536 the next Pope issued the bull which established the Portuguese Inquisition. However, in 1544, under strong pressure from Portuguese New Christians who lobbied at the Vatican, the Pope suspended all the sentences imposed by the Portuguese Inquisition. Consequently, in its early years the Portuguese Holy Office was relatively inactive: one *auto de fe* in Oporto in 1543, where four Judaizers were burnt at the stake, others in Tomar in that and the following year, one in Evora in 1542 and six more in the following fifteen years, and one *auto* in Lisbon in 1540, is the sum total.[28] Lea, the great American scholar of the Inquisition, gives the figure of 1,998 people punished, 168 burnt at the stake and 51 burnt in effigy, from the foundation of the Inquisition until 1580.[29] This is the only calculation made for the period. Nevertheless, Lea gives the figure of 31,398 reconciled or burnt at the stake or in effigy until 1720, a figure markedly larger than the one given by the Marquis de Pombal, the Portuguese minister who abolished the Inquisition, for the period 1536 to 1732: 24,068 and 1,447 burnt at the stake, a total of 25,515. But even supposing that Pombal's figures include merely the Judaizers and not the others punished by the Inquisition, his figures do not appear sufficiently high. In any case, they go up only to 1732, while the last *auto de fe* with Judaizers took place in 1765.[30] A more recent calculation produces 40,026 trials in the documents preserved from the courts of Lisbon, Coimbra and Evora. There were 760 *autos de fe* with 31,353 people reconciled or burnt at the stake between 1536 and 1794 in the Inquisition courts of Lisbon, Evora, Coimbra and Goa.[31]

Refugees in Italy and Turkey: Gracia Mendes

By the time the Inquisition was set up in Portugal in 1536, the New Christians had enjoyed nearly forty years without Catholic catechization or inquisitorial pressure, more than a generation in which they had been able to develop a particular form of secret Judaism which had taken deep root among them.

When the Inquisition in Portugal finally began to act, the Portuguese crypto-Jews began to seek ways out of the country with their property and families. They went to Antwerp, London, Venice, Ferrara and other cities where, though their Jewish practices were an open secret, either there was no local Inquisition or, if there was one, it was less fierce than in Portugal. The secret Jews were tolerated although, at times, it was not until they arrived in Moslem territory that they felt secure from the long arm of the Holy Office and could venture to practise their Judaism openly. This was the case with the Mendes or Nasí family, the most famous in the history of the *Marranos*.

Beatriz de Luna (1510-1569) was born into a *converso* family in Portugal. At the age of 18 she was married to Francisco Mendes. With his brother Diogo, Francisco built up a business in precious spices, which became a great financial house. Beatriz was widowed young and at the age of 27, when the Inquisition was established in Portugal, she left for Antwerp, where there was an important branch of the family firm, accompanied by her nephew João Micas or Míguez (1524-1579), her sister Brianda de Luna, and her daughter.

Beatriz, known from 1552 onwards as Gracia Nasí, devoted her talents and the wealth of the House of Mendes to bringing Portuguese crypto-Jews out of Portugal and the clutches of the Inquisition. When her brother Diogo died in 1543, the pressures on the Mendes family became intolerable, and Gracia and her nephew fled to another centre of ex-Marranos, this time in Venice. When the situation there turned against them, they fled to Ferrara.

Italy had been a favoured refuge for secret Jews from the Iberian peninsula, at least while they drew breath before moving on to somewhere they could settle permanently. Most of the exiles from Spain and Portugal who reached Italy went to Naples, such as the famous Don Isaac Abarbanel, once a great statesman both in Portugal and in Spain, as well as a noted Jewish scholar.

Expelled by inquisitorial pressure from Naples in 1541, the Jews were received by Ercole d'Este, Duke of Ferrara, a city which became one of the most important ex-Marrano centres, where so settled was Jewish life that in 1551 a press began to publish Hebrew works. This publishing house belonged to Abraham Usque and Yom Tob Atias, and brought out books in Hebrew or in Spanish or Portuguese translation for the liturgical and educational use of the ex-secret Jews who, having been brought up as Catholics, had only the most cursory ideas about Judaism.

In Ferrara, Gracia Mendes began to use the historic pre-conversion name of her family, Nasí or 'Prince'. With the wealth of her trading and banking house she financed the publication of two famous works: the Bible in Spanish, published in 1553, for the use of the ex-Marranos, and another work, one of the most famous of those written by the Spanish and Portuguese Jews who fled from the Inquisition, Samuel Usque's *Consolaçam as tribulaçoens de Israel* (Consolation for the Tribulations of Israel).

In the publishers' dedicatory page to their Bible translation they wrote:

Prologue to the very magnificent lady Doña Gracia Nasí:

It did not appear proper, most magnificent Lady, that having been translated word for word from the Hebrew into our Spanish language (an extraordinary feat never before seen),[32] it should end up in the hands [only] of persons whose favour was of no value to it, but of someone so noble and magnanimous to whose nobility it would be a further ornament. For this reason we wish to dedicate it to Your Ladyship whose merits have always been granted the highest place among us. Your Ladyship's greatness merits this honour as much as our nationhood and love for the land of our birth lays this great obligation on us. May Your Ladyship accept it with the willingness with which we offer it, and may she favour it and aid it with the goodwill with which up to now she has always helped all those who pleaded for her succour. And since Your Nobility is well accustomed to this role we feel safe from any hostility which may arise from the diversity of opinions [about our translation], and we beg Your Lady-ship not to forget our desire to be at her service. May Our Lord keep your person and prosper your magnificent state for many years to come.

Servants of Your Ladyship, Yom Tob Atias and Abraham Usque.[33]

So despite the fact that there was at least one of the publishers who was Portugese, it was the language of 'the land of our birth' — 'our Spanish language' — into which the Bible was translated, for the tradition was that the nobility of Spanish came second only to that of Hebrew, even though the vernacular tongue among the ex-Marranos of Ferrara was probably Portuguese. Generally speaking, in the coming centuries, the Spanish and Portuguese Jews would write their religious works in Hebrew, Latin or Spanish. Portuguese was used for convenience, for community registers and for summoning men to honours in the synagogue service. Spanish, however, was the language for written instruction and religious life, though as soon as the ex-Marranos learnt to read Hebrew they were expected to pray in that language. Spanish had great political importance and was also the language of the rabbinical authorities who served the new communities, descendants of the 1492 exodus to Algiers, Salonika and Constantinople.[34] The Ferrara translation of the Bible, issued many times, would acquire a standing almost as high as the Hebrew text itself.

Circumstances in Italy became less favourable to the ex-Marranos just at the time the Bible was in press, and Gracia Nasí left Ferrara for Constantinople where she dedicated herself to re-establishing Hispanic Jewish life on the shores of the Bosporus. Known as the Lady (*la Señora*) she also reconstructed the silk industry of the abandoned city of Tiberias in Ottoman Palestine, where she died in 1569, one of the most distinguished women in Jewish history.

Her nephew, João Micas or Míguez, had accompanied his aunt when they left Portugal in 1537. Throughout the next twenty years he helped to prosper the activities of the House of Mendes, negotiating with the Emperor Charles V (King Charles I of Spain), with the king of France and with many major political figures. In 1554 he settled in Constantinople with his aunt and married his cousin Reyna. João had, in his dealings with European royalty, become an accomplished diplomat and, ennobled by the Sultan Bajazet, became ambassador extraordinary in the service of the Ottoman empire, with the title of Duke of Naxos. Like his aunt, João financed the publication of literary works and works of Jewish erudition. With the defeat of the Ottoman fleet at Lepanto in 1571, João Míguez's influence declined. He died in 1579, but his widow Reyna, Duchess of Naxos, continued to extend generous patronage to works of Jewish learning until her own death in 1597.[35]

When Ferrara passed under the rule of the Church in 1597, the uncertainties of their position led many Jews to leave for Venice, while others formed one of the most famous of ex-Marrano communities: Leghorn, where they lived in peace until modern times.

3

Portuguese New Christians Move into Spain

The frequency with which pardons were issued – in 1533, 1535, 1547 and 1577 – to Portuguese New Christians who were widely suspected of Judaizing suggests that the authorities preferred to leave them in peace in order to allow their commercial activities to fructify and enrich the country. The exchange worked in reverse also. The offer of money by the New Christians to a permanently needy treasury smoothed the path to the granting of pardons. The pardon of 1577 was conceded by the Crown in exchange for a quarter of a million ducats. The converts were promised ten years free of pressure. Even if convicted by the Inquisition for the crime of Judaizing, their offence would be considered as the first one, so that they would not lose their property, an additional punishment almost always imposed on a second offender. Furthermore, the Portuguese converts were given permission to leave the country, in the hope that their trading, from Brazil, Antwerp or Seville, would enrich Portugal.

The Portuguese Church protested unsuccessfully against the granting of a pardon. So did Philip II of Spain, but to no avail, for the Portuguese king, Dom Sebastian, was badly in need of funds for the military adventure which would end so tragically with the death of almost all the cream of the Portuguese aristocracy and the young king in the deserts of Morocco.

The Portuguese New Christians lived lives of constant uncertainty and anxiety. The pardon granted on 21 May 1577, which was to have been in force for ten years, was revoked in 1579. During the two years of its validity many Portuguese New Christians crossed into Spain. It is from this time that the records of the Spanish Inquisition courts begin to include the names of Portuguese Marranos.

The Portuguese crypto-Jews were attracted to Spain by the apparent somnolence of the Spanish Inquisition, which had so thoroughly destroyed the Judaizing heresy earlier in the sixteenth century. By this time, the Portuguese commercial empire was beginning to decline under the competition of Holland and England. Moving to Spain promised Portuguese New Christians the chance of developing large commercial enterprises in the Spanish empire in America, as well as the traditional occupations of the New Christians such as tax farming royal and private revenues, skilled crafts and the commerce associated with them. Some New Christians would rise to the heights of international finance as money factors, bankers, and suppliers of naval and military stores, although the lists of the occupations of the majority of convicted Judaizers show that they were people of modest means attracted by the apparently greater freedom and prosperity of Spain at the time.

The great age begins

In 1598, Philip III succeeded his father on the thrones of Spain and Portugal. Up to that date, New Christians had been able to leave Portugal only with difficulty. They bought – once more – the right to leave Portugal with a contract to lend the king 170,000 cruzados, raised to 200,000 in 1601. In exchange they were conceded freedom of movement and the right to be appointed to all offices and to receive all honours without being obliged to endure an investigation into their *limpieza de sangre* over more than the previous two or three generations.

The Portuguese Church wanted to restrict the movements of the New Christians, but failed although the three Portuguese archbishops humbled themselves so far as to pay a special visit to Spain to beg Philip III not to grant the New Christians what they wanted. On 2 December 1600 the Portuguese Inquisition declared its own reasons for not conceding the freedoms that the converts had pleaded for. Such were their offences, said the Inquisition, that they could not be wiped out with money. In any case, money thus obtained was tainted and would harm the moral standing of the monarchy. Nor did anyone have the right to alter canon law as it applied to heretics. Besides, added the Portuguese Inquisitors, to pardon the heretics would be an offence against God, especially when it involved Judaizers, who were obstinate and repeated their sin even after begging forgiveness and receiving absolution. All the New Christians, said the bishops in some panic, were like lepers in society. They went abroad to Judaize, but returned to enrich themselves. They went into hiding. Their confiscated property never remained long out of their hands for 'they are cautious and crafty people'. They knew everything, even in the secret prisons of the Holy

Office 'using cyphers which only they understand'. In all, the king should not believe the New Christians when they said that they were asking him to concede the pardon with the intention of living as good Christians from then on. If their goods were given back to them, concluded the Portuguese bishops, they would assume that God had rewarded them for their fidelity to the Law of Moses.[1] As for those New Christians whom the bishops well knew did not Judaize, the prelates of Portugal quoted Scripture: '*Omne animal quod tetigerit montem, lapidabitur*' ('Every animal which touches the mountain must be stoned').[2] That is to say that the innocent would suffer with the guilty by association, just like the animals which might innocently graze near Mt Sinai when God gave Moses the Ten Commandments.

The prelates protested in vain. On 23 August 1604 the Portuguese New Christians handed over 1,700,000 cruzados in exchange for a pardon granted by the Pope at the request of the king, advised by his favourite, the Duke of Lerma, whom the New Christians had bribed heavily. The papal brief allowing the New Christians to leave Portugal was published in Lisbon on 16 January 1605. One hundred and forty prisoners, charged with Judaizing, emerged from the dungeons of the Inquisition, to be received with a hail of stones from the Lisbon and Coimbra mobs.[3] In Seville, an *auto de fe* was planned for 7 November 1604, and many Portuguese Judaizers were due to appear at it. They had come to live in the Andalusian capital which was wealthy from the profits of its monopoly on trade with the Indies. People had travelled long distances to witness the impressive spectacle. However, influential friends of the Portuguese Judaizers had managed to obtain a bull from the Pope which admitted the Judaizers to reconciliation with the Church without the lengthy process of investigating every aspect of their lives. Fast riders brought the bull to the Spanish Court, resident at the time in Valladolid in Old Castile, from where further couriers rode to the castle of Triana on the banks of the Guadalquivir, headquarters of the Inquisition of Seville, bearing an order to cancel the *auto de fe*, which was now imminent. When the Supreme Inquisition Council heard the news, it protested fiercely. Never before had royal authority been used in this way. Not only was riot threatened in Seville but the Inquisition pointed out that its prestige was seriously damaged. The king gave in and the *auto* was held, in the words of the Inquisitors' report, 'to the great contentment of the people. The *auto* was watched by the largest crowd that had ever been seen.' The reason for the excitement and the consternation of the Inquisition when they feared the *auto de fe* would be cancelled emerges in the next sentence of the report: 'The prisoners released to the secular arm gave us no cause to act mercifully towards them.'[4] This means that the victims were people of great moral strength. Condemned irrevocably to die at the stake, they refused to ask for absolution even as they choked in the smoke and as the accompanying monks thrust their crucifixes into their faces to make them beg for absolution. With a word they could have been instantly strangled by the public executioner, who stood ready with his garrotting cord, but they refused.

Some of the New Christians wanted complete freedom of movement so that they could go and live where they would be free of persecution, particularly in Amsterdam, where Jews had been able to live at liberty since 1585 and where, in approximately 1603, the municipal authorities began to tolerate the private practice of Judaism.[5] Suspicion that the New Christians were seeking to leave the Iberian peninsula to be able to Judaize freely led to a royal decree of 8 June 1605 recommending the authorities at frontiers and ports to be extremely vigilant in tracking the movements of suspected Judaizers.

In all these complicated details of allowing or forbidding New Christians to leave or not, there was of course no question of freedom of conscience. It was merely a matter of whether overmuch harshness or excessive leniency towards the New Christians would be less or more likely to retain and encourage their contribution in services, loans and the production of wealth for Spain. A Portuguese historian puts it succinctly: 'Under the urgent pressure of financial stringency, religious prejudices had to be set aside, and the proposals of the Marranos had to be taken into consideration.'[6] Like the Jews of earlier times, the New Christians were tolerated only when they were needed.

Were all New Christians Judaizers?

There were great difficulties in collecting the huge sum that the New Christians had guaranteed to provide. The official list consisted of 6000 families, many of whom tried to leave Portugal without paying their share. Consequently the Pardon was revoked on 13 March 1610.[7]

The difficulty in collecting the required sum arose because, even more than a century after the forced baptisms of all the Jews in Portugal, families descended from them were still identifiable as New Christian, but not all the members of those families Judaized. The evidence suggests that for the Portuguese ecclesiastical authorities a descendant of *conversos* was, by definition, a Judaizer. Therefore, in order to collect the promised sum of 1,700,000 cruzados, a tax was imposed on all the

New Christian families. One very powerful group of wealthy Lisbon merchants refused to pay, claiming that they needed no pardon because they were not Judaizers.

The general political context of the early seventeenth century tended to favour the New Christians, especially those who were merely *suspected* of Judaizing or descended from convicted Judaizers. Following an *auto de fe* held in Madrid in November 1618, the Council of Portugal advised King Philip III to sequester the property of all suspects and then expel them. The king replied that abjuration of heresy when the victim had been merely strongly *suspected* of that crime – known as abjuration *de vehementi* – did not in canon law bring with it loss of the heretic's property, so that if the victims left Spain they would take their wealth with them.[8]

Martín González de Cellorigo's *Alegación*

One of the best guides to the situation of Spanish and Portuguese New Christians in the first third of the seventeenth century is the *Alegación* of Martín González de Cellorigo.[9] The author had been an advocate at the Inquisition court of Valladolid. In 1619, the date of his essay, he was acting judge in charge of sequestered property at the Toledo Inquisition court. He wrote the *Alegación* and had it printed for the private use of Friar Luis de Aliaga, the recently appointed Inquisitor-General of Castile, who may have wanted to make an impartial study of the question of the large number of Portuguese New Christians then flocking to the cities of Spain.

To the reader of his essay, Cellorigo appears to be an original thinker. He stresses that the majority of New Christians were descended from Jews who had lived in Spain since before the death of Jesus Christ. Thus they could not be accused of deicide. Cellorigo demonstrates that while Portugal, with its fewer than three million inhabitants, possessed a large and homogeneous population descended from converts from Judaism, all baptized in 1497, in Spain the situation was not the same. In that country there was a minority population which had Jewish ancestors. Therefore purity of blood (*limpieza de sangre*) that is, the requirement to prove the absence of Jewish or Moslem ancestors before one could hope for certain posts or honours, had a very important role in Portugal where it could discriminate successfully between those of Christian descent and those descended from converts. This was becoming more difficult, however, in Spain, where families had been inter-marrying for over two centuries. In addition, wrote Cellorigo, the

Inquisition in Portugal was more youthful and vigorous; its judgements were harsher and its procedures often more severe than in Spain.

This point was confirmed in 1621 in a document signed by another person who played an important advisory role. This was the King's confessor, Friar Antonio de Sotomayor, who was asked to chair a committee set up to discuss how to treat the New Christians. Although Friar Antonio thought that the New Christians were complaining more than they had reason to ('it is true they make no little complaint and tend to exaggerate the wrongs done to them.'), he admitted that in Portugal 'they persecute them more than is just or more than what Christian charity permits.'[10]

The Inquisition remained highly suspicious. Even Catholic priests had been known to flee the Iberian peninsula and help to found Spanish–Portuguese Jewish communities abroad. Christian devotion was no proof that one was not a Judaizer. When an important financier, Manoel Gomes da Costa, who had complied loyally with the contract he had signed to build ships for the King, applied to be granted the Order of Christ and a title of nobility (*hidalguía*), the Council of Portugal insisted, on 13 August 1621, that it was dangerous to grant such an honour to a descendant of converts because there was always the risk that he might be a secret Jew. To give this New Christian what he was demanding would, wrote the Council, encourage

the people of the New Christian Nation to persevere in their false belief . . . so many people of this Nation appeared at *autos de fe*, some of them canons and parish priests, friars and monks . . . that with all due submission and humility the Council could not fail to point out to His Majesty . . . that such a precedent could cause great damage to religion . . . [11]

At the time that these questions were exercising the minds of members of royal councils, the case of Antonio Homem was being tried in Portugal. Homem (1564–1624) was a descendant of New Christians. He appeared before the Portuguese Inquisition in 1621 charged with spreading the Judaizing heresy at the University of Coimbra, of which he was chancellor and professor of Canon Law, as well as confessor and preacher at the cathedral. According to the charge, Antonio Homem was the leader of a group of Judaizers among the university professors. He was said to organize services and other ceremonies over which he presided, dressed as a priest in the Temple as described in the Bible. The ceremonies at the time of the Great Fast of September (*Yom Kippur*) saw the congregation,

> barefoot and bareheaded, uttering laments and raising their eyes heavenwards, placing the palms of their hands together and lowering their heads to their breasts, bowing to the left and the right, while the prisoner repeated some Psalms of David, without the *Gloria Patri* at the end.[12]

Whatever his intentions may have been, Homem's acts were very distant from Jewish liturgical practice. Nevertheless, he was trying to perform Jewish ceremonies, as is shown in the descriptions of the group's celebration of the Fast of Esther and the Passover. His case is an example of the arbitrary and corrupt practices of the Portuguese Inquisition of which the New Christians regularly complained, for one of the inquisitors, Simão Barreto, was related to one of Homem's many enemies at the university, and was found to have exercised excessive pressure on some youths, with whom Homem was accused of the *pecado nefando*, the Inquisition's codeword for homosexual practices. In the event, however, the general council of the Portuguese Inquisition ordered the youths to be examined again. Despite some evidence of corrupt Inquisition dealings with Homem's valuable property, the evidence of his Judaizing was convincing.

The importance of Cellorigo's *Alegación* in favour of the New Christians is that his awareness of the economic and financial interests of the kingdoms of Spain and Portugal led him to propose solutions that were not as cynical as the ones devised earlier when pardons were granted in exchange for money. He recognized that the presence of the New Christians would be beneficial for Spain. A more appreciative attitude towards the merchant and commercial class in general would exercise a valuable influence over Hispanic minds, whose hostility to commerce had created grave problems for the economy since Spain had become a world power.

Certainly Cellorigo was not appealing for freedom of religion, but only on behalf of those New Christians whom he was representing. We do not know, however, if those New Christians who had asked Cellorigo to appeal on their behalf were genuine Christians or whether they were secretly Jews. Were they perhaps pulling the wool over his eyes?

The Supreme Inquisition Council had previously discussed the recommendation of its Portuguese colleagues that convicted heretics or those strongly suspected of heresy should be expelled.[13] The problem, they concluded, was indeed a serious one. 'Neither with clemency nor with severity did they [the New Christians] cease to persist in their perfidy and evil.' In a simile which compared the Judaizers to the bad humours of the body, they continued:

> evil people are necessary to preserve the good, as happens with the human body. Though it has many bad humours they cannot be all removed because if they are the body will be subject to and brought near to death.

The Inquisitors' recommendation was to 'retain these people with the least damage possible' (*conservar esta gente con el menor daño que sea posible*). It was better to keep them in Spain. There were now so many Portuguese New Christians living in Madrid that a special delegated office of the Inquisition should be set up in Madrid.[14]

Philip IV

Cellorigo was speaking on behalf of men such as Manoel Rodrigues d'Elvas and Duarte Fernandes, delegates of the New Christian merchants who claimed that they did not Judaize. At the beginning of the reign of Philip IV (March 1621) they went to Madrid and offered a loan of 150,000 ducats on favourable terms, asking the king in return to forbid the custom of accepting anonymous denunciations of Judaizing against New Christians.[15] It was because of this, they alleged, that many Portuguese New Christians had fled the country to settle in the Netherlands, contributing to the wealth of Holland and impoverishing Portugal.

This question was uppermost in political discussion.[16] The Church, however, was unwilling to grant any pardon for previous offences or to relax its pressure on the descendants of the converts. The Portuguese Inquisition and, perhaps with slightly less vehemence, the Spanish Inquisition, did not trust the New Christians because active nuclei of secret Jews were still being uncovered. Furthermore, it was well known that the New Christians left Spain and Portugal to go and live as Jews wherever they were tolerated. Thus neither Inquisition was prepared to give up its power to investigate the family history of a New Christian when he solicited a post or honour which required purity of descent.

Papal complaints arrived about the 'multitude of synagogues that they have in Asia, Africa and Europe, and the most recent that they have just constructed in the rebel States'.[17] A Portuguese theologian opposed to any concessions wrote that a pardon could, nevertheless, be granted to those New Christians who paid large dowries to marry their daughters into Old Christian families when with a smaller dowry they could have found a bridegroom among their own people. Effectively, the tradition of endogamous marriage, which as has been seen was taken by the rabbis as a proof of authentic Judaism, was seen similarly by the Inquisitors. The writer went on to say that people arrested for Judaizing were not like the simple Moorish peasants, labourers or at the most craftsmen, whom they had investigated for continuing some Islamic practices earlier in the century and who in the end had been expelled, but monks, friars, lawyers, jurists, doctors and theologians. Expulsion was the only solution, he thought.[18] The Spanish Inquisition, however, recognized that the proposal to exile New Christians was unjust for the innocent and would have no effect on the hardened Judaizers.[19]

These documents of 1621 and 1622 preserve some of the views of interested parties about how to behave towards the New Christians. Freedom of movement into Spain from Portugal had encouraged a substantial number of businessmen and others to flock to the prosperous cities of Spain. The most important of them were at court, where their services as financiers were becoming indispensable.

Olivares and the New Christians

Philip IV, barely 16 years of age, had come to the throne in 1621 with a favourite adviser already in position. This was Don Gaspar de Guzmán, Count and later Count-Duke of Olivares who would be the dominant figure in Castile until his fall from favour in 1643. Determined to find solutions to Spain's problems of empire and finance, energetic and intellectually rigorous, Olivares bore in his character perhaps some traces of his *converso* great-grandfather Lope Conchillos, secretary to the Catholic Monarchs. This Jewish ancestry was ignored when in 1624 Olivares was admitted to the Military Order of Alcántara. He was now *limpio* – of pure blood – for how could a noble *caballero* be otherwise?[20] Spanish converts could move in three or four generations, as did the family of the famous St Teresa of Avila, from being reconciled Judaizers to becoming distinguished Catholic noblemen, simply by marrying into Old Christian families and falsifying their ancestries.[21] The Inquisition was aware of what was happening. It was known, for example, that the great-great-grandson of a victim of an *auto de fe*, whose penitent's robe was still hanging, to recall the shame of the family, in the parish church, held a senior Church post and was an Inquisitor in Seville. This information was written down in an Inquisition file, though whether anything was done about it is not known.[22]

The foreign policy of Olivares was openly expansionist. One of his first decisions was to launch the famous Spanish infantry regiments – the *tercios de España* – against the rebellious United Provinces of the Netherlands, after the peace which had lasted since 1609. His decision would lead to twenty-seven further years of brutal war and to intolerable costs in maintaining the armies and rebuilding the Spanish fleets. Such an aggressive policy required a vigorous economy, which in its turn demanded the cooperation of the bankers and army contractors, many of whom were New Christians. This, logically, demanded some relaxation in the rigour with which the statutes of purity of descent were applied in granting honours and making appointments, together with some moderation in the severity of the Inquisition.[23]

In the summer of 1621 and again on 7 May and 18 October 1622, a group of important Portuguese New Christian financiers – Melchor Gomes d'Elvas, Rui Dias Angel, Isabel Gomes, widow of Juan Rodrigues d'Elvas, and her son Antonio Gomes, and several others – energetically protested to the Holy Office in Lisbon against the request for a pardon made by the representatives of other New Christian families. They insisted that, since they did not Judaize, they had no need of any pardon.[24]

The problem was not one which allowed of easy solutions. It was not merely a question of what was true, but of the impression of the truth that was received. Not everybody agreed that liberating the New Christians from the discrimination they suffered would be beneficial for Spain and Portugal, for they were suspected of harming Spain's interests as much as of favouring them.

One example of this was the currency question. The Spanish Crown minted huge amounts of copper coinage. The resulting inflation meant that the cost of the silver which Spain needed to meet its overseas obligations rose continually. It was calculated that 5 million ducats of silver went abroad annually to pay for the armies in Flanders and Italy, together with naval expenses, while 4 million ducats were spent on imports of wheat. There was a steady drain of illegally exported silver. This is shown by the accusations against the New Christians contained in a paper from the Council of Finance (*Consejo de Hacienda*) dated 24 July 1622, which mentions

the bad opinion held of people of this nation who deal in tax farming and trade and are reputed to use these activities to export much gold and silver from these kingdoms and send it to others of their nation who, in flight from the Inquisition, reside in La Rochelle and other parts of France and in other kingdoms and States, with whom they correspond, and who in the same way place large quantities of copper coinage which their correspondents in La Rochelle, Holland, Germany, England and elsewhere send them.[25]

Counterfeit copper coinage, smuggled into the country and exchanged for silver, depreciated an already inflated currency still further.[26]

How to treat the New Christians presented a serious problem for the Inquisition and the statesmen of the time, as well as for the historian today. The issue is not clear-cut. Most descendants of converts no longer Judaized, but they were clearly identifiable as New Christians and, since some of them, even people who appeared to have led exemplary Christian lives while still in the Iberian Peninsula, did Judaize and indeed lived openly as Jews once they could, how should the State and the Church behave towards people like those who signed the protest? If they were indeed genuine Christians, it was unjust to behave towards them as if they were not. But who could be sure?

Faced with the protest by the New Christians, the royal confessor, Friar Antonio de Sotomayor, wrote to the king on 18 October 1622, recommending extreme caution in the matter.[27] The Gomes d'Elvas group did not want to be included in the pardon requested by the New Christians. Yet, wrote Friar Antonio to his sovereign, presumably giving the young Philip IV the best advice he could summarize from his committee, 'I recommend they be treated with caution lest they get hold of some document which they then use to excuse themselves from their share of any payment . . .'[28] That is to say, Sotomayor suspected that the Gomes d'Elvas group were protesting at having been included in the number of New Christians who had to make the special payment in exchange for a pardon, and that they were not necessarily to be considered as innocent of at least potential Judaizing.

As has been seen, the Spanish Inquisition was not in favour of expelling the New Christians. False converts would be permanently lost. The Holy Office would not be able to use them as witnesses, an important aspect of the method of the Inquisition courts. The answer to the problem was to increase the severity of the Inquisition, continued the document. All Judaizing apostates should be sent to row in the galleys, which was probably the harshest sentence after burning at the stake that the courts ever imposed. Judges ought to ensure that convicted Judaizers, even after serving their sentences, should not practise as lawyers, doctors, apothecaries, surgeons, spice merchants, goldsmiths or silversmiths, nor wear silk or jewels, carry arms or ride on horseback.

The other extreme is apparent in the case of Manoel Gomes da Costa, who also preoccupied the Inquisition. Far from being persecuted by the Holy Office, this man, referred to as the 'Factor of the Atlantic Ocean', who had built ships for the king strictly according to contract, had, as has been seen, applied for the Order of Christ and a title of nobility in his native Portugal. Despite objections made on 13 August 1621 by the Council of Portugal because Gomes da Costa had 'defects of ancestry', other influential voices pointed out that honours had been granted in the past ignoring the ancestry of the person in question. One example they mentioned, which goes to show just how irregular and subject to the pressures of the moment this whole question was, was Diogo Lopes Soeiro, honoured despite the fact that his mother had been condemned by the Inquisition. Finally the king granted Gomes da Costa the honour he requested. Nevertheless, one of the points most in his favour was that he had paid large dowries to marry his daughters into Old Christian families.

Documents, pleas and counterpleas rained down on the king from both New Christians and Sotomayor's committee. On 23 November 1622, a group called The Hebrew Nation in Portugal' ('La Nación Hebrea en Portugal') sent a petition which provides a picture of the clear identity of New Christians in Portugal and the discrimination which they suffered:

> The people of the [Hebrew] nation of Portugal, greatly afflicted and suffering . . . sent Your Majesty a plea which Your Majesty ordered to be considered in a committee chaired by the royal confessor . . . [asking that] in Portugal the Inquisition should proceed as in Spain . . . [the New Christians should enjoy] freedom of movement and the right to sell their real estate . . . and to go to the conquered territory of the Kingdom [i.e. the Indies].[29]

The petition asked that the Judaizers among the New Christians should be allowed to go abroad as well: 'If the bad go, they will free the good ones from their infamy and contagion.' (*Yendose los malos dejaran libres de su infamia y contagio a los buenos.*)

The genuine Christians among the descendants of the converts thought that the presence of Judaizers caused the discrimination to which they were all subject. They asked for all who were descended from Catholic ancestors, by now as far back as their great-grandfathers, to be entitled to be considered for all honours and offices, as in Spain. There, wrote the Portuguese New Christians in a document important for what it conveys of the real meaning of racial discrimination statutes, 'if they do not ask for purity of descent in Castile they should not ask for it in Portugal either, for those who have Catholic great-grandparents.'

Of course, 125 years after the forced baptisms, almost all the New Christians had Catholic great-grandparents, so that by the term 'Catholic' must be understood people whose ancestors had no record of conviction by the Inquisition for Judaizing.

This febrile activity took place during the first 2 years of Olivares's ministry. The new minister had the Inquisitor-General replaced in 1632 by Friar Antonio de Sotomayor, who had taken a diplomatic view about how to treat the New Christians. He was, after all, the king's confessor, and his appointment as Inquisitor-General reflects perhaps an attempt to bring the Inquisition more under royal, and therefore Olivares's, control.[30]

Olivares employs the New Christians

Olivares understood Spain's need to profit from the financial and commercial abilities of the New Christians. Employing them would reduce Spain and Portugal's dependence on the Genoese bankers. Since the twelve years' truce with the United Provinces had come to an end in April 1621, the need to pay armies on time had become the major concern.

Whether Olivares felt some friendliness towards Jews, as his enemies alleged, is hard to say. How important was it that in 1624 the Inquisition gave him a permit to 'possess and read any books written by rabbis who have translated, paraphrased or written commentaries on the Old Testament or any part of it' or that the statesman's library included many Hebrew works?[31] Significance has also been seen in the presence on the Council of Finance between 1636 and Olivares's fall in 1643 of Manuel López Pereira, who had been in the capital since 1623 and would be the future executor of Olivares's will. He was a New Christian, born on the island of Madeira, who had been convicted of Judaizing and had appeared at an *auto* in Lisbon. He had lived for many years in the Jewish community of Amsterdam, where two of his brothers still dwelled, but had come to make his fortune in Seville.[32] His personal religious views and behaviour, however, probably did not matter as much as the value of his advice, for Olivares had a single-minded agenda based on *raison d'état*.

4
Commercial Activities of the New Christians

The Spanish economic crisis of the early seventeenth century had been caused by the intolerably extended burdens of the joint Spanish and Portuguese Crown and by the exhausting war between Spain and the rebellious Dutch. The Spanish monopoly of trade with the West Indies was under threat from British and Dutch intrusions into the Caribbean.[1] To produce more money, the multitude of imposts had to be collected more efficiently and commerce had to be expanded.

Spain had suffered two major setbacks. The catastrophic defeat of the Armada of 1588 had demonstrated that she could not invade England; nor could she assert her dominance over the insurgent Dutch. At the same time, the stagnation of Spanish agriculture and the plagues of 1599–1600 had weakened Spain at home. The consequence was disillusion, the suspension of debt repayments to the Genoese bankers and, in 1609, a truce between Spain and the recalcitrant Dutch.

Olivares understood that Spain needed New Christian help to finance her grand strategy. If the New Christians were to serve Spain and Portugal, some lessening of inquisitorial pressure would have to be tolerated. This was beginning to chime with the spirit of the age, for a more liberal attitude towards Europe's Jews was not limited to the Iberian peninsula. As part of the search for the supreme interest of the State, from the second half of the sixteenth century onward the Jews, previously expelled or forcibly baptized in most countries, had begun to make an appearance on the international mercantile stage. Among the principal participants in the economic expansion which followed the explorations and colonizations of America, Africa and Asia were the Iberian New Christians, many of whom were crypto-Jews, or Marranos.[2]

The change in *realpolitik* in the direction of a more tolerant attitude towards the Jews led to settlements of New Christians in a number of commercial cities. A dozen Portuguese Marranos came to live in Hamburg in 1590.[3] Earlier, the Duchy of Ferrara, the Senate of Venice, the papal authorities in Ancona, the Grand Duke of Pisa and the Duke of Urbino had allowed Jews, mostly of Iberian origin, to settle in their domains. While the right of Jews to live in these areas was never absolute, and they were not infrequently admitted to one Italian city-state only to be expelled from another, from the 1570s onwards the Republic of Venice, which dominated Mediterranean trade, granted rights of residence and became a powerful magnet for Iberian New Christians. Other cities – Pisa, Mantua and Leghorn – followed the example of Venice. As early as 1550 rights of residence in Bordeaux and Bayonne had been granted to the '*marchands portugais*' who were known to be secret Jews. So long as they did not publicize their practices or cause offence to Christians they were tolerated. Groups of secret Jews lived in Rouen and in London.[4]

In 1595, the Dutch blockade of Antwerp, the great entrepot through which the New Christian merchants of Lisbon distributed the sugar, precious stones, woods and spices which they imported from the Portuguese and Spanish colonies, led the New Christians to move to Amsterdam. In 1603, the private practice of Judaism was permitted by the burghers of this city, which would become the most famous of all the European ex-Marrano centres.

The New Christians took advantage of the immense changes which were coming about in the mercantile panorama as a result of trade with the Spanish and Portuguese colonial empires. In the middle of this energetic activity stood vibrant cities, open to the oceans: Seville, Lisbon, Bordeaux, Antwerp, Amsterdam, Hamburg and later London, growing modern centres through which goods passed to and from the distant colonies. The New Christians were active participants in this trade. The Duke of Lerma himself, principal minister of Philip III, wrote as follows in a letter of 16 September 1605, whose exaggerated tone may have been justified by the need he perceived to employ the New Christians: '[I]t is well known that it is the Portuguese merchants who run most of the trade and commerce of Europe. They live in all the main commercial cities, of which the most important is Lisbon . . . '[5]

A New Christian commercial elite appeared and flourished in these centres of international trade. From Lisbon the New Christians sent their relatives to open branches in Goa in Portuguese India, and in Brazil. These agents bought precious woods, jewels, sugar and spices and sent them to Europe. The customs duties on the import of this merchandise had risen, by 1619, to 1.4 million ducats a year.[6] The great

New Christian trading-houses of Lisbon and Seville sent agents through-out the Portuguese empire. They exchanged goods for slaves which they then dispatched to Mexico and Cartagena de Indias, the massive walled harbour on the Caribbean coast of Colombia. Other members of the New Christian clans, beginning as clerks in the counting-houses of Lisbon and Seville, went to Amsterdam, Bayonne, Bordeaux, Nantes, La Rochelle, Rouen, Venice and Leghorn, which were the sea and river ports of western Europe. Their energy multiplied commercial inter-change and the movement of money. They became experts in the trans-fer of large sums of cash, no easy task in days when roads were poor and unpoliced. This particular capacity was of vital value to the king of Spain who had to place massive amounts in cash in countries where his armies were fighting and where his fleets required victuals and stores. *Asientos* or the placing of huge quantities of coin became a speciality of the New Christians. Others did business in Spain itself, importing colo-nial produce and exporting luxury goods to the rich colonial market. Like their Jewish ancestors in the Middle Ages, the New Christians of the Iberian Peninsula developed the manufacture of cloth, silk and lace, as well as occupying themselves with farming royal, noble and ecclesi-astical taxes and collecting rents, as can be seen in any list of profes-sions of the victims of an *auto de fe*.

The grand financiers

Whatever the doubts of the Church and the Inquisition, the realities of war and politics meant that the rulers of Spain had to use the financial opportunities offered to them by the presence of men who understood the mechanisms of international trade and the movement of money. Spain needed loans secured by mortgaging future income. She also required efficient collection of revenues together with facilities to place enormous sums, provisions and war materials in specific places abroad at precise moments.

As well as the armies of Spain in Italy and Flanders, the New Christian merchants provisioned the great fleets of galleons which sailed from Lisbon and Cadiz. To negotiate the contracts, New Christian financiers flocked to Seville and to the Court in Madrid:[7]

> [The New Christians] played a role which was altogether out of proportion to their numbers in the trade of Western Europe. The same language and the same essential culture prevailed among a larger or smaller circle in every port. It was possible for a man to go

from Hamburg to Bordeaux, and from Bordeaux to Leghorn, without any violent sense of change. Correspondence could be conducted over half the civilized world in the same tongue. Most of the important families were international, members being settled in each of the greatest centres. Thus 'credit', in the literal sense, was a social reality, which automatically assisted social intercourse... A commercial nexus was thus formed which has perhaps no parallel in history except the Hanseatic League of the Middle Ages. Certain branches of commerce were almost entirely in the hands of these Marrano settlements. They controlled the importation of precious stones into Europe, both from the East Indies and from the West. The coral industry was a Jewish, or rather a Marrano, monopoly. Trade in sugar, tobacco and similar colonial commodities rested largely in their hands.[8]

In the sixteenth century and at the beginning of the seventeenth, then, the Portuguese New Christian merchants had created the commercial routes through the Mediterranean and the Atlantic and Indian Oceans. As yet they were not involved in the *asientos*, the annual contracts to lend funds and transfer large sums of cash to Flanders, central Europe and Italy.[9] In the financial year 1598–1599 the Treasury of Castile paid interest rates and charges of 14.67 per cent to the Genoese bankers for these services.[10]

The rise of Olivares, chief minister to Philip IV, led to the renewal of war against the rebel Dutch. Olivares was determined to fight this war with a healthy economy, which inclined him towards the New Christians, towards systems of compulsory saving, drastic reductions in overblown officialdom and any mechanism which would stimulate trade.[11]

On 11 August 1622, the first meeting of a very powerful reform committee was held. This was the *Junta Grande de Reformación*. Among its members, besides Olivares himself, were the presidents of all the royal councils, the Inquisitor-General Andrés Pacheco and the royal confessor Friar Antonio de Sotomayor, six further delegates from the royal councils, Olivares's own confessor, the Jesuit Hernando de Salazar, and another Jesuit, Jerónimo de Florencia, confessor of the king's two brothers.[12] Thus men who depended for their positions on the favour of the king and of Olivares formed a powerful bloc together with the Jesuits. The followers of St Ignatius of Loyola had always been rivals of the Dominicans, who had spearheaded the earlier campaigns to baptize the Jews and now ran the Inquisition.

A few months later this junta circulated its proposals on how to treat the New Christians. It sent a letter to all the cities which had a vote at the Castilian parliament, the Cortes de Castilla. The cities replied favourably to proposals that anonymous denunciations against a person's *limpieza de sangre* should not be accepted, that investigations of *limpieza de sangre* should stop after three of them had not proved any Jewish or Moorish ancestry and that family trees in private hands should be destroyed.[13]

If a New Christian's ancestors had not appeared in an *auto de fe*, the fiction was to be that he possessed purity of descent. The recommendation that private family trees should be destroyed had as its purpose the concealing of the Jewish descent of so many New Christians who were always at risk from a blackmailer. Certainly there was no proposal to abolish the application of purity-of-descent statutes altogether, and, as has been seen, those New Christians whose parents or grandparents had been in trouble with the Inquisition were permanently marked by the Holy Office as potential Judaizers, which in many cases they were.

There was, therefore, an apparent attempt at liberalizing the way New Christians were treated. Such a change was politically essential. A report from the Council of Finance in the summer of 1626 revealed the desperate straits of the Treasury. Nobody could be found to accept the contracts to make funds available and supply war material. Olivares had been unable to persuade the cities of Castile to accept a reform of the taxation system. It had taken six months to negotiate the *asiento* of 1625 with the Genoese bankers. The sum involved was 3,250,000 ducats, but the Spanish Treasury would have to pay out an extra 930,000 or 28 per cent in bribes and losses on the exchange, without counting the intolerable interest rates charged. The Council of Finance described the contract as one of the most onerous in many years.[14]

On 31 January 1627, the Crown of Castile was obliged to suspend the payment of interest on the *juros*, the long-term State bonds with which the Genoese bankers were usually repaid. In addition, Olivares devalued the currency. Since the profits arising from the finance contracts included sizeable gains from exchanging Spanish money for other currency, and from issuing and accepting bills of exchange, the suspension of payments was a hard blow for the Genoese. The door was opening for the New Christian bankers of Lisbon and Seville.

State bankruptcy was imminent. On 16 August 1626 a consortium of Portuguese bankers, Nuno Dias Mendes de Brito, Duarte Fernandes, Manoel de Paz, Simão Soares, João Nunes Saraiva and Manoel Rodrigues d'Elvas, had offered to place 421,000 escudos in Flanders. With the exception of Manoel de Paz, all were *hombres de la nación*, that is New Christians, though not necessarily crypto-Jews.[15]

Two months before the Council of Finance accepted this offer to finance the *asientos*, an edict of 26 June 1626 allowed the New Christians
to leave Portugal. At the request of the king, prompted by Olivares, the
Pope granted an amnesty of three months for the secret Jews to confess,
if necessary, without incurring penalties. This was about the most that
could be granted, and a long way from the tacit tolerance current in
many European cities. The Portuguese Inquisitors had been discon-
certed. They insisted that though heretics were treated with great mercy
in Portugal, they suspected that

> Your Majesty has given credit to the complaints and appeals sent by
> those of the Hebrew Nation who are seeking in this way to remove
> the authority of the Inquisition and discredit those who serve it, as
> they have tried to do many times before . . . [The King, they added,]
> would do well to silence them for good, just as Your Majesty's ances-
> tors and the Supreme Pontiffs did when they were convinced of their
> false claims.[16]

Despite the subscription of 240,000 ducats in exchange for permission
to sell their goods and leave the Iberian peninsula, in 1630 the New
Christians were still submitting appeals complaining that obstacles
were being put in their path.[17] A committee headed by the king's confessor reported on 30 July 1630 that the New Christians were legitimate
objects of suspicion, since there were good reasons to suspect that they
not only practised secret Judaism but committed acts of sacrilege also.

Effectively, at that time the Inquisition court was judging the notorious case of the Patient Christ (*Cristo de la Paciencia*), which would end
in a long-remembered *auto de fe* in July 1632. This was probably the case
which encouraged a view not previously evident in all these high-level
discussions. On 27 September 1630, the king's confessor wrote that he
had received yet another petition from the Portuguese New Christians.
Sotomayor commented, in a deterministic tone that he had not used in
the past, that the Jews carried their sin within them, despite baptism.
This was not a very Christian view, but was a common one in anti-
Jewish polemics. And so, wrote Sotomayor, it was still right to hold
suspicions against even genuinely Christian descendants of Jews. It was
a strange view for an important Christian cleric to hold.

A few weeks later, he wrote that even penitent Jews, reconciled with
the Church, could not be trusted. There were so many Judaizers and
apostates among the New Christians that one could rightly suppose
that they were all secret Jews. Nevertheless, Friar Antonio could not

recommend expulsion, because '[T]he kingdom will lose population and will be impoverished because they enrich our enemies with their property.'[18]

After another loan secured by mortgaging future revenues for 240,000 ducats, the movements of the New Christians were further eased. Naturally the king's letter of 25 March 1631, announcing the concessions, underlined the positive aspects of the changes:

> With equal sincerity they [the New Christians] have sought the religious life. It is true that from their baptism until now the religious orders have been and are full of monks and nuns from this people, heedless of cost [of dowries for nuns?]. They appear to join religious orders with such fervour that, even though the doors are sometimes closed to them because of private statutes [of purity of descent], they request dispensations in order to overcome the problem and they even leave their homeland to enter religious orders abroad.[19]

These arguments, based on confused premises – Did they Judaize or not? If they did not Judaize, what reason was there not to treat them as equals? – reached no clear conclusions. As Pilar Huerga Criado, who has studied crypto-Judaism in an area of Spain close by the Portuguese frontier, writes:

> Sotomayor clearly expressed the contradiction implied in accepting the argument of infected blood and rejection of the convert as such, while at the same time the New Christian was considered indispensable, and formulae for retaining him were sought, even at the cost of opening the doors to honourable status.[20]

Perhaps the appeal to the deterministic argument against New Christians was paralleled in the lengthy conclusions of the assembly of Portuguese bishops and theologians, held at Thomar from May to August 1629. Despite nearly a century of efforts by the Portuguese Inquisition, they wrote in their report, crypto-Judaism persisted to such a degree that any Portuguese living outside Portugal was considered to be a Jew. In desperation, apparently, the Portuguese bishops brought up the old anti-Jewish calumnies, such as the killing of Christian children and the poisoning of wells. They even alleged that the offspring of unions between Old Christians and New Christians were effeminate.[21] Probably, they said, the only solution was expulsion. In any case, those New Christians who lived in the Iberian peninsula should not be allowed to take Holy Orders, matriculate at the university to study theology, law or medicine, or practise as doctors, apothecaries or surgeons, since the Portuguese bishops still believed that New Christians with medical knowledge killed their Old Christian patients. Racial fear clearly emerges from the recommendation to ask the Pope to ban 'mixed' marriages.[22]

Nevertheless, the Olivares view dominated decisions; another committee concluded that the Portuguese bishops' recommendations were unjust and unchristian. To ban marriage between *conversos* and Old Christians went against both Canon Law and Natural Law. The recommendations of the Portuguese bishops may be taken, therefore, as important subterranean views, even though they were not put into effect.[23] As Philip IV noted on 25 March 1632, in the present circumstances, an amnesty could not be denied to the New Christians. A general pardon for heresy already committed was essential, because reasons of State so demanded, given Spain's financial difficulties. In the face of the usual opposition to this proposal, the king established yet another committee to look into the question.

One interesting point in this torrent of written documents presented at the highest levels, is that they rarely describe the New Christians as such. Whether the document was written in Spanish or in Portuguese, the New Christians were called 'Jews', 'Men of the Nation', 'Those of the Hebrew Nation', 'Portuguese people of the Nation' or 'Portuguese men of business'. This must mean that many New Christians over the 120 or so years since the mass baptisms of 1492 and 1497 had not married into Old Christian families. One reason for this may have been the unwillingness of the latter to associate with the descendants of Jews precisely because the purity of descent statutes would impede the access of later generations to offices and honours, but obviously endogamy would be essential among those New Christians who were concerned to preserve their Jewish status and the secrecy of their practices.

Matters now seemed relatively satisfactory for the New Christians. Between 1627 and 1629 more Portuguese financiers – Simão and Lourenço Pereira, Duarte Dias Henriques, Marcos Fernandes Monsanto, Garcia d'Ilhão and Pedro da Baeça da Silveira – took a share in the *asientos*. By 1630 the amounts involved had risen to two million ducats.[24]

All this activity led to a significant movement of population. By the middle of the seventeenth century seventy thousand Portuguese had migrated to Castile, and of these forty thousand had flocked to Madrid.[25] The financiers and merchants came to the Spanish capital with their wives, children, relatives, bookkeepers, cashiers and clerks. Many of the employees were people in positions of trust and were, like their employers, secret Jews.[26]

Calculations based on the number of Portuguese described as such in the lists of those who had to undergo Inquisition penances show that 43 per cent of the victims of the Spanish Inquisition in the seventeenth century were Portuguese.[27] Probably most of the others were of Portuguese parentage. The presence of Portuguese was even more marked because they settled in cities or specific areas, and in groups, like most immigrants, and involved themselves in commercial and financial occupations, ranging from the international banker with his private carriage and lackeys, to the humble street vendor of home-made lace, and from the farmer of the *millones* tax on household essentials to the simple tobacconist in a small town. Nevertheless, 71 New Christians shared in the annual *asientos* from 1631 onwards. Meanwhile, as many as two thousand Portuguese merchants lived in Seville, exporting wool to Venice, Leghorn and Flanders, trading with the Indies, importing cloth from Antwerp, France and Italy, bringing spices from the East, and creating a source of capital and credit.[28] Others who had lived earlier in Lisbon and Seville, moved to Madrid and transferred their interest from pure trade to high level public finance. Olivares raised New Christians to influential positions in the Treasury office – the *Contaduría Mayor de Cuentas* – where they had a say in jobs, contracts and financial privileges and where the Count-Duke allotted them major tax farms and collectorships.

Inevitably some New Christians surrendered to the temptation to display their wealth, their importance and in some cases their titles. Manuel de Cortizos, for example, rode in his own coach accompanied by uniformed lackeys. Attended by an army of servants, he lived magnificently in the Carrera de San Jerónimo in Madrid, in a house adorned with Flemish tapestries, furniture from the Far East and silver dinner services. Here, on 16 February, 1632, he offered the king and queen a gala reception with supper and a play.

It is hardly surprising that the rise of such people, Portuguese New Christians suspected of crypto-Judaism, should have provoked some discontent. For the time being, however, Olivares's power prevented any demonstration of protest, which was restricted to scribblings on the walls.

The Inquisition, however, feared nobody and continued its inexorable attack on the Judaizing heresy. The ever-increasing arrival of Portuguese New Christians led to a corresponding increase in the number of *autos de fe*. In three held in Córdoba on 2 December, 1625, 21 December, 1628 and 4 July, 1632, 157 heretics faithful to the Law of Moses were forced to abjure or die at the stake.[29]

In Portugal, the calendar of *autos de fe* had been particularly full. In Coimbra, two hundred victims appeared in 1623. On 18 July, 139 stood on the public stage, and ten were relaxed to the secular arm to be burnt. 75 were dispatched on 26 November, eight being relaxed in person and two in the form of cardboard effigies. A year and a half later, on 14 May 1625, an immense event took place. 189 heretics filed past the Inquisitors, and nine went to their deaths.[30] June 1628 saw 168 victims at Evora, two of whom were relaxed, while in April of the following year 202 appeared at an auto in the same city. Four went to the flames while thirteen effigies of dead or escaped heretics were also burnt. The following month, Coimbra was the scene of another colossal auto, with 210 victims, including eight who were burnt. In Lisbon, in September 1629, 127 heretics were reconciled with the Church.

The issue, not merely of secretly observing the Law of Moses but of committing sacrilege against Christian religious objects, came to the fore in a notorious trial held in Madrid between 1628 and 1632. This was the matter of the Patient Christ, or *Cristo de la Paciencia*, as it came to be known, from a religious house built on the site of the dwelling where the sacrilege was supposed to have taken place. The trial concluded with an *auto de fe* on 4 July 1632 and the burning of the victims at the *quemadero* (burning-place) – the place where the stakes were erected, just outside the Alcalá gate.[31]

Were the accusations of sacrilege a method of preparing the ground for some well-known cases against powerful bankers and important royal contractors? In 1632 the Inquisition arrested Phelipe Dias Gutierres, Henrique Nunes and, most importantly, João Nunes Saraiva.

The case of João Nunes Saraiva

This 50-year-old financier, born in Troncoso in Portugal, who arrived in Madrid in 1606 and began his career peddling in the street, had with others contracted an *asiento* for the Treasury of 1,852,000 ducats, which with interest and other charges totalled 2,159,438 ducats. In 1629 he agreed to make a personal loan to the Treasury of a quarter of a million ducats and to reduce from 24.3 per cent to 15 per cent his commission for exchanging copper ducats for silver escudos. He was denounced to the Inquisition, probably for some personal enmity, by a New Christian woman, Juana de Silva, and, despite his political importance, was arrested in the spring or summer of 1632. Saraiva was suspected not only of Judaizing, of which there was abundant proof, but also of financial manipulations connected with his heresy.[32] He was charged with aiding

New Christians who had been tried and had fled Portugal and needed funds to bring their families out to safety. Saraiva had placed silver and gold with ex-Marrano bankers in cities of the Marrano diaspora such as Amsterdam, Rouen and Bordeaux, where his father had lived until his death in 1631. This was probably true, for Saraiva maintained a network of New Christian agents in Bordeaux and Rouen. He was also accused of importing counterfeit currency and of massive smuggling operations through customs posts also controlled by New Christians.

The trial was lengthy, and Saraiva did not appear at an *auto de fe* until 13 October, 1637. Probably through powerful friends and many statements in his favour, even from Jesuits – rivals of the mendicant orders which controlled the Inquisition – with whom he had commercial dealings, he did not go to the stake. He had been tortured but had kept silent. It is even possible that some Inquisition functionary passed on to him the names of hostile witnesses, normally anonymous, so that Saraiva could identify his enemies. According to Inquisition procedure, the court was obliged to discount their testimony. Apart from evidence of his Catholic loyalties demonstrated by almsgiving and gifts to churches – he claimed that Olivares consulted him at critical moments. Even so, the Inquisitors strongly suspected that Saraiva observed the Law of Moses. The gaoler reported that Saraiva had not eaten some of the prison rations, which made the court suspect that he was obeying the Jewish dietary laws. It was assumed, therefore, that he must have been Judaizing before.

Saraiva's wife, María Nunes, in despair when she saw how ill her husband was after six years in prison and the torture he had suffered, appealed to the Supreme Inquisition Council. She claimed that her husband had lost so much credit and wealth that she and her children no longer had the wherewithal to keep body and soul together.[33]

The accusations proved at Saraiva's trial were, however, grave. The court accepted that he had brought a rabbi from Amsterdam to Bordeaux to circumcise his father before he died. He had helped another who had come to Madrid from Salonika to collect funds to ransom captives from pirates. He paid for lamps to burn in Amsterdam synagogues in memory of his dead relatives. Despite these proofs of Judaizing, however, he was forced only to abjure *de vehementis* – grave suspicions of heresy – and to pay a fine of 20,000 ducats.

The Portuguese of Rouen

João Nunes Saraiva had a correspondent in Rouen. This was Antonio Rodríguez Lamego, whose son, Bartolomé Febos, lived the life of an elegant man about town in Madrid. But the Inquisition had him under observation and arrested him on the night of 13–14 April 1633 in his house in the Calle San Bernardo.[34] On 6 August the prosecutor published the charges against young Febos: he had Judaized while living in Rouen with his father, he demonstrated lack of respect for the Christian religion and he entertained crypto-Jews. As was usual in these trials, Febos denied the accusations. The first witness, an arrested Protestant, had been detained while carrying a draft for 480 silver ducats drawn on Febos and signed by Lopo Ramires (the ex-Marrano David Curiel) in Amsterdam. The witness referred to Febos as 'a Portuguese Jew'. If Febos accepted drafts signed by Ramires/Curiel in Amsterdam, he probably Judaized like him also. Other witnesses spoke of a crypto-Jewish 'mass' and a priest who elevated the Host asking if the Messiah had already come or if he was *going to come*. This sort of evidence, much of it second- or third-hand, was not too convincing. Another witness was Manuel Correa, the lover of a woman, Marta Pegada, who apparently frequented the Febos circle. He claimed that she had said that

> when she went to Judaize with the others they met in a certain house and a Portuguese priest performed the ceremonies of the Law of Moses in Mosaic vestments and in a glass case he had Moses and that the said priest read the Law and ordered her to fast all day and she said she would do so and went to her house and ate very well and that the meat eaten by those who met to Judaize had to be washed several times and all the fat and the blood had to be removed and it had to be mature mutton slaughtered according to the rites of the Law.

This account recalls the ceremonies described at the trial of Antonio Homem in Coimbra. They were a sort of artificial construction based on a reading of the ceremonies conducted in the biblical Temple, very confused with Catholic rites. What, for example, was the meaning of 'Moses in a glass case'? Was it a statue or a picture in a frame, as if Moses were to be compared to a holy image? The clearly Jewish part of what Manuel Correa remembered that his lover Marta had told him was the slaughter of the animal, the washing of the meat to rid it of blood, and the removal of the fat (though Scripture requires only the intestinal fat to be cut away). The important point was that Marta had mentioned Febos and João Nunes Saraiva in association with these rites.

Another witness alleged that he had heard Febos deny the existence of Purgatory, say that he preferred the Old to the New Testament, boast of his Jewish origins and spit three times on a crucifix.

These charges do not seem very convincing. Nevertheless, they were the most appropriate actions if one wanted to 'declare oneself' as the phrase was, and to inspire trust in another New Christian whom one suspected was a crypto-Jew.

The witness Pedro Fernández Correa informed the court about Antonio Rodríguez Lamego, Febos's father, and provided details about the secret Jews of Rouen. Antonio de Acosta, the Madrid commercial agent of both genuine Christians and crypto-Jews in the same Rouen community of Portuguese merchants, provided a list of observers of the Law of Moses in that city.

Febos defended himself, claiming that accusations of Judaizing arose from commercial rivalry. He gave the court a list of enemies of his family in Madrid, mostly people to whom he had refused loans. He hoped that the anonymous denouncers were among them.

The court had difficulties in making up its mind, but it was sure that Febos was not being frank and that he was hiding a great deal. On 4 April 1635 they ordered him to be taken down to the torture chamber. Febos must have realised that the Inquisition did not have enough proof of his guilt. He resisted the immense pain and shock of torture. Unable to condemn him completely, the court imposed a moderate fine of 1500 ducats and required him to abjure de *levis*, that is, acts of which he was lightly suspected. He escaped the shame of a public appearance at an *auto de fe*, abjuring in the hall of the court itself. As for Antonio Rodríguez Lamego, however, Febos's father, whose Judaizing the court found proven, but who was either dead or living in Rouen, the court decided that his effigy should be displayed at an *auto de fe* and burnt.

Rouen, evidently, required an investigation by the Holy Office.

5
Lives of Secret Jews Inside and Outside Spain: Splits in the Rouen Community

Rouen had been one of the earliest refuges for New Christians fleeing the Inquisition.[1] Henri IV of France recognized the commercial advantages that would accrue from their presence and allowed them to reside in this river port which traded with the Iberian peninsula.[2] This early community of Marranos collapsed when the General Pardon was announced in Portugal on 16 January 1605. An era of tolerance seemed about to begin in the Peninsula, and so the Marranos returned. Unfortunately the atmosphere in Portugal soon changed and many of them were arrested the following year. 75 appeared in the *auto de fe* held in Lisbon on 5 April 1609.

Later that same year, fleeing New Christians again settled in Rouen, but this little group would be riven by internal feud and suspicion. The peculiar procedures of the Inquisition meant that reconciled (genuinely or not) Marranos lived outside the Peninsula side by side with New Christians who probably had not Judaized but were in danger because of their association or family ties with those who had.[3] An unpleasant atmosphere of mutual suspicion arose.

In the case of Bartolomé Febos and the references to his father Antonio Rodríguez Lamego (see Chapter 4), a well-known Judaizer of Rouen, two of the prosecution witnesses were Catholic priests who knew the Rouen community well: Diego de Cisneros and Juan Bautista de Villadiego.

Cisneros had been living in Rouen since 1630. His account is preserved in a memoir he wrote for Philip IV, dated 9 April, 1637.[4] In it, he explains that he had had a lot to do with the conversion of Jews, by which he means Judaizing New Christians, in Flanders and in France where refugees from the Inquisition lived who were not necessarily convinced Jews and could be swayed by a persuasive cleric. Cisneros pointed out that there were many such Christians among the Portuguese of Rouen. His memoir describes a world of concealed struggle between New Christians who were now 'New Jews', as Cisneros called them, and others who had been in trouble with the Inquisition or may have been living in Rouen for commercial reasons, but certainly had not readopted Judaism completely. Given that Cisneros was a priest, he naturally explained the tension between the two groups of New Christians as a reflection of what he called the historical hatred of Jews for Christians. 'It seems', he wrote to Philip IV, 'that Judaism finds its greatest satisfaction and achievement in persecuting the Church.'[5]

Cisneros busied himself in Rouen separating the 'Catholics' from the 'Judaizers' and even sending letters with questions to the rabbis of the Spanish and Portuguese Jewish communities elsewhere, presumably to be able to prepare rejections of Jewish arguments. Among the twenty-three questions he sent to Saul Levi Morteira, a rabbi in Amsterdam, were basic issues of theology such as: How could it be proved, as the Jews insisted, that God cannot exist as a trinity, and that the Messiah will be a man and not divine? Other questions showed that Cisneros was unable to comprehend Judaism outside the ambit of his own vision of the truth.

Rabbi Morteira answered Cisneros's questions, adding some more of his own.[6] Cisneros responded with a publication whose title clearly explains its content: *Christian antidotes to the poison of the Jewish replies given to my written questions by the Jews of Amsterdam in September 1631 when I was in Rouen trying to convert them.*[7] Despite his tendency to challenge Judaism in Catholic terms, Cisneros did make an effort to absorb the ways of thinking of his opponents. In his memoir addressed to Philip IV he even cited important Jewish sources such as the *Mishnah* – the first codification of applied Jewish law – and the *Mishneh Torah*, the twelfth-century code of Maimonides, in connection with the attitude taken by Jews towards a Jew who adopts another religion. However, he misread Jewish sources for his own purposes. Cisneros insisted that when a New Christian returned to Judaism and was circumcised, he swore an oath to kill all apostates. This is an example of how an ancient and probably minority rabbinic opinion could be taken out of its context, when the important point was the practice rather than the theory. Of course, Cisneros could never have produced an example of such a murder. In this sense his statement was irresponsible, for he must have known that what he was insinuating – that the 'New Jews' of Rouen murdered those who remained Christians – was a plain lie.

Cisneros, nevertheless, gives an interesting picture of the real situation in Rouen. Unlike in Amsterdam, where the Jews were allowed to live as Jews, in Rouen they still had to appear officially as Christians. Cisneros writes that many Portuguese who did not Judaize dealt on a daily basis with Judaizers but were unwilling to denounce them to the local bishop's Inquisition. 'But in public,' writes Cisneros, 'they keep quiet, dissimulate and dare not accuse them or bear witness against them.' In reality, Cisneros's words can be interpreted as describing not a community riven by hatred where the true Christians dared not denounce the Jews but rather one where people rubbed along together in peace. Perhaps the very presence of the trouble-making Cisneros contributed to awakening the fears and suspicions of the Marranos of Rouen.

Cisneros gave useful information to the Inquisition about other refugee communities. He explained that there were three synagogues in Amsterdam and three in Hamburg, with a total of twelve thousand Jews. Venice had five synagogues, of which the two largest were Spanish and Portuguese. There were others in Leghorn and Pisa. In Cisneros's words, this was intolerable. The Hamburg and Amsterdam communities were in places with 'freedom of conscience', that is to say where the Jews did not need to simulate a false Christianity in order to live in peace. For the Spanish priest, as might be expected, 'freedom of conscience', especially for those who had been baptised, as was the case with the New Christians, was a pejorative expression. These synagogues were widely supported by other Jews, especially other ex-peninsular communities such as Antwerp, Paris, where there were ten or twelve families, Rouen with 22 or 23, Bordeaux with forty, Bayonne with over sixty, Dax with ten or twelve, Peyrehorade with over forty, La Bastide with over eighty and Nantes with a handful. That is to say that Cisneros calculated the Marrano population of France at about three hundred families.

Cisneros's opinion was, in broad terms, similar to the views that the New Christians were putting to Philip IV at the same time, protesting about the suspicions that the Holy Office had of them because of the behaviour of some. Besides, some, if not many, genuine Christians certainly were living among the Marranos of Rouen. The Marrano poet João Pinto Delgado castigates them. In 1631 or 1632, one of them publicly repented having returned to Judaism in Amsterdam. To celebrate the event a banquet was given by a leading real Christian, Antonio da Fonseca, which all the others attended, while Pinto Delgado wrote that the new *converso* 'had returned to the blasphemy in which he had been born'.[8]

The Antonio da Fonseca who gave the banquet was, nevertheless, accused of Judaizing by his son. Another son, Jerónimo, who lived in Madrid, appealed to the *Suprema* against his father's condemnation and offered to pay the expenses of a visit to Rouen by an Inquisition official who could establish his father's innocence. This official, Juan Bautista de Villadiego, visited the city and wrote a report headed *Report by the Licentiate Juan Bautista de Villadiego, secretary of the Inquisition of Seville, on behalf of the Portuguese Catholics of the Hebrew Nation who have come from France, against the Judaizers of the same nation.*[9]

When Villadiego finished examining Antonio da Fonseca, he returned to Spain taking with him 62 New Christians. If the community had 22 families, as Cisneros reported, and if each family comprised, say, 6 persons, Villadiego would have persuaded about half the New Christians to return to Spain.

Actually, he had another mission. Before he left for Rouen, the Inquisition gave him his instructions. He was to find out as much as he could to answer the following questions:

1. Were the New Christians of Rouen, other French towns, Flanders and the Low Countries, Christians or Jews?
2. Did they travel into Spain? If so, which routes did they use? When did they travel? Did they change their names when they came to Spain?
3. Who were their agents and commercial correspondents in Spain? Were they Jews or Christians?

Villadiego left for France at the end of 1632 and reached Rouen early the following year. As he crossed the frontier and stopped briefly at an abbey in Saint Jean de Luz, the abbot told him that all the Portuguese New Christian merchants who lived in the district of Saint Esprit in Bayonne were Judaizers.

As soon as Villadiego reached Rouen he found himself involved in a dispute with the French authorities when the Judaizers accused Cisneros of being an agent of the Inquisition and having brought Villadiegos to Rouen to confiscate the property of the local Portuguese merchants, to the detriment of the general prosperity of the town and of course the royal tax revenues. Consequently, the two Spanish priests and the Judaizers were arrested and only after long and complicated negotiations and the offer of a sizeable sum by the Judaizers for charitable purposes were the latter freed in 1633. Their goods were restored to them and the Royal Council forbade anyone, in particular the Rouen authorities, to trouble them.

The episode at Rouen allows some conclusions to be reached about the real conduct of the New Christians. Were they Judaizers or merely the descendants of Jews, suspected unjustly by the Inquisition? Of course all the so-called 'Catholics' among them had been persecuted by the Inquisition. They cannot all have been innocent. There were three possibilities: that the conflict in Rouen may have reflected nothing more than commercial rivalry; second, that some may have hidden their Judaism more than others; third, that the persecution they had undergone in the Peninsula may have persuaded some to think they had sinned by Judaizing, so that their hostility against the Judaizers reflected their own self-hatred.

Was the latter the psychological path of, for instance, Estevão Arês da Fonseca, born in Coimbra in 1598 of a family whose members had appeared at *autos de fe* generation after generation? He was arrested for Judaizing and reconciled with the Church in Lisbon on 28 November 1621. He left Lisbon for Seville, and from there reached Amsterdam where he joined the Jewish community and was circumcised, though under pressure.[10] He visited the cities – Leghorn, Venice and Salonika – where there were ex-*Marrano* communities. In 1631 Arês da Fonseca reached Rouen where he and his family continued to observe the laws of Judaism. Yet when the Spanish priests Cisneros and Villadiego arrived he asked to be reconciled with the Church and finally returned with Villadiegos to Spain where he gave evidence about Judaizers living abroad.[11]

Meanwhile, Rouen continued to be an important city where the Marrano poets Antonio Enríquez Gómez and João Pinto Delgado published their work.[12] The former was born in Cuenca in 1600 of a New Christian father and an Old Christian mother. His father was accused of Judaizing and fled to Nantes. When his wife died, he married Caterina da Fonseca, a New Christian.

Establishing himself in business in Madrid, Enríquez Gómez travelled to Nantes and Bordeaux. In May 1634 he gave evidence at the trial of Bartolomé Febos. Apprehensive that the Inquisition might arrest him, he left for Bordeaux and then Rouen. In France he devoted his talents to the cause of Portuguese independence, which would be achieved in 1640, and to literary composition. Returning to Spain in 1649, under the pseudonym of Fernando de Zárate, Enríquez Gómez underwent the disturbing experience of seeing his own effigy burnt at an *auto de fe* at

Seville in 1660. The following year, however, image nearly became reality, for he was arrested. He died in prison on 18 March 1663 and, since he was deemed to have showed signs of repentance, his effigy was reconciled in the 1665 *auto*.

He most obviously Jewish work, which was not published, is the Ballad to the Divine Martyr, Judah the Believer, done to death for his faith by the Inquisition in Valladolid.[13]

This refers to the execution of Lope de Vera y Alarcón in 1644.[14] As this was an exceptional case of an Old Christian who had been convinced of the truth of Judaism, Enríquez Gómez was particularly moved by Lope de Vera's martyrdom at the stake, about which he wrote:

> the most wonderful of martyrs,
> the most perfect of believers,
> the most brilliant of beacons,
> the most divine of intellects
>   the sun has seen, the world has known,
> soldier of the ancient army
> of Sinai, suffered so many
> intolerable tortures
> that he recalled the bravery
> of the steadfast Maccabees.
>   He circumcised himself in jail,
> as Abraham had before him, writing himself
> in his own blood
> the letters of the highest bond.[15]

As commercial conditions changed, the Marranos moved from city to city, particularly to Amsterdam and London where probably one of the reasons that induced the Lord Protector Oliver Cromwell to allow Spanish and Portuguese Jews into England in 1656 were the services given by the Marrano Antonio Fernández Carvajal, who left Rouen probably at the time of the conflict created by the priest Cisneros. In England Fernández Carvajal supplied the Parliamentary forces with wheat during the English Civil War of 1642–1646. During the Commonwealth years he provided Cromwell with secret information from his contacts in the Low Countries about the invasion of England plotted by Spain and the exiled Charles II. Another agent was Manuel Martínez Dormido, who began formal talks with Cromwell about the re-admission of the Jews.[16]

How the Marranos of Bayonne prayed

From the evidence of the priests who visited Marrano communities and from what other witnesses told the court, the Inquisition built up large files of information about Judaizers living outside Spain. The purpose was twofold: to provide evidence for prosecutions if anyone from such a community was arrested in Spain, and to learn about Jewish practices in order to be able to charge New Christians with following them. They provide fascinating data of how Marranos, newly returned to Judaism, tried to follow its commandments and, in particular, its prayer customs.

On 23 November, 1661, Diego Núñez Silva, a Portuguese tax farmer accused of Judaizing, was giving evidence before the Inquisition court in Toledo. He mentioned Diego Rodríguez Cardoso, who lived in Bayonne.[17] Núñez Silva said that in 1656 he had stayed in Bayonne with another Judaizer, Rodrigo López Núñez, and a group of Portuguese New Christian merchants who were all 'Observers of the Law of Moses'. Núñez Silva told the court, honestly or not, that he did not care if the others were Judaizers but he had preferred not to declare himself as one because it was 'quite a serious matter in Spain'. When the Inquisitors asked him if he could remember the names of the Judaizers in Bayonne, Núñez Silva mentioned Rodríguez Cardoso and gave a complete physical description of him. He was about fifty and spoke Portuguese, but the witness did not know if he ever visited Spain. He also mentioned a number of others: Diego and Enrique Núñez Cardoso, Manuel Cardoso, Antonio López de Castro, Luis Gómez Silvera and Jorge de Figueroa, names the secretary took down carefully in case they came up again in some other interrogation.

The witness told the court that he used to go to their homes 'to pray and carry out the other customary ceremonies'. The first house he visited was precisely that of Diego Rodríguez Cardoso. The witness remembered the names of up to seventeen people who were present, adding that there were more whose names he had forgotten, and several women.

This group of up to forty Marranos used to meet at seven in the morning to pray in the room on the first floor of Rodríguez Cardoso's house. Each had a prayer-book in a literal Spanish translation, following Hebrew syntax. This must have been one of those published in Venice or Amsterdam for the use of newly arrived New Christians who did not know Hebrew. Rodríguez Cardoso, as master of the house, began with the morning psalms.

Diego Núñez Silva must have attended many times, because he was able to repeat to the court one of the principal morning prayers of the Jewish liturgy:

Oh my God, the soul which thou gavest me is pure; thou didst create it, thou didst form it, thou didst breathe it into me. Thou preservest it within me and thou wilt take it from me.[18]

This was followed by silent recitation of the morning psalms. Rodríguez Cardoso was evidently familiar with the Jewish rite, and waited for them all to finish before beginning the main prayer, the *Shema,*[19]

which must be said and was said by everyone sitting down and without anybody talking about anything else. Diego Rodríguez Cardoso began it and he and the others continued, since it is the custom that one who is older or has more authority begins the recitation of the psalms and until all the others have finished saying them he does not begin that prayer, and when he begins to say it (the *Shema*) all the others begin to recite it also . . .

The court asked the witness if he could say the *Shema* in Hebrew. He said he could, but either he or the Inquisition secretary produced a few words of gibberish which is just recognizable as the first two lines of the *Shema.*. However, he continued to recite this scriptural passage in Spanish, which is almost certainly how the marranos said it:

And thou shalt love the Lord . . . when thou sittest in thine house, and when thou walkest by the way, and when thou liest down, and when thou risest up.

The witness's memory failed him as he tried to complete the *Shema,* but he remembered that when they reached the sentence, 'Blessed art thou, O Lord, who hast redeemed Israel', they all rose to recite the central prayer of the Jewish liturgy, the *Amidah,*

'which is to be said by all standing and with the feet together . . . '

O Lord, open thou my lips and my mouth shall declare thy praise. Blessed art thou, O Lord our God and God of our fathers, God of Abraham, God of Isaac, and God of Jacob, the great, mighty and revered God, the most high God, who bestowest loving kindnesses, and art Master of all things: who rememberest the pious deeds of the patriarchs, and in love wilt bring a redeemer to their children's children for thy Name's sake

The witness continued to quote by heart almost the whole prayer, as if he had actually spent more than the few days in which he had recited it. He particularly remembered the end:

He who maketh peace in his high places, may he make peace for us and for all Israel, and say ye, Amen.

Having finished the *Amidah*,. they took three steps backward, as is the custom.

From all these details given to the Inquisition court by Diego Núñez Silva, one may conclude that the Marranos of Bayonne, newly returned to Judaism, ignorant of Hebrew and probably without a rabbi to guide them, were maintaining the tradition of reciting the daily services, morning, afternoon and evening as the witness said. They all observed the Sabbath and wore clean clothes on that day, a fact which the court secretary underlined.

These Jewish descendants of the converts of 1492–1497 were now living in lands where they could pray and behave as Jews more or less without hindrance. Yet even the secret Jews in Spain had some ways of learning how to observe the religion of their ancestors.

Jews in Spain

There was regular interchange of visits between communities of Marranos outside and within the Iberian peninsula. In particular, people who had enjoyed a Jewish education were vehicles for the transmission of basic information for Judaizers who wanted to learn more.[20] For example, in 1628 the Inquisition was informed that there were circumcised Jews in Madrid from Pisa and Turkey: '[T]hey are in Spain making trouble . . . as is their custom . . . '[21] – that is to say that the person who reported them suspected that they were associating with New Christians and suborning them. Specifically, the report mentioned a young Jewish man from Pisa called Andrés de la Peña, living with a certain Leonor Jorge in Seville. Leonor had left for Madrid with another Pisan Jew named Antonio de Lucena. They could all be arrested in one fell swoop in Madrid if the raid was carefully planned, wrote the agent. In this case the informant had been one Pedro de la Vega, who gave the Inquisition a description of how the Marranos of Pisa prayed. He repeated the *Shema* and explained that, during morning prayers, the Jews wore 'narrow strips' (*corriones angostos*),. that is to say the phylacteries, bound round the arm and the forehead,

> and each one with a strap around his head in that way and another around the left arm, with the end of the strap twisted around the middle finger, and wearing a white shawl over their shoulders... which they call *tallit*, and all those whom he has mentioned here and in other statements and said are circumcised, have been seen by him wearing those straps on the foreheads and arms and that white serge shawl around their shoulders.

The Inquisition rightly feared that such Jews as these, who were Spanish or Portuguese in origin and who knew the religious customs of their faith, would be a dangerous influence on the New Christians of the Peninsula. One of them was Francisco de San Antonio, whose arrest gave rise to a long and complicated investigation.

Francisco de San Antonio

The real name of this adventurer was Abraham Ruben. He came from Fez, in Morocco. Arrested in Madrid, he was judged in the Inquisition court of Toledo in 1624–1625.[22]

Francisco de San Antonio had been reported by Pedro Gómez de Sotomayor, a 19-year-old servant of the Count of Alaguas. What Pedro told the court shows there were Jews in Spain who met New Christians and tried to persuade them to return to the Judaism of their ancestors.

One day, Pedro had been in the first courtyard of the royal palace. This was a place which was frequented in particular by businessmen discussing their affairs, doing deals, and trying to solicit favours or payment from the government offices in the palace. Pedro got into conversation with a man who said his name was Juan Alvarez. When Alvarez learned that Pedro came from Portugal,

> drawing him away to the quieter part of the courtyard, the man told this witness that Portuguese who lived in Spain were strongly suspected of being Jews. This witness replied that it was true, but the reason was that in Portugal the Holy Office harassed those who were not [Jews] so much that they ran off to Castile, and they punish

them here and find that they are Portuguese, and this was the reason for the bad opinion. And then the other man said: 'Of course the Portuguese must have some Jewish blood because there are so many of them [descendants of converted Jews] and nobody can deny that he has some and Your Honour must have some Jewish blood in him because all of us who come from there have some.'

Evidently, the man who had approached Pedro thought that the young man was a New Christian and probably a secret Jew who was afraid to admit it to someone he did not know. 'Juan Alvarez' continued, still according to Pedro's evidence:

Your Honour should know that the Hebrew People were the most prized by God, a people to whom he had been so merciful and whom he had greatly favoured, so every one should appreciate what he was.

Then 'Juan Alvarez' asked Pedro Gómez directly if he had 'Jewish blood' (*raza de judío*) and what his name was. When Pedro had said that the Portuguese Inquisition persecuted genuine Christians he had suggested what he was. Now he gave 'Juan Alvarez' a false name, Méndez, a much more Portuguese and New Christian sounding name than his own, Gómez de Sotomayor. It is difficult to work out the truth through the rather bald statements produced by the Inquisition secretary, but the episode begins to be suspicious. Was Pedro Gómez de Sotomayor an *agent provocateur*?

When 'Juan Alvarez' heard the name 'Méndez', he asked Pedro why he denied what he was, and openly stated that he himself was Jewish: 'Now look, I belong to the Hebrew nation [underlined in the text] and I dearly love the Portuguese because most of them belong to the Hebrew nation.' And he assured Pedro that he could 'declare himself' to him without fear, that is, say he was a Jew.

Walking to a quieter place. Pedro said that he knew very little about Judaism. Whether he said this to 'Juan Alvarez' or for the benefit of the court to which he was telling his story cannot be stated for sure. Nevertheless, he told the other that he knew the Marrano custom of sweeping the house from the outside inwards instead of the reverse. 'Juan Alvarez' told Pedro that they ought to call each other by the familiar '*tú*', 'because all those who belong to the Nation do so', and went on lecturing him: 'You should know that up to now you have lived ... with your eyes closed. You should know that your salvation requires you to make a great effort to learn all the prayers and ceremonies of our Law.'

In his somewhat disordered account, Pedro remembered that 'Juan Alvarez' had told him about the way the Jews of Florence dressed and how in Jewish communities everyone helped each other and especially those who had just arrived from Spain and Portugal. These latter were taught a trade for, unlike in Spain, nobody was dishonoured because he worked with his hands as a cobbler, blacksmith or carpenter.

Pedro told the court that 'Juan Alvarez' showed him some prayers to be directed to 'saints' of the Old Testament, such as Susana, Daniel and Jonah. This would seem to be an elementary way of inclining people towards the Hebrew Scriptures if they habitually prayed to Christian saints for intercession, though of course the whole concept of praying to Bible characters is unknown to Judaism.

Next, they spoke about names. What name would Pedro like to be called? He said he would like to be called Joseph (almost always spelt thus in documents of the time). 'Juan Alvarez' told him that his own name was really Abraham.

They went into a church where Mass was being said. Abraham asked Pedro if he really believed in the Eucharist:

And what about the wine? . . . [T]hey say that the Messiah has already come and that he is really the Son of God and that we crucified him and that is why they persecute us, but all that persecution is to get our property and our money.

'If they catch you,' said Abraham to Pedro,' the best thing is to ask for mercy. You'll lose your property but you'll save your life.' And, using a metaphor which echoed the Christian discourse which the Marranos used, he told him, 'All the affronts are crowns [of thorns] which it [the Inquisition?] puts on each of us.'

Pedro told his master everything that had happened with 'Juan Alvarez' that morning. The count took him straight to the Inquisition, which decided to use Pedro as a spy. So, if he was not an *agent provocateur* before, he certainly was now. They ordered him to associate with 'Juan Alvarez' or 'Abraham' and get more information, obviously with the aim of capturing an entire group of Judaizers.

At his next audience, on 9 November 1624, Pedro told the Inquisitors that he and the secret Jew, whom he now knew as Abraham, had walked together under the trees behind the royal palace. In their conversation, Abraham had brought up the subject of circumcision: '[T]hat little piece of skin you have on your member, the hood, is the worst and most accursed thing you have.'

As they strolled, Abraham told Pedro about the Israelites crossing the Red Sea as they fled from Pharaoh, how Moses drew water from rocks and how the manna which the Israelites ate in the desert tasted of whatever they wanted. He explained Jewish death rites, washing the private parts, cutting the nails and burying the body in virgin earth. He stressed that the Jewish people had received the law on Mount Sinai personally.

Pedro, intelligent as he was, would be a great rabbi, said Abraham. However, great caution had to be employed: 'Speak very quietly, Jew, for the plants and the stones have ears.'

Pedro recalled for the court that as he and Abraham walked through the Lavapiés district towards the river Manzanares, they talked about the great community of Spanish Jews in Salonika. Abraham, who had apparently told Pedro more about himself than the court record reveals, including probable untruths about his employment, said: 'Here we are prisoners . . . you see how they call me Mr. Secretary and show me great respect . . . I shit on it all. I'd rather be in a free land with my head covered where I could serve God as I should . . . '

The next day, the two men met in the busy second courtyard of the Palace. Pedro recalled for the court Abraham's minor comments that indicated suggestions of Judaizing. They went into a church and Abraham said, 'I only come here because the ordinary people expect it.' On another occasion he repeated a rhyme which must have been used by the secret Jews, with its mixture of rejecting the divinity of Jesus with faith in the coming of the divine Messiah: 'God has not come but God will come, God who made me, God will save me.'

By November 1624, Pedro had acquired teachers for Jewish religion and for Hebrew. In the courtyard of the Palace, Abraham had introduced him to a soldier named Francisco de San Antonio, who knew Hebrew. On another day, accompanied by an agent or *familiar* of the Inquisition, Pedro searched for San Antonio and a Hebrew textbook which San Antonio said he lent out for twenty reals a month. Pedro spoke to San Antonio's wife, who offered him a sheet with a printed Hebrew alphabet for twelve reals, a sum which the *familiar* gave Pedro. Consequently the sheet has been preserved among the case papers in the Inquisition archive. It consists of a double folio with a Hebrew alphabet with vowel points. Lower down are several Hebrew phrases taken from the Bible. On the back of the sheet is part of the commentary of Abarbanel (Venice, 1579) to the chapter in Leviticus dealing with the temple sacrifices. The printer may have used the blank side of a spare double folio. Alternatively, the Abarbanel text may have been intended for advanced students once they had mastered Hebrew reading.

San Antonio read over the Hebrew letters with Pedro, recommending he learn them carefully. He taught him some prayers that he had to recite when he got up, went to bed or ate. Among other comments, San Antonio said that 'Juan Alvarez' was happy not to have any children by his wife who was an Old Christian (presumably because the children of a non-Jewish women are not Jewish in Jewish law). He himself was married to an Old Christian, from Santarem, but was thinking of leaving her. 'Accursed be anyone who does not marry one of his own people!' he exclaimed.

The Inquisition was not yet satisfied that it had a firm basis to bring charges, and that it would be able to unmask a network of Judaizers. On 14 November 1624, the Holy Office ordered the detention of Francisco de San Antonio. He was arrested on the corner of the Calle de Teatinos, searched and found to be in possession of a little book 'like a closely ruled notebook' with Latin, Greek and Hebrew words. When his room was searched, an exercise book with the Hebrew alphabet was found. The Inquisition suspected that it had caught a dangerous and daring person.

In his first appearance before the court, on 23 November 1624, Francisco, whose clear and elegant signature betrayed a certain level of education, said his name was Francisco de San Antón or San Antonio. He was 45 years old and had been born of Jewish parents in Fez. Three years earlier he had married a certain María de los Reyes, but there had been no children. Francisco had been baptized in 1616 by the bishop of Antwerp. He insisted that he was obedient to the Church's demands and confessed and took communion regularly. He admitted that he knew Hebrew well, for he had learnt it as a child in Fez.

He had been an adventurous youth and had left home to go to Leghorn and then to Constantinople, where he had engaged in business for many years and travelled in Greece, Turkey, Hungary and Portugal. He had spent three or four years in Amsterdam. In that flourishing Jewish centre he had taught the children Hebrew and Bible.

The court asked him why he had himself baptized in 1616. He answered that God had enlightened him. The Inquisition did not enquire whether his conversion reflected true Christian belief, if he had a difference with the Jews in Amsterdam or if his baptism had been simply opportunistic, but the court certainly suspected something of the sort. San Antonio moved to Brussels and then to Portugal. Here he met María de los Reyes, who had been abandoned by the man who had abducted her from her parents' home. Fearful of her father's anger, she begged Francisco to take him with her. The couple went to Madrid, where he persuaded her to say she was a Jewess, to request baptism and to marry him in church. Evidently, the baptism of a Jewess was an important event, and the ceremony was performed by no less than the Patriarch of the Indies, who proceeded to marry the couple. Francisco and his new wife returned to Flanders where they remained until 17 May, 1621. There Francisco repented having persuaded his wife to undergo a ceremony of baptism when she was already Christian. He confessed his sin to the papal nuncio and was absolved. All this might be true or not. Someone as resourceful as Francisco de San Antonio would tell the story which most suited him, though it would not have been difficult for the Inquisition to discover the truth. The couple came back to Madrid where they had been living for two years when Francisco was arrested.

When asked by the court, according to the usual formula, 'whether he knows or presumes the reason for his arrest', Francisco said it was because he had forced María to go through a baptism ceremony when she was a Christian already.

The court did not take Francisco's statements too seriously. They realized that he was trying to put the Inquisitors off the scent by drawing their attention to something less important than teaching Hebrew and Judaism to New Christians. They told him to go back to his cell and think again. He realized that the Hebrew alphabet sheet was the evidence that was going to condemn him, so he told the court that he had been given it by one Luis de Fuentes, a translator, who lived near the Plaza de Antón Martín. Francisco claimed to have asked Fuentes for the alphabet because he intended to give Hebrew lessons if he and María returned to Flanders.

On 27 and 29 November, 1624, Francisco was given the required two standard warnings or *moniciones* that he should tell the truth. He was advised that the prosecutor had charges ready. These were read to Francisco, including all the details reported by Pedro Gómez as told to him by the talkative 'Juan Alvarez' about the New Christians in Madrid. 'Alvarez' had also mentioned that Francisco de San Antonio was skilled at carrying out the highly specialised art of Jewish slaughter. The court suspected that Francisco was butchering animals for the secret Jews of the capital. Convinced that Francisco knew much more than he had confessed, the prosecutor demanded that he be put to the torture.

Alone before the feared court, Francisco had recourse to all his capacity for inventing stories. He claimed not to have returned to the faith of his boyhood. Quite simply, one day, as he went to the palace with some applications and appeals, he had been hailed by two men. One was called Abraham (this would have been 'Alvarez') and the other was a student, presumably Pedro Gómez de Sotomayor. Francisco told them that he no longer remembered the Hebrew language and therefore would be of little use as a teacher. This implies that in some way the two men had recognized him as a Jew brought up outside Spain. Francisco said that he told them to go and seek out Luis de Fuentes, the translator.

The court then had the famous Hebrew alphabet brought in and shown to Francisco. Despite his feigned inability to remember Hebrew, Francisco translated the printed phrases, taken from the Bible and the Jewish liturgy. The court asked the prisoner if the sheet was used to teach children the laws or ceremonies of Judaism, to which he answered that it was not, which was strictly true. Asked what the Hebrew phrases were for, he said that he did not know. He could have said that they were reading exercises, but he may have wanted to deny any knowledge of the sheet. Teaching the Hebrew alphabet, of course, was not a sin; teaching Judaism and Jewish doctrines was quite another matter. Francisco denied point-blank having taught Pedro Gómez de Sotomayor any Hebrew prayers. He admitted telling the young man that he was married to an Old Christian but denied having stated, as Pedro had reported, 'Accursed be anyone who does not marry one of his own people!' He also denied having slaughtered animals in the Jewish manner in Madrid, though he admitted having done so in Fez, which proved that he possessed the requisite training and demanding skills.

Seeing that Francisco was tying himself up in his lies once more, the court sent him back to his cell to think his answers out again. In Francisco's case this may not have been such a good idea, given his ability to weave tales. After the interval, he appeared in front of the Inquisitors. Now, for the first time, his defending advocate made an appearance and asked the court to absolve his client on the basis of what he had already confessed. The prosecutor, however, opposed this and claimed that he had further evidence. But María de los Reyes, Francisco's wife, who would have been the most important witness, could not be found, despite the public appeals of the Inquisition.

Francisco spent December 1624 in prison. On 10 January 1625 he was brought up into the courtroom where an anonymous statement was read to him. Francisco, however, must have realized that it had been made by another prisoner whom the Inquisition had put into his cell. According to this man, Francisco had told him that he was very worried. He thought that his wife had been arrested. Would she give him away? He told the spy that he knew many Portuguese secret Jews. The other told him that he ought to report them, to which Francisco had retorted,' 'Let the Devil report them. I don't want to.' He then said he had heard of a sodomite whom the Inquisition had burnt in spite of having promised him his freedom if he confessed.

This testimony said little, except that Francisco knew Judaizers and did not denounce them, which was in itself a religious crime. So on 14 January 1625 the court asked him if he knew Judaizers in Madrid, to which he answered that he knew a certain 'Francisco', also from Fez, and that they had spoken of returning there. Another recent convert, 'Pedro de Santa María' had bitterly regretted having accepted baptism and had talked about going to a Jewish community in Italy because he did not want to be buried without a white shroud and unwashed, as he had seen happening to other converts.

Pressed by the court, which knew the answers to the questions it asked but wanted Francisco to confess, he admitted that he had appeared twice at *autos de fe* in Lisbon. It would seem that, despite the alleged severity of the Portuguese Inquisition, he had not been forced to abjure at all at one ceremony and at the other only from slight suspicion – *de levis*.[23]

The evidence was, nevertheless, mounting up, and Francisco realised that he would have to confess something. So he admitted that he and his wife had fasted for the soul of the crypto-Jew Gaspar Fernández, who had died in gaol. Although neither fasting to celebrate a holy day nor as in this case in supplication for the soul of a person who had died was a Jewish custom or requirement, each was nevertheless recognized by the Inquisition as characteristic sign of Judaizing. Francisco and his wife had also fasted on Mondays and Thursdays – how many times is not clear – and Francisco recited what he could remember of the three daily Jewish services.[24] Asked why he did this, Francisco gave the only reason which occurred to him: he did not know that it was a sin to fast on days other than those laid down by the Church. He also confessed that he had wanted to show (to the other Judaizers?) that his wife was Jewish – though she was not – and had taught her to say the *Shema*.

Francisco further admitted the very serious offence of having offered to circumcise Pedro Gómez de Sotomayor. The court told Francisco that he could not be a Christian and at the same time offer to circumcise another for religious reasons. Francisco could only plead ignorance, and admit even more. He had taught Pedro two Hebrew blessings, the standard Jewish way of praising God. He repeated them before the court.

It had been so long since Francisco had prayed with real Jews that his Hebrew pronunciation had suffered some interference from Spanish. Here are the three blessings as the court secretary heard Francisco recite them:

On washing one's hands before eating, a Jew said: '*Baruj atta adonay eloenu meleh haolam, haser qidessano bemisvotav besibano al netilad yadaim*' (Blessed art thou, O Lord our God, King of the Universe, who has commanded us regarding the washing of the hands). Secondly, before eating bread, one said: '*Baruj atta adonay, eloenu meleh haolam, amosi lejem min ha ares*' (Blessed art thou, O Lord our God, King of the Universe, who bringest forth bread from the Earth).

Perhaps an even more serious offence was that, as Pedro Gómez had testified, at the end of Mass, Francisco had repeated the rhyme '*Pan y vino veo, en la Ley de Moisés creo*' (Bread and wine I see, in the Law of Moses I trust). In other words, he had said he did not believe in the Eucharist.

Having heard all this the Inquisitors told Francisco that it was clear that at least two people considered him a Judaizer, so he would be best advised to make a complete confession. But Francisco was a strong and clear-minded man. He asked to be heard by the court, which usually meant that the prisoner was going to confess. He gave the Inquisitors an account of his vicissitudes after he had left the city prison – why had he been in it? – in Madrid in October 1623. He had no money so, together with a fellow ex-prisoner called Mezquita Pimentel, who may have also been a Judaizer, he went to the Calle Fuencarral to visit a certain Manuel López de Montemayor and ask for help. They spoke to the woman of the house who asked him his name and if he had been in Portugal. According to Francisco, this was to discover if he was a New Christian.

One November day in the following year, continued Francisco, the woman called him from a window as he was walking down the Calle Fuencarral. She asked him why she had not seen him again, since 'they were all one'. She knew that Francisco had appeared at an *auto de fe* in Lisbon and that he had been a 'rabbi', a word which seems to have been used among the Marranos merely to mean someone who knew more about Judaism than the others, not an officially qualified teacher and giver of legal decisions. What did he think, the woman asked him, of the rumour that the Messiah was to come that year? This seems probably an invention of Francisco, so that he could tell the court that he had answered the woman that Jesus was the real Messiah.

The court, however, composed of sober canon lawyers, was hardly convinced, and on 8 August 1625 the prosecutor brought further evidence. The detective work of the Inquisition was efficient. Yes, it was true, as Francisco had confessed, that he had been baptized in Antwerp. In Lisbon the Inquisition had been suspicious and had required him to appear at the *auto de fe* and abjure *de levis* on 5 April, 1620. Even though he had been required to undergo a period of intense Catholic instruction, he had still Judaized, which was why he had been expelled from Portugal after the *auto* of 10 January 1625.

The court also knew about his second baptism, which had taken place in the royal chapel and in the presence of the king and queen of Spain. The Inquisitors knew that María de los Reyes had been baptized, though she had been christened at birth. They knew about her marriage to Francisco, which was probably bigamous, since there was some evidence that the man who had eloped with her from her home had married her.

From this it appears that Francisco de San Antonio wanted to begin a new life. If he and María presented themselves for baptism as two Jews who wanted to live as Christian man and wife, this would be a triumphant moment for the Catholic faith, and attract the favour of the king and a ceremony in the royal chapel. A prosperous future awaited the couple.

Francisco, stunned by what the court knew, answered that he had always been a sincere Christian. He knew nothing of María's first marriage. He denied having presented himself for baptism a second time. It was she, not he, he insisted, who had been baptized in Madrid. Nevertheless, the prosecutor had even more to say. According to what Francisco had told him, the Patriarch of the Indies had baptized the couple before marrying them. Then the prosecutor dropped the bomb. María de los Reyes had been found.

How could Francisco have been able to make María say she was Jewish, have herself baptized and married though she was a Catholic and already married? She told Francisco that he was suggesting sinful actions, but he explained to her, with the persuasive assurance typical of him, that if they said they were Jews who wanted to be baptized and live in Christian matrimony, the impression created would be so great that the king would help them. They would surely be able to go to Flanders where nobody would know their secret. She was probably deeply in love with this persuasive and self-confident man. Having run away from home and been abandoned by her first lover, she probably feared that Francisco would do the same if she did not fall in with his wishes.

Francisco was now reduced to denying everything, in the hope that the prosecutor could prove nothing. He again denied that he had been baptized a second time. This may well have been true, and perhaps Francisco thought that, if this could be shown, the court would wonder about the truth of the other accusations.

To strengthen his defence, he listed the names of ten or eleven persons who could vouch for him. His defending advocate asked for the court to question them. The answers certainly confirmed Francisco's insistence that he had not been baptized twice, but they also said that they had not seen him at Mass.

The court accepted, finally, that Francisco was not guilty of having himself baptized twice, but it found all the other charges proven. On 13 September, the Inquisitors decided that, as he was a reluctant confessant – *confitente diminuto* – he should be tortured to force him to tell the whole truth. On the 18th he was taken down to the torture dungeon. As was frequent, the secretary's handwriting becomes shaky and difficult to read as he tried to take down the screams and begging of the victim. This file does not contain the usual word-by-word – *de verbo ad verbum* – fair copy of Francisco's confession, so the reader must try to decipher the scribbling done during the torture session itself.

One may assume that Francisco was semi-delirious as a consequence of the ropes that had been tightly twisted around his limbs. He confessed that in the Palace courtyard he had met somebody called Sotillo (this must have been Pedro Gómez de Sotomayor), who had told him he wanted to be a Jew and had asked Francisco to circumcise him. In the hearing of a certain Abraham, Francisco agreed to teach him the Law of Moses. He also admitted having gone back to Judaism after his baptism in Antwerp. He said

> because he was poor he had wanted to go to Holland to be a Jew and keep the said Law of Moses. He had done so for three years even as he confessed and took communion . . . All his troubles had come upon him for having abandoned our Holy Catholic Faith in which he insisted he wished to live and die.

Francisco ratified his confession on 19 September and admitted also that he had instructed María de los Reyes to say she was a Moroccan Jewess named Cafira. Both had lied at the highest levels, in a statement to the king announcing that the couple wanted to be baptized and married. The point of the lie was, evidently, worldly advantage.

Francisco had lost his defiant battle. Surprisingly, this bold adventurer was not sentenced, as would be expected, to be burnt at the stake, even though he had abjured in Portugal and had resisted confession until forced by torture to admit his offences. Perhaps the Holy Office recognized that Francisco had not received any Christian instruction when he was baptized in Antwerp. The court imposed the maximum sentence below death. On 24 December, 1625, one month after Francisco had appeared at an *auto* as a penitent in the Plaza de Zocodover in Toledo, Miguel Rodríguez, notary of the Inquisition court, signed that he had handed Francisco over to Ambrosio Navarro, governor of the Toledo town gaol, to await the convict gang in which Francisco would walk to Cartagena on the Mediterranean coast to begin the six years in the galleys that he would have to serve, before returning to the Inquisition's own open prison, dressed in the yellow robe of penitence, the sanbenito.

A tough man like Francisco might survive the six years chained to the oar. In the Inquisition prison he might not have to serve more than a year or two. So he could well be free again in seven or eight years and could restart his life. His file, however, contains no more information.

What emerges from the long trial is that there were born Jews in Spain who had had themselves baptized voluntarily for reasons which are not always clear. When they came to know secret Judaizers, they offered them the chance to learn Hebrew prayers and more details about their religion.[25]

The Cansinos

There were also cases of real Jews who had diplomatic status and were thus allowed to live in Madrid despite the Edict of Expulsion of 1492. The best known examples belonged to the Cansino family, which came from Oran, a Spanish fortress in North Africa.

During the sixteenth century, the Jews of Oran were tolerated because they acted as interpreters between the Spanish and the Moroccans. Among them were Isaac and Haim Cansino, whose son Jacob came to Madrid in 1625 to act as interpreter for the Count-Duke of Olivares, the king's chief minister. He lived in the Calle del Olivo, and enjoyed special permission to talk to 'all persons suspect in matters of faith', though he dressed as what he was: a Moroccan Jew. Described by a contemporary as 'very friendly to Spain', he negotiated a substantial loan in 1656.[26] So marked was the mutual confidence and affection between Olivares and Cansino that the latter dedicated his edition of Moshe Almosnino's *Extremos y Grandezas de Constantinopla* to the Spanish statesman[27].

These extraordinary privileges extended to Cansino worried the Inquisition. Rumours flew about that the Jews were going to be allowed to return to Spain. On 19 November, 1643, for example, Juan Ponce, an assessor to the Holy Office and ex-commissioner of the Inquisition in Oran, advised the *Suprema* of the imminent arrival of Jews from Oran, including Jacob Cansino, a 'powerful magician' ('*mágico poderoso*'), whose intention was to use powders and herbs against Spain. Another Jew, Salamon Saporta, was about to come to Spain to sell slaves. Ponce recommended he be expelled immediately after completing his business. If not, he would be seen in Madrid eating unleavened bread on the Passover, killing animals in the Jewish style, 'sneering at our religion and praying for our destruction'. The Supreme Inquisition Council paid scant heed to these alarms. All the same, it recognized that if real Jews were in Spain they might have a harmful effect on the Catholicism of New Christians, and ordered the Valencia court, in whose jurisdiction the Moroccan Jews would disembark, to examine passengers closely and expel any Jew who did not have specific royal permission to land.[28]

If indeed the handful of Moroccan Jews who received permission to enter Spain were able to associate with New Christians, they would constitute a fruitful source of Jewish knowledge. Yet there were very few Moroccan Jews in Spain: Jacob Sasportas and his father-in-law Isaac Cansino were in Spain in 1598; Samuel and Joseph Palache had been in the country in 1579, while Salomon Pariente came in 1620 as the Sultan's emissary. Nevertheless, in 1583 Philip II decreed that any Jew in the Peninsula with special permission would have to wear a yellow cap. In his *Breve discurso contra a heretica perfidia do Iudaismo*, of 1623, Vicente da Costa Mattos assumed that any unconverted Jew had a religious role to play, and insisted that Pariente had been present in 1620 at the deathbed of a New Christian.[29] Furthermore, when Estevão Arês da Fonseca testified to the Inquisition in 1635, he claimed that in 1630 Isaac Farque, an expert *mohel* or circumciser from Amsterdam, had been in Spain.

6
The Decline of Spain and the New Christians

By 1640, the Hispanic crisis was approaching its peak. The renowned Spanish infantry had suffered a series of defeats. In June 1636 the 'Spanish Road', which linked Spanish territory in the north of Italy with Flanders, was cut. In September, 1639 the Dutch admiral Van Tromp destroyed a Spanish fleet. Finally, the expedition sent from Lisbon in 1638 to recover the colony of Pernambuco, occupied by the Dutch, failed. The king's powerful chief minister, Olivares, found it impossible to deal with the situation:

> The Count-Duke was beginning to look like a fireman desperately running from one corner of the building to another with his bucket of water as the flames leapt from place to place.[1]

Both Catalonia and Portugal now raised the flag of rebellion and secession from the Spanish monarchy. On 16 January, 1642, Catalan independence was proclaimed, while in Lisbon in December the Duke of Braganza was placed on the throne of Portugal as João IV.

Olivares falls

Spain was close to bankruptcy, despite desperate efforts to find more money to meet the Empire's insatiable demands, and Philip IV had no alternative but to dismiss Olivares. The Count-Duke, exhausted, aged and sick, left Madrid a beaten man on 23 January 1643. He lived long enough to know of the humiliating rout of the famous Spanish infantry at Rocroi on 16 May 1643. Surviving two years in retirement, he died on 22 July 1645.

The Portuguese rebellion swelled the general suspicion in which Portuguese were held in Castile, especially the financiers, the *asentistas* – those people who guaranteed to provide money when and where the king required – plus the always unpopular tax farmers and, given the suspicions of Judaising, even those Portuguese, from high administrators to mere retailers, who ran the royal tobacco and other monopolies. Castilian xenophobia was aroused. Many believed that the union of the crowns of Portugal and Castile had benefited only the New Christians and Judaizing Portuguese. And this was despite the remittance, between 1641 and 1642, of twelve million ducats to the Castilian Treasury by those same Portuguese financiers.[2]

Those who attacked and brought down the mighty Olivares accused him, among other crimes, of favouring the New Christians. On 7 December, 1639, the provocations of the writer Francisco de Quevedo, author of one of the best-known Spanish picaresque novels – *La Vida del Buscón* – had led Olivares to order his arrest. Quevedo had written a satire against the Count-Duke, entitled *La Isla de los monopantos*, about a fictional island governed by 'Pragas Chincollos', an obvious anagram of Gaspar, Olivares' Christian name, and Conchillos, referring to his convert ancestor Lope Conchillos. According to the satire, Olivares had favoured a camarilla of Portuguese crypto-Jews, who had ruined Castile with their financial manipulations.

The Jews, enemies of Spain

Quevedo's attack exemplified the conspiracy theory constructed to attack the New Christians. Spanish society did not understand that general wastefulness together with the immense cost of war were the real cause of the nation's financial difficulties. Nor did it appreciate that the Portuguese New Christians had stepped in to supply money when in 1627 Castile had suspended debt repayments to the Genoese bankers. Of course the New Christians had sniffed profit in the air. They financed the Castilian Treasury because they hoped to protect themselves against the Inquisition and to overcome the discrimination they suffered. But they had no intention of taking vengeance on Spain for expelling their ancestors in 1492, a myth created by the anti-Jewish writers of the time and maintained in the continuing legend of the Jewish conspiracy against Spain, which was a part of Spanish right-wing writing until recently.[3]

Nonetheless, suspicion fell on the secret Jews and their commercial and family links with Jews abroad and particularly in Amsterdam.[4] The very existence of these communities of Judaising heretics – for all had been baptized – was an offence to the Spanish Christian conscience. Ideas appeared sometimes which could be called racist, in the sense that they assumed that the descendants of Jews, even baptized ones, were irremediably bad. A Portuguese manuscript, for instance, dated in Madrid in 1671 and signed by Dr Roque Monteiro Paym, commenting on a sacrilege committed in a church, insisted that the criminals had to be 'the men of the Hebrew Nation', who were known to be bad because of the curse laid on their ancestors:

> These assumptions are valid generally against all those who are descended from and infected by the Hebrew Nation, because the curse includes all of them. They all have the same blood, and because of their blood and nature, they all have the same characteristics.[5]

The learned theologian suggested expelling all Judaizers who 'after seeing the light of the Church, return to the perfidious blindness of Judaism'.[6] As for those New Christians who did not Judaize, the author proposed the completely unchristian remedy of refusing them any public honours or noble status, as well as maintaining rigid separation in order to prevent 'mixing of blood', that is, intermarriage.

The real problem was that Christian society in Spain was hostile to the very principle of innovation, particularly if it was foreign in inspiration. Castilian values were those of battle and chivalry, and not those of commerce and the lending of money, seen as typical of the Protestant Dutch and the despised Jews.[7] Now, by the Treaty of Munster of 1648, Castile was forced to recognize the independence of the United Provinces where the most important ex-Marrano community lived. Since the Count-Duke had forced new ideas on a reluctant Spain, the reaction to his fall was conservative and traditional. The attacks on Olivares for favouring the Judaizers were unfounded, for the latter had not been protected against the Inquisition during his rule, as the statistics show. But now they were defenceless. Within a few decades, there would be no more great New Christian financiers in Spain.

Spain's losses outside the Iberian Peninsula continued. By the Treaty of the Pyrenees of 1659, she lost Artois, Roussillon and Cerdagne. Other territories were steadily peeled away from the Empire, ending in 1714 with the complete loss of what was left of the Spanish Low Countries and many territories in Italy.

The triumph of the Inquisition

Even during the years of Olivares's maximum power, the Inquisition attack had been relentless. Of the many New Christians who had participated in the *asientos* since 1627, only three were left by 1634, and this despite the favour of the Count-Duke and of Philip IV, who at one stage intervened to protect the New Christians from ill-treatment, as this order shows:

> Considering how well I am served by these people and how satisfied I am with their good behaviour, I order that they be treated like other natives of these kingdoms and as they have been treated up to now. They must not be vexed or harassed.[8]

The services of New Christian financiers were, however, no longer needed. In June 1643, some months after Olivares had fallen from power, the king's confessor, Friar Antonio de Sotomayor, who was considered too tolerant in his stance towards the New Christians, was forced in his turn to leave his post as Inquisitor-General. He was replaced by Diego de Arce y Reinoso, a devout, methodical, disciplined and inflexible ecclesiastic who would preside over the Supreme Inquisition Council until 1655, when both he and his sovereign, Philip IV, died. During Arce y Reinoso's control of the Holy Office, seventeen major *autos de fe* were held, together with many more smaller ones. Thirteen thousand people were made to do penance for their sins, and the biographer of the Inquisitor-General calculated that twelve thousand crypto-Jewish families left Spain.[9]

The rout of the Spanish infantry in 1643 plunged the financial markets into chaos. The bankers worried about the security of their loans, and refused to grant any more. Capital fled to Venice and Amsterdam. When in 1648 Spain recognized the independence of the Dutch provinces, the empire could no longer fulfil its obligations to its creditors. The Spanish Treasury suspended payments, ruining about sixty major financiers in the process. Most of these were Portuguese who were interrelated by marriage and ancestry, so one investigation would pull in large numbers of suspects.[10] Further suspensions of payments of the *juros*, Treasury bonds, in 1662, ruined almost all the Portuguese financiers. Hardly any New Christians took up contracts to supply money in 1670 and 1680.

Large numbers were ruined as the domino effect brought down small businessmen and their creditors in turn. Many denunciations to the Inquisition must have been motivated by rancour. The wealthier New Christians, harassed on all sides, saw no future in Spain and moved to the new communities in Amsterdam, Venice, Hamburg, Leghorn and, from 1656, London.[11] Others, less fortunate, were arrested in droves. Jerónimo de Barrionuevo, observing Madrid from his house in the Calle Real de Lavapiés, noted in his diary:

Nobody trusts the Portuguese, because they go bankrupt every day and disappear, fleeing from the Inquisition. Since the *auto* at Cuenca I am assured that over two hundred households with all their people have sneaked off overnight.[12]

In subsequent entries in his diary Barrionuevo commented that the Inquisition had arrested fourteen Portuguese businessmen since, as he observes some pages later,

there is no Portuguese, high or low, who does not Judaize in Madrid, [and again] not a tobacco retailer has been left at liberty by the Inquisition. Recently [he was writing on 23 October 1655] they have taken two whole families away, parents and children, and many others are running away to France.

A year later, Barrionuevo noted that Fernando de Montesinos, who had been forced to appear at a public *auto de fe*, to abjure and to pay a fine, had left for Amsterdam,

to live in peace, for he fears they will burn him if they arrest him again. He has given his sons their inheritance while he is still alive. It is thought that they will transfer it over there little by little, and that one day or other they will do the same as he.[13]

Barrionuevo was writing in 1656, the year when Oliver Cromwell allowed the Portuguese Marranos who were living in London to shed the mask of Catholicism and establish a Jewish community. However, one hopes that Barrionuevo's notes on events in Madrid were more accurate than what he had to say about England. On 28 June 1656, he wrote that the ultra-Protestant Cromwell had sold three Catholic churches to the Jews, and an entire Irish city which he called 'Galbea' (Could this be Galway?), for the Jews to open a seminary for the training of rabbis.[14] Barrionuevo's absurd exaggeration about the handful of Marranos then in London shows how fearful Spanish Catholics were of these small groups of Judaising New Christians, now living full Jewish lives, who had fled in terror from the power of the Inquisition.

Autos de fe ... month after month

As Barrionuevo, the diarist, had noted, the well-known Portuguese New Christians Méndez Brito, Montesinos and Blandón had appeared at an *auto de fe* in Cuenca on 8 January 1656, while forty-two Portuguese were publicly shamed at the *auto* at Seville on 15 May of the same year. On 24 August, 1660, Barrionuevo noted the penalty of flogging and galleys imposed on a ship's captain, a man of noble ancestry – which made the penalty even more shameful – for having helped some Judaizers to escape.[15] On 11 August 1663, he noted the second arrest of Francisco Díaz Méndez Brito, Grand Chancellor of the Court of the Cruzada (this was not quite as historically dramatic as it seems; the Cruzada was a tax which had originally financed crusades, and which still bore the name). On 10 November Barrionuevo wrote that eleven families had been arrested with four of their sons, who were royal guardsmen, which shows that this was a possible path of upward mobility for New Christians.[16] On 18 July 1665, he wrote that seventeen families and four single men had been arrested the previous week, and that so many people were in the Inquisition cells that a new prison was being built in the Calle Almirante 'capacious enough to hold all those people who fall into the trap every day'.

The numbers of Judaizers who appeared at *autos de fe* in the seventeenth century are impressive. In Toledo alone, from the beginning of the century until 1665 there were 1,906 trials, of which 674 or 35 per cent were for Judaizing. The average, however, obscures a marked increase in the percentage of Judaizers among those tried during the rule of Olivares. This figure rose until in the five years 1636–1640 it reached 40 per cent of all trials, only to fall sharply on the Count-Duke's resignation, to rise again between 1651 and 1665 to an average of 70 per cent of all those punished for offences under Inquisitional jurisdiction.

Inquisition Court of Toledo: Trials 1601–1655

Years	Trials	For Judaizing
1601–05	162	22 (14%)
1606–10	188	17 (9%)
1611–15	122	23 (19%)
1616–20	138	20 (14%)
1621–25	141	16 (11%)
1626–30	87	18 (21%)
1631–35	161	62 (39%)
1636–40	83	33 (40%)
1641–45	144	53 (37%)
1646–50	149	21 (14%)
1651–55	240	183 (76%)
1656–60	150	115 (77%)
1661–65	141	91 (65%)

Total (1601–1665): 1,906 trials of which 674 or 35% were for Judaizing.[17]

In Seville, a peak was reached with the *auto* of 13 April, 1660, when 92 Judaizers appeared in person or in effigy. There were 34 more in the *auto* of 30 November 1673.[18]

In the seventeenth century, Judaizing was the Inquisition crime by definition. Two hundred and ninety-eight of those punished in the 1650s were New Christians. In Cuenca in the twenty years from 1650 to 1670 the average percentage punished for secret Judaism was 61 per cent of all victims.[19] In Granada, the *auto* of 30 May 1672 condemned seventy-five Judaizers out of a total of ninety prisoners. In Córdoba, thirty-four of the forty-eight victims of the *auto* of 29 September 1684 were Judaizers.

Following the most recent and thorough calculation, based on the registers catalogued as *Legajos* 666, 667 and 668 of the Inquisition section of the National Historical Archive in Madrid, Michèle Escamilla-Colin has concluded that in the twelve Spanish courts in the period 1659 to 1739 there were 2,317 sentences for Judaizing out of 3,260 cases in all (that is, 71 per cent). In Cuenca over 97 per cent of those charged were accused of Judaizing.[20] In the seventeenth and eighteenth centuries, Judaizing was the major crime judged by the Inquisition. Unlike most of the other crimes punished by the Holy Office, Judaizing was a crime of persons of high rank and social class. In any case, most of the other religious offences, leaving aside bigamy and sorcery, were often petty and were frequently dealt with by relatively minor penances.

One of the most distinguished victims of the Holy Office at this time was Rodrigo Méndez Silva.

Rodrigo Méndez Silva

Cisneros and Villadiego, the priests who created divisions in the New Christian community in Rouen, were not the only ecclesiastics to spy among the Marranos. Francisco Páez Ferreira also pursued his investigations in Amsterdam and Bordeaux, announcing in consequence that Rodrigo Méndez Silva, royal chronicler to Philip IV, had fled after killing an Old Christian child in Portugal.[21] Méndez Silva was a renowned advocate of patriotic causes. At a time when the kingdoms of the Peninsula were breaking apart, he wrote a work on the subject of national unity, and dedicated it to Manuel Cortizos, an important financier and Judaizing New Christian, who was under Inquisition suspicion though perhaps too powerful to be touched for the time being.

Arrested by the Inquisition in Cuenca, Don Rodrigo appeared with his wife at an *auto de fe* on 25 June, 1662, where the couple were reconciled with the Church. His trial revealed that he had used his genealogical knowledge to construct family trees (perhaps ones which concealed Moorish or Jewish ancestry). He even possessed a copy of the famous and scandalous work, the memoir presented to the king by Cardinal Mendoza y Bobadilla in 1560, known as the *Tizón de la nobleza española* (*Smudge of the Spanish Nobility* or, perhaps, *Blot on the Spanish Escutcheon*), which revealed that many of the noblest families in Spain had Jewish ancestry.[22]

The court, to its credit, ignored the accusation which the probable blackmailer Páez Ferreira had brought against Méndez Silva of taking part in the ritual murder of an Old Christian child. This was the difference between the Holy Office of the Spanish Inquisition and some Churches in other countries, particularly in Eastern Europe. Without really believing in such 'blood libels', they have been unwilling to condemn them, even in the twentieth century. The Inquisition was honest according to its own lights. Its power and independence guaranteed that its prisoners had thorough trials and were not abandoned to the violence of the mob.

Under torture, Méndez Silva confessed that he had Judaized with several others, especially Fernando Cardoso, later to write a celebrated Jewish apologetic, *Las Excelencias de los Hebreos*.[23] He was sentenced to appear at a public *auto de fe* in Cuenca on 25 June, 1662, and to life imprisonment wearing the penitential Sanbenito. Clara Feijóo, his wife, refused even under torture to implicate her husband, but her courage was pointless, for he had already incriminated her in his crypto-Jewish life.

Imprisonment for life, without the possibility of pardon – *perpetua e irremisible* in the standard expression of the Spanish Inquisition – was anything but that. The penitential prison was not the solitary cells of the secret prison in which the suspects were immured during their interrogations. *La Penitencia* had no bars; it was rather like an open prison. Prisoners had to go back to it every night. They seem often to have spent the day begging in the street or doing a little trade to keep body and soul together, for this prison did not provide food for its inmates. Even so, accommodation often became crowded and the Inquisition had to rent houses at its own expense. So normally, after a year or two of perfect Catholic conduct, attendance at Mass and other religious obligations carefully supervised by friars appointed as overseers of the Judaizers' conduct, the *Suprema* would free the captives.

Nevertheless, they had to watch their step. They were still subject to the permanent restrictions on wearing fine clothes and jewels placed on convicted heretics; they had to obey the sentence of internal exile if it had been included in the penalty. In Méndez Silva's case, he told his supervisors that a canon of Saragossa had asked him to come and investigate his genealogy. Méndez Silva went to Saragossa, the Aragonese capital, and, taking great risks, for his sentence had forbidden him to approach the frontiers or ports of Spain, from there escaped to Italy.[24]

His confessions to the court reveal something of the mind of an intellectual Marrano, who owned 1,200 books and manuscripts, as well as numerous paintings.[25] He said that he had been visited in 1656 by a certain Francisco del Hoyo or Enríquez, who told him that he was wrong to believe in Christianity, and this had plunged him into a profound spiritual and intellectual crisis, which had induced him to practise both Judaism and Christianity at the same time. As he told the court, in those two and a half years, sometimes he firmly believed in the Law of Christ, and at other times he hesitated about which of the two Laws was better.[26]

Could this Francisco del Hoyo or Enríquez, who taught Hebrew, have been another born Jew, like Francisco de San Antonio, who functioned as a secret missionary among the New Christians of Spain?

As was the case with not a few New Christians, Rodrigo Méndez Silva, the questioning intellectual, came to be unsure of which faith to hold. Thus he seems to have ended as a sceptic. His flight from Spain took him to the important ex-Marrano community of Venice. He allowed himself to be circumcised but was never seen in the synagogue. Apparently he could not divest himself of the Spanish habit of taking off his hat on hearing the names of Jesus and Mary.[27] As for his heroic wife, there is no evidence whether she escaped with him or not. Perhaps, given her suspicion that he had betrayed her, she was happy to see him go. He decided to take advantage of the rule current in the ex-Marrano communities that his Christian marriage was not Jewishly valid and that he could remarry under Jewish law without the need for Jewish divorce. He married an 18-year-old girl, which at his age was looked on with ridicule.

Flight over the frontier: flight over the sea

At least Méndez Silva solved his problem. Flight ensured his physical safety from the Inquisition. The long lists of fugitives' effigies burnt at *autos de fe* shows how frequently suspects did escape. Yet flight was very difficult in those days of long journeys when to go from Madrid to Bayonne, for example, in a litter or by mule train could take two or three weeks and was expensive because of the nights which had to be spent at inns and the cost of food, not to speak of the peril from bandits and natural disasters. In contrast, the Inquisition maintained an efficient post system which linked the courts and the dense network of lay agents, the familiars, and sent them the descriptions of people the Holy Office wanted to trace, with their height, skin colour, style and colour of hair and all sorts of physical details, including for instance whether a suspect breathed with difficulty because of nasal polyps or if he had a distinctive limp, was pockmarked or squinted. People assumed different names with ease, but they do not seem to have made much attempt to change their physical appearance by, say, shaving their beards and moustaches, or wearing wigs.

Fugitives would probably aim first for Bayonne, just over the French frontier, especially if they were coming from Madrid or the North and East of Portugal. Fugitives from Andalusia might take ship from Cádiz for Italy, and from Lisbon many sailed to England.

There were routes also through Saragossa, Logroño and Pamplona which would take refugees to France. The journey was dangerous, especially for those already posted as wanted, given the web of familiars, agents and busybodies who took pleasure in doing their duty in inquisitorial Spain, with its atmosphere of suspicion and denunciation of those who did not conform. One did not travel alone, of course. The guides and muleteers themselves were not always trustworthy, especially when the Inquisition interrogated them. Were they not to make a full confession, they would be liable to punishment for having aided heretics to flee and continue to practise their heresy abroad. In any case, the guides, Navarrese or Basques, who were usually Old Christians because neither Moors nor Jews had reached the fastnesses of the northern mountains of Spain, had no reason to keep quiet.

On 18 May 1727, an *auto* held in the Castilian city of Valladolid tragically illustrates what could go wrong with an expedition of fugitives. 38 Portuguese Marranos had crossed the frontier into Spain and were making their slow way towards the French border, when they were arrested in Salamanca.[28] One of them, Ana Enríquez Núñez, a 56-year-old widow, who had been reconciled in Lisbon once already in 1703, had found that the Inquisition was still on her heels and had decided to join a party making for France. Judged by the Inquisition court of Valladolid, she was condemned to the stake. The Inquisition's files were well kept, and the court discovered that Ana's travelling companion, Margarita Navarro, had been reconciled at an *auto de fe* in Seville in 1693. She accompanied Ana to the flames. Another widow, Guiomar Gómez Enríquez, who was 71, died in prison. Her effigy was consigned to the flames at the same *auto*, because she had not shown signs of penitence.

Little of the documentation has survived. One would wish to know more of these widows. Had they decided to live Jewish lives in a tolerated community only after their husbands' deaths? Had the latter perhaps been afraid to try to leave Portugal or were the women in fact more inclined towards Judaism than their spouses? And what of their families? Did the women leave sons and daughters, and grandchildren? Or, on the contrary, were they widows who had no family, and now perhaps sought a second husband in Bayonne?

In the same travelling party was Héctor Méndez Lisboa, a 34-year-old bachelor businessman and rental agent. He, together with his friend or perhaps brother, Manuel Freyre Lisboa, suffered harshly though they were not relaxed to the stake. They received two hundred lashes each and five years in the galleys. However, galley service was now being abandoned and the Inquisition decided that the two men were not in a fit state to row. They went to the Penitential prison and were sentenced to internal exile for eight years.[29]

Given the onerous restrictions placed on the Judaizers once they had experienced arrest, interrogation, long imprisonment, *auto de fe*, possible flogging and public shame and then further imprisonment, it is hardly surprising that while some must have been convinced that they had been wrong to Judaize, others took the risk of trying to leave Spain for a freer life in a tolerated Jewish community. Manuel Gómez de Acosta, for example, and his family were reconciled with the Church in Toledo at an *auto* held on 15 June, 1669. Accompanied by his wife Isabel and his three daughters Isabel María, Ana and Angela, Manuel was later arrested in Saragossa from where he was trying to go to France, according to the charge, which was based on evidence from the carters who were taking them.[30]

In front of the court, Manuel admitted that he had been sentenced to exile from Madrid and Toledo. He had chosen Burgos as his place of residence. He had, nevertheless, to support his family. Burgos did not offer very much in the way of commercial opportunity, which was the only skill he possessed, so he told the Inquisitors that he was on his way to Saragossa, not intending to cross the frontier to France, but making for Barcelona, where the opportunities were, he thought, better. The court asked him whether he had not been forbidden to approach any port. He replied that his memory was bad and that the prohibition had not been given to him in writing. In any case, he repeated, he was not intending to leave the country. Nevertheless, he could not explain why the carters had said that they were taking him and his family across the frontier. The court did not believe him, but since it had no convincing proof that Gómez de Acosta and his family did intend to cross the frontier or take ship in Barcelona, they sentenced him to an extra year of internal exile, to be served in Guadalajara, about as far into central Spain as the jurisdiction of the Saragossa court reached. He also had to pay two hundred ducats in costs. When the *Suprema* verified the sentence, it reduced the costs, which Manuel probably could not pay, but they awarded this 55-year-old man two hundred lashes for disobeying the original order to go to Burgos.

Isabel, his wife, claimed that the Inquisitors of Toledo had not imposed any sentence of internal exile on her, or if they had she did not hear it because she was partially deaf. Nevertheless, she had believed that the party were travelling towards Burgos rather than Saragossa. However, the witnesses testified that she knew the wagons were making for Saragossa. She had no answer to this. The court therefore punished her like her husband.

A doctor living in Atienza, in the jurisdiction of the Cuenca court, Antonio de Céspedes, his sister Leonor, widow of Francisco Fernández Pato, and his mother Angela de León, did manage to reach France. The three were burnt in effigy as fugitives at an *auto* held in Cuenca on 22 November 1722.[31] The *Suprema* had ordered the arrest of Fernández Pato and Leonor his wife on 28 May 1718, but when the Cuenca court sent for them they were found to have fled four years earlier. Francisco had died and Leonor was living with her children in Atienza with her brother and her mother. Fortunately for them, Dr Céspedes had made arrangements for flight.[32]

Miguel de Robles's attempt at escape was less successful. He discovered that the Toledo Inquisition was looking for him, since he was one of the most important teachers of Judaism to a substantial group of Madrid Marranos. He decided to leave for Saragossa and from there make his way to Bayonne, where he had been born and brought up. Robles had to abandon his wife and children. She had to stay in Madrid 'both through lack of money and because she was encumbered by four children'.[33] What is to be understood by this apparently selfish and cowardly flight is that Miguel de Robles had to be protected by all means from arrest. If he were forced to confess, he would reveal the entire structure of the crypto-Jewish group in Madrid. Miguel de Robles did manage to avoid the mass arrests of secret Jews in Saragossa also, when several very important people running the tobacco monopoly were caught, including his eldest son Francisco, who had fled from Madrid with his father. He was cruelly punished with two hundred lashes and seven years in the galleys as a 'delaying and insufficient confessant' (*tardo y diminuto confesante*). Manuela, Robles's wife, was sentenced in Toledo on 13 February, 1721: life imprisonment and two hundred lashes as she was led on a donkey through the streets of the city. However, her exemplary conduct in prison inclined the court, in November of the following year, to commute her sentence for penitential exercises. Other details suggest that Francisco may not actually have gone to the galleys, since Manuela was sentenced to be separated from her Judaizing friends and family in Madrid and to live in Saragossa where, either by chance or by her choice, her son was in prison. In June 1727, the *Suprema* gave her permission to accompany him to Granada where, for some reason, he was serving his sentence. Did Manuela ever rejoin her husband, Miguel de Robles?

Judaizers escaped from Lisbon also, even though the Portuguese Inquisition insisted on its right to search ships to check that no suspects were smuggling themselves out. In 1703, Britain and Portugal signed a commercial treaty, which included a clause freeing British ships from customs inspections in Portuguese ports. A probably unforeseen consequence was that Inquisition agents could not search British ships. The Marranos took advantage of this and paid passage to England even in ships of the Royal Navy. The Portuguese government protested against what it considered an abuse of the concessions included in the treaty, alleging that the refugees owed money to the Royal Treasury. However, British traditions of tolerance and ships' captains' eye to a quick profit meant that nothing was done. Some destitute refugee Judaizers even travelled for free, since captains knew that the Spanish and Portuguese community in London would pay up to three pounds for each passage.[34]

Gonzalo Báez de Paiba: the Inquisition mills grind slowly . . .

This businessman arrived in Madrid in 1648 with his wife and first cousin Catalina. Born at Jumilla (Murcia), he had worked his way up in Ciudad Real until he felt ready to take on the opportunities that the capital offered. His file describes Gonzalo as 'a handsome, tall, upright, black-haired and thinnish fellow of about 30' (actually he turned out to be 35), while Catalina is described as beautiful with a good figure, a pale complexion and light chestnut hair, also about 30.[35] Following the usual procedure, the court asked for a potted autobiography (the *discurso de su vida*). Gonzalo and Catalina listed the different addresses in Madrid where they had lived. Gonzalo farmed the income of the salt-pans in Espartina and Murcia. However, when the eastern provinces of Spain had been desolated by plague, he had gone bankrupt and been unable to meet his obligations. On 29 March, 1653, with debt-collectors after him, he took refuge in the Nuestra Señora del Buen Suceso hospital, which offered him sanctuary against his creditors. When the Inquisition sold his property at auction to provide for his upkeep in prison, this realized only 3,250 copper reals, and no cash had been found when his property was inventoried. So, with no money and imprisoned, his fortunes were at their lowest ebb.

Gonzalo had been mentioned in evidence given to the Inquisition by a woman, Beatriz Rodríguez, who had been arrested and threatened with torture during the roundup of the family of the important late financier Manuel de Cortizos. Beatriz, however, revoked her evidence when required to ratify what she had revealed under torture. The point of ratification was to ensure that the victim was giving the information freely. However, if one revoked one's confession one might be taken down to the torture chamber again. Furthermore, a *revocante* risked extra punishment just for denying the truth of a previous confession. However, although a modern court would reject her evidence out of hand, the revocation did not necessarily mean that Beatriz had named Gonzalo spitefully and then had suffered pangs of conscience. She explained to the court that she had not been able to think straight in the torture chamber; she had been confused and demoralized, as was understandable. She claimed she had meant to say that she personally had no evidence that Gonzalo was a Judaizer, only that her brother had told her that Gonzalo had told him he was an observer of the Law of Moses. Gonzalo's guilt was not certain and his case is an example of the Inquisition's thoroughness and persistence.

Like almost all the New Christians arrested by the Inquisition, Gonzalo answered the standard questions in the preliminary interrogation by claiming to be an Old Christian and insisting that nobody in his family had ever been arrested by the Holy Office. Perhaps there was some point to these questions in cases of people charged with offences other than Judaizing. Judaizers, however, committed an offence at once by lying, because the court nearly always knew who they were and quite a lot about their families. Furthermore, while obviously not all descend-ants of converts, who must by the mid-seventeenth century have been numbered in tens of thousands, had ancestors who had been in trouble with the Inquisition, by long experience the court knew that it was rare for somebody to Judaize without having Judaism in the family tradition. So when Gonzalo said that none of his ancestors had been punished by the Inquisition he was telling his second lie.

The accused had the right to offer names of people who would vouch for their Christian conduct. Gonzalo mentioned the priest at the Buen Suceso Hospital, Don Dionisio de Salas, who told the court that indeed he had often seen Gonzalo with his rosary in his hand. Gonzalo also called his own confessor, Friar Simón de Castilblanco. Unfortunately for the Judaizers, putting forward witnesses to guarantee one's pious Christian conduct carried the risk that, if convicted of Judaizing in the end, one would find oneself condemned for performing one's Christian duties hypocritically, and this only added to one's crimes.

The court does not seem to have taken much heed of the defence witnesses, probably because it was not very difficult to find such advocates, given that the Marranos lived a normal Catholic life in public. However, Gonzalo made a mistake when he named Francisco Rodríguez Vejiga, a bookkeeper and administrator of the salt-pans of Granada. Instead of defending him, this man said that Gonzalo tended towards violence, even with women, and alleged that Catalina and Gonzalo were separated for this reason.

Nevertheless, the prosecution witnesses did not seem very impressive either. The most important one of these was 20-year-old Miguel Díaz Jorge, son of the Beatriz Rodríguez who had first mentioned Gonzalo to the Inquisition as a Judaizer. Miguel gave evidence for the first time on 21 April 1651 at another trial. When Gonzalo had gone bankrupt four years earlier, he said, he had been looking after the books of Pablo de Saravia and Jerónimo de Fonseca. While Miguel did not say that these two men had been ruined by Gonzalo's bankruptcy, this may well have led to mutual rancour, which in a court other than the Inquisition would have invalidated most of Miguel's evidence.

Another prosecution witness, the soldier Fernando de Castro Ciudad Real, recalled having stayed with his father among the Portuguese New Christian merchants in Bayonne. He had seen Gonzalo praying three times a day with the other Judaizers. Gonzalo, presented with this evidence, alleged personal malice on the part of the witness and presented an alibi for the time he was said to have been in Bayonne. He said that on the dates in question he had been on a business trip in Andalusia. Fernando de Castro Ciudad Real had not been arrested, but obviously had knowledge of Judaizers because he frequented them. He was offering to tell the court what he knew because he must have been concerned for his own fate. His evidence was suspect to say the least. But so were Gonzalo's witnesses who gave him his own alibi. The court, therefore, sent Gonzalo down to the cells again while it made further enquiries.

Gonzalo was a young man, courageous and high-spirited. Despite having gone bankrupt he was energetic and optimistic. He refused to obey the disciplinary regime of the Secret Prison, despite warnings and punishments. In the secret cells one could, by making an effort, communicate with the other prisoners. The court was told that Gonzalo communicated at all hours of the night and day with Violante de Acosta, Isabel de Silva, Beatriz López, Luisa Rodríguez and other Portuguese women accused of crypto-Judaism. He teased and flattered them in Portuguese, recited poetry to them and advised them about their cases. All of this was, of course, strictly forbidden. Alonso de Cañizares, the gaoler, admitted that he was unable to impose the rule of silence. They all talked to each other ([s]e comunican todos), he said. Even more serious, when he searched Gonzalo's cell, the gaoler found ink, a pen, paper and a rope, all made by the enterprising prisoner from articles and material he was allowed to have. The gaoler threatened him with one hundred lashes, changed his cell and put him in chains and leg-irons.

The regulation of the Inquisition prison, very much milder than the town gaol, allowed flogging in the case of serious infractions of prison regulations. This punishment was inflicted on 20-year-old Manuel López, who managed to escape from the Madrid prison – which stood approximately on the corner of the present Calle San Bernardo and the Gran Vía – but got only about three-quarters of a mile away when he was caught in the olive grove of the convent at the end of the present Calle de Atocha. He was given one hundred lashes in the corridors of the gaol. The prisoners were instructed to open the windows in the doors of their cells, something normally prohibited, in order to witness the punishment.[36]

Báez de Paiba's trial revealed serious irregularities in the running of the Toledo prison. Bartolomé Arias, for example, a young merchant under arrest for Judaizing, managed to get away in October 1651 by letting himself down from the roof of the prison by a rope which he had made from silk stored by Cañizares, the gaoler, in one of the empty cells.[37]

The regulations appear not to have permitted Gonzalo Báez de Paiba to be chained and shackled for long, since the gaoler was soon telling the court again that Gonzalo was saying 'lewd things' (*cosas deshonestas*) to the women, and asking each of them to place a lighted candle in the spyhole of her cell door so that he could look at them. The gaoler was shocked at the loose language, laughter and even singing encouraged by Gonzalo in the secret cells, where terror and guilt were supposed to be augmented by the deathly silence which should have reigned. The gaoler told the court that the prisoners could even exchange messages when they went out into the yard to collect their food from the kitchen or to empty their chamber-pots.

Cañizares appears to have exaggerated the indiscipline of the prison in order to get rid of his assistant, and replace him with his own son-in-law. Still, from what other witnesses said about Gonzalo one may assume that the gaoler's description of him as self-reliant, to say the least, was true. Cañizares told the court that Gonzalo managed to communicate with his wife Catalina and to give her a message

> that she should not worry about the charges, which were nothing, that she should blame everything on him, and that if she did not do what he said . . . as soon as he got out he would stab her.

She replied 'that he need not worry, for she would stand firm and do what he told her even if they broke her into little pieces.'

Before the court stood a man of spirit, accustomed to getting his own way, and a brave woman. While Gonzalo defended himself in the courtroom, Catalina, naked, embarrassed, fearful but not demoralised, endured torture silently. She admitted nothing. The court could do no more. It recognized that the evidence of Beatriz Rodríguez, her son Miguel Díaz Jorge and the soldier Fernando de Castro Ciudad Real was unreliable. So Catalina and Gonzalo heard their sentence in the courtroom itself, without being required to undergo the shame of appearing at the public *auto de fe*. Husband and wife would be, in the formulaic language of the Inquisition, 'severely reprimanded, admonished and warned'. In addition they would be expelled from Toledo, where they had been judged, from Madrid and from Ciudad Real, where they had lived.

Gonzalo and Catalina emerged from prison on 27 January 1657. Gonzalo had not been mistaken when he assured his wife that so long as she kept silent under torture they would have nothing to fear.

People who lived in an age when pain, hunger, sickness and death were always close, had different attitudes towards such vicissitudes of life. Gonzalo enjoyed two years of freedom. He seems to have been free of his debts and was now administering the *millones* tax in Medina del

Campo. He took an over-confident attitude towards matters in general and on 23 March 1659 found himself once more in the Inquisition gaol. Gonzalo appears to have Judaized when he felt most safe doing so, that is when he was among the New Christians of Bayonne. That is where he and Catalina had gone after leaving prison and where Catalina had died in childbirth, a pregnancy which had resulted perhaps from their first amorous encounter after their release. Denounced by people who evidently acted as Inquisition spies in Bayonne, this time Gonzalo confessed. He said that in 1657 he had left Catalina, who was ill, possibly as a result of torture or perhaps because of the early weeks of her pregnancy, with a Portuguese doctor in the Calle de Alcalá in Madrid. Gonzalo had decided to go to Rome. On the way he decided to settle in the Saint Esprit district of Bayonne, where the Portuguese merchants lived. This may have been true, but Gonzalo may have lied about his intention to go to Rome in order to suggest that he settled in Bayonne by chance. Catalina followed him and, according to Gonzalo, told him that she had been Judaizing for years. He, Gonzalo, had not Judaized before his first trial. In this way he cast the blame on Catalina, who was now dead and beyond the reach of the Holy Office. Fortunately for Gonzalo, the Inquisition's doctor and surgeon had established that Gonzalo had not been circumcised and did not even have a scar to show that any operation had been performed on his member. Gonzalo explained that, though he did Judaize – the witnesses were trustworthy at this trial and he could not deny their evidence – he had not had the courage to undergo the operation. Given Gonzalo's personal valour, he probably meant that he had not decided to take the final step. It was a grave risk to run if he ever returned to Spain.

Indeed, he did return to Spain from Bayonne, convinced that he had erred – so he told the court – and was about to approach the Inquisition to make his confession when the post of administrator of the *millones* tax in Medina del Campo came up. He went to this centre of Castilian trade, changing his name to Gonzalo Pacheco de Luna. Presumably this was because somebody who had been found guilty of heresy could not occupy a post of profit under the Crown.

By now the court realized that it had before it a man with considerable capacity of invention. There was no point in tackling the prisoner on his own stories. But the Inquisition went into all the recondite details of a person's life, and here they asked Gonzalo a question for which he was unprepared. Why had he concealed the fact that his mother Clara Enríquez had been reconciled by the Inquisition court in Murcia in 1621? Taken aback for a moment, Gonzalo gave the only possible answer in the circumstances. He said he did not know, though it is unclear whether he meant that he did not know she had been reconciled or he did not know why he had not admitted it.

This time, Gonzalo's punishment was greater. However, since his first sentence had not required abjuration, he could not be said to have relapsed. The sentence, read at a public *auto de fe* on 21 December 1659, sentenced Gonzalo to life imprisonment wearing the sanbenito, which meant that he would remain in the Penitential prison until the court considered him cured of his tendency to Judaize. He was also sentenced to those civil disabilities which were also imposed on heretics: to internal exile and to prohibition from approaching the coasts or frontiers. He should not even think of going to Judaize in Bayonne. Aware of the ingenuity of this enterprising man, the court forbade him to change his surname.

A year and a half later, on 25 May, 1661, he was allowed to remove his penitential robe, and this allowed him to go round and about his new place of residence without everyone sneering at him as a convicted heretic. Not long before this concession, he had been brought up again before the court. Joseph García de León, another suspected Judaizer, had mentioned Gonzalo Báez de Paiba as having taken part in prayers in Bayonne. There was some discussion about whether Gonzalo had been *diminuto* in his previous confession but, fortunately for him, the court dismissed this and Gonzalo's third trial was stopped.

Nevertheless, this foolhardy man was arrested again in 1664. He was now inspector of the *millones* tax in Jaén in Upper Andalusia, calling himself Gonzalo Pérez de Villagarcía. The change of name was cause for suspicion alone and, moreover, had been specifically prohibited as part of his earlier sentence. This time he was betrayed by some details which emerged from his correspondence with another Portuguese Judaizer, Diego Gómez de Salazar. In this, Gonzalo's fourth trial, held in the Madrid delegated court of the Inquisition, Gonzalo admitted having disobeyed the order of internal exile imposed by the 1661 sentence. Now, the Inquisition produced a long list of witnesses against him. He was accused of having drugged himself so as to endure torture at a previous trial. His sentence was read on 7 June 1669. Perhaps because Gonzalo had defended himself spiritedly and because, despite the witnesses, it was hard to prove anything against him definitely, he was sentenced only to abjure *de levis*. Nevertheless, the court was outraged by his defiance when it was accustomed to frightened submission from those who appeared before it, so they awarded him two hundred lashes and, what was worse, eight years in the galleys. If he had been born in

1619 as he said, he was now fifty. The sentence would be hard to survive.

It was the Catholic Kings, urgently in need of rowers for their royal galleys, who persuaded the Pope to allow Inquisition convicts to be sent to the galleys for the first few years of a life sentence. Thus heretics and bigamists, blasphemers, false witnesses and those who pretended to be priests when they were not, especially if they had behaved defiantly or insolently to the court, could be punished without cost to the Inquisition's frequently depleted coffers. Between 1660 and 1739, in the Inquisition courts of Castile, a third of those punished with the humiliating and shameful penalties of flogging and galleys received some years on the rower's bench. Normally, five years was the sentence; three was the minimum, but some people received eight, after which they were to be brought back to serve their 'life' sentence in the Inquisition gaol. Medical examination, however, frequently showed that age, illness, the effects of torture or, with surprising frequency, a hernia, made a man useless for the galleys. By the eighteenth century, 'galleys' usually meant a spell of forced labour in a convict prison or military fortress. Galleys as a punishment was finally abolished in 1748. All the same, as late as 1745, in Valladolid, two Judaizers, Miguel Gutiérrez, 64, and Francisco García, 55, who had both been reconciled many decades earlier in the same city, were sentenced to ten years in the galleys, as well as two hundred lashes.[38] One hopes that the *Suprema*, which examined all sentences at this time, excused them the galleys, a sentence imposed on 61 Judaizers as mentioned in the published *Relaciones* in the eighteenth century.[39]

Flogging was a more frequent punishment and considered as a public humiliation. Those sentenced to the galleys were almost always flogged as well, but the lashes were given also to people who had delayed their confessions (*tardos confitentes*), revoked them (*revocantes*) or not confessed fully (*diminutos*). Here also, the court, or the *Suprema*, tended to pardon people whose age or physical condition advised against the punishment. In the *auto* held in Granada, for instance, on 30 November 1721, Nicolás Jerónimo de la Peña, a 45-year-old tobacco retailer from Málaga, was sentenced to two hundred lashes for having sworn falsely and delaying his confession. Nevertheless, he was excused the flogging '*por accidente*', which suggests some kind of medical condition. Yet he had to suffer the 'public shame' (*vergüenza pública*) of being paraded round the town mounted on a donkey, amid the jeers of the populace.[40] The same sentence was imposed – at his 75 years of age – on Gaspar Manuel Cabello, punished with his wife, brothers and children, in

Seville two weeks later. He was sentenced to two hundred lashes as a delaying confessant, but this was commuted to public shaming on the back of a donkey.[41]

Gonzalo Báez de Paiba did, however, go to the galleys. He sent three appeals to the *Suprema*, however and, on Christmas Eve 1672, the Inquisitor-General remitted his sentence. He had rowed for three and a half years. Had prison and his sufferings at the oar calmed the spirits of this New Christian, whose Judaism, though doubtful at first, had been clearly demonstrated during his fourth trial? Was this the end of his Judaizing or did he manage to escape from Spain? The court assumed that Gonzalo would soon be back to his old tricks, so it forbade him even to go within ten leagues of the Inquisition prison, since he was guilty of the offence known as *fautoría*, that is hindering the task of the court by advising and encouraging the prisoners.

7
Under the Rod of the Holy Office

The Cortizos family

Manuel Cortizos was one of the most important financiers of the reign of Philip IV. Born in 1605 in Valladolid, his parents' first stop on their way from Portugal to Madrid, he began by farming the taxes on Castilian wool. Successful and enriched, he was ennobled as a knight of the Military Order of Calatrava and became secretary of the Royal Treasury or *Contaduría*,[1] under Olivares, who refused to allow questions of *converso* descent to create difficulties when he wanted to make appointments and grant honours which he judged necessary for the national good.

Between 1630 and 1650 Manuel Cortizos and his younger brother Sebastián negotiated enormous loans for the Royal Treasury. In February 1637, at the peak of his fame and wealth, Manuel Cortizos entertained the king and queen at a reception on which he spent unheard-of sums, an event which must have been extraordinary even in the atmosphere of conspicuous spending characteristic of the age. In 1642 and 1643, during the campaign in Catalonia, Cortizos lent eight hundred thousand escudos to the queen and refused to take interest or the jewels which the sovereign offered as security for the loan.

Manuel died young in 1649. He may even have been too powerful for the Inquisition to touch him. Nevertheless, his death coincided with the upsurge in the repression of Portuguese crypto-Jews living in Castile, and many members of the Cortizos family fell foul of the Inquisition, among them Manuel's widow and cousin, Luisa Ferro, and her mother, Mencia de Almeida, arrested in Madrid in 1654 and imprisoned in Cuenca. From the evidence given at their trials, the Holy Office learned many details about the private life of this family.

Soon after her husband's death, Luisa Ferro told her cousin Serafina de Almeida, according to the latter's evidence, that

Her husband had died and she was so well off that she wanted to help his soul by giving alms at her door to everyone without exception, during the nine days of *horras*. She did this and gave her steward the job of distributing charity.[2]

Horras, which means something like 'empty' or 'pointless', were the days after the funeral when in Jewish custom the close relatives of the dead person do not work, while relatives or neighbours keep them company and attend to their physical needs. Normally there are seven such days. However, when Francisco de Torres testified in 1717, he told the court that the period of intensive mourning lasted nine days.[3] This was an ancient custom, mentioned already in the fourteenth century.[4]

Manuel Cortizos's brother Sebastián was temporarily short of funds, so he asked another Portuguese financier, Fernando de Montesinos, to lend him one thousand silver ducats to give as charity for the soul of his brother. The witness explained that the death of Manuel de Cortizos had stirred his family to make five distributions of alms. Cortizos himself had been very generous during his lifetime. As Father Páez Ferreira, who occupied himself spying among the New Christians, said:

accepted and commonly known among them was that the said Manuel Cortizos ... was a Jew who observed the Law of Moses and as such he sent very large sums of alms every year to Amsterdam to be distributed among poor Jews there.[5]

Of course, giving charity in exchange for prayers for the soul of a dead person is more familiar to Christianity than to Judaism, although in Jewish tradition mourning is an emotion which should stimulate almsgiving. Given the Catholic upbringing of the crypto-Jews, it is hardly surprising that they should want to give charity in such circumstances. However, what mattered for the Inquisition was the intention, and this is clearly described in the evidence. The mourners drew up 'lists of people to whom alms were to be given, and they were all observers of the Law of Moses'. Other sums were sent to Seville and Granada as well as to the ex-Peninsular communities in Venice, Florence, Leghorn and Pisa and to Jews in the Holy Land who devoted themselves to the study of sacred texts and to prayer in the holy cities of Safed, Jerusalem and Hebron. Furthermore, the mourners fasted for the soul of Cortizos 'according to the observance of the Law of Moses'. Fasting was the principal form of religious devotion among the crypto-Jews. That it reflected Catholic self-mortification more than Jewish custom is less important than the fact that the Marranos practised it with Jewish intentions and at times when the Church did not require it.

On 2 March 1651, the trial of Luisa Ferro, widow of Manuel Cortizos, began before the Inquisition court of Toledo.[6] The prosecutor had assembled 32 items of written evidence against her. Most of the depositions had been taken from poor Portuguese immigrants who had received alms from the heirs of Cortizos. The court accepted, however, that there was no formal evidence of Judaizing on Luisa's part, only suspicions and conjecture. That Manuel and she had sent money to Venice was not conclusive. There was no proven religious crime – no *delito de fe* – and so the trial was stopped.

Luisa's mother, Mencia de Almeida, also escaped the full rigours of the Inquisition. She had a powerful son, Sebastián Ferro, ex-royal Paymaster-General in Flanders, who used his circle of influential connections to help his mother. In any case, it did not suit the Holy Office that the old lady, who was unwell, should die in prison before confessing. So on 20 April 1656 she was set free, and was required only to abjure *de levis* and to stay for four years away from Madrid, Cuenca and other places where she had lived.

Manuela de Almeida: constancy of a 22-year-old woman

Not all the family were dealt with as lightly as Cortizos's widow and her mother. His cousin, Manuela de Almeida and her husband, Thomas Gómez, were arrested. The couple had the tobacco concession in Ciudad Real, which came under the jurisdiction of the Toledo Inquisition court.[7]

The procedure of arrest was subject to well-established rules. The local constable or *alguacil*, or the local lay representative of the inquisition, together with a notary whose job it was to take an inventory of items sequestered, arrested the couple, taking careful note of everything they had in their possession and their clothes.[8] Anybody else living in the house had to vacate it. If there were children and nobody to care for them, an Inquisition familiar would take them in.

The couple were escorted to the prison, put in separate cells and kept in complete isolation to prevent them colluding in their statements to the court.

Given the bureaucratic uniformity of the Inquisition, it seems likely that one prison was similar to another. Toledo was probably like

Cuenca where the cells measured about 3.5 metres square. They had a double door, a fireplace, whitewashed walls, a high window and some minimum furniture.[9] However, the inventories of possessions show that, in comparison with the relatively abundant personal clothing and objects of value, people were not used to much comfortable furniture in their homes. The comparative absence of such comfort may explain why the physical condition of the prisoners does not seem to have deteriorated much in the months and even years that some of them spent in the cell.

Under questioning, Thomas confessed that his wife obeyed the dietary and other laws of the Bible. She removed blood from the meat by a process of salting and washing. She cooked with oil rather than lard. She cut the throats of poultry instead of wringing their necks. She respected Saturday as the Sabbath by putting clean cloths on the table and not cooking. Thomas tried to disassociate himself from his wife by saying that when he was away from home he ate everything. He worked on Saturdays and did not know much about what his wife did. The perceptive inquisitors, however, sensed that Thomas's ignorance of what Manuela did was feigned and that she must have told Thomas more than he was admitting about her faith and her habits.

Manuela was questioned on 23 February 1649, the day after her arrest. She gave her personal details and the names of her family. She was 22 and had been born in Guadalajara. She said that her late father was a soap manufacturer called Diego de Almeida. Her mother was Beatriz del Campo, who still lived in Guadalajara and ran the soap factory with Manuela's brother. Manuela told the Inquisition the names of her grandparents, uncles and aunts. Thomas was her cousin, whom she had married after obtaining the necessary ecclesiastical dispensation. They had been together for four years, and had no children. Thomas had obtained the tobacco concession in Ciudad Real a year before.

The court next asked her, as it always did, whether there had ever been any Judaizers in her family, 'because people of impure blood – that is those descended from Jews – are more likely to offend against the Faith', according to the *Manual of Inquisitors*.[10] Manuela answered that she came from 'a very good Portuguese family' of Old Christians. Did she know why she had been arrested? Manuela answered with the usual denials, which were errors because the court knew about the families of people it arrested. The court always advised a prisoner that 'the Holy Office does not arrest anyone without due cause', which in effect meant that the court had already decided that the prisoner was guilty. All that remained was for her to confess and name her Judaizing accomplices.

Manuela was probably accustomed to an easily satisfied regular confessor. In gaol she had nobody to advise her on how to tackle the sophisticated Inquisitors. After her first interrogation she was left alone, probably very apprehensive, for three days, and then she asked to be heard, as was her right. She was brought up from the cells on 26 February 1649 and asked what she had to say. She said that she remembered that once, as a child, an old Portuguese woman called Cardoso had told her to leave a rasher of bacon that her aunt had given her and do penance for having eaten some of it. Manuela hoped that the Inquisition would be satisfied with this confession of some half-forgotten event concerning a person who was almost certainly dead. She was mistaken; the inquisitors were never satisfied with some unimportant admission. On the contrary, they would worry at it until the whole story came out. To Manuela's surprise, they kept asking her about her aunt and the Cardoso woman. Manuela said that Cardoso had mentioned nothing about Judaism, only telling her not to eat the bacon. But did Manuela not know, asked the court, from the proclamations often made – the *edictos de fe* – that it was sinful to abstain from pork and that people who did not eat it were called Hebrews or Jews? Manuela admitted that she did know that. So why, asked the inquisitors, had she obeyed Cardoso? She should go down to her solitary cell again, think very carefully and relieve her conscience. Manuela realized that she had made a mistake in bringing up the story. Far from serving as a way out, it had pushed her further into trouble. She was literate and signed her statement, but this time with a hand that was shakier than after her first interrogation. Nevertheless, over the next few days, as Manuela received the three required warnings, she insisted that she had nothing more to say.

When the prosecutor read out the tremendous and terrifying accusation, he normally had a long list of written testimonies of the accused's guilt. In the end, the latter would have to confess. Manuela, however, may well not have thought that was the case. Even if other members of her family had gone through the Inquisition court and prison, people who had survived were threatened into silence by terrifying threats of what would happen to them if they breathed a word of the procedure. Manuela may have thought she could defy the court. How would she have reacted when the Prosecutor uttered the thunderous accusation?

a Judaizer ... perjured and excommunicate, a baptized Christian ... setting aside the fear of God and salvation of her soul ... an apostate and heretic ... passing to the superseded and dead Law of Moses, performing its rites and ceremonies...committing the following enormous crimes.

Specifically, the Prosecutor accused Manuela of the whole list of Jewish acts: on Friday she prepared food so as not to have to cook on the Sabbath, which she honoured with clean table linen and by not lighting the hearth. 'Continuing in her perfidy', she abstained from pork, from blood, certain parts of the fat and the back legs of the animal (which contained the forbidden sciatic nerve). She always used oil to cook with, and had reproved a maid for having basted a partridge with lard. Once she had broken plates in which a servant had inadvertently put blood sausage. She had the poultry killed in the Jewish way by cutting their throats rather than throttling them. Lest Manuela say that she had medical reasons for all this or that it was merely a matter of personal preference, the prosecutor thundered that she did these things 'solely to observe the Law of Moses' (*sólo en observancia de la Ley de Moisés*) or at least to obey that Law as far as she could (*por conformarse en cuanto puede con dicha Ley de Moisés*). To deny the birth of the Messiah, she ate little at Christmas time. 12 years previously, continued the prosecutor, she had fasted on the Great Day of September, as the Marranos called *Yom Kippur,* the Day of Atonement. It might be objected that she had only been ten-years-old, but, said the prosecutor, she could have remembered and ought to have confessed the episode. He had a long list of testimonies of Manuela's behaviour, but she insisted on confessing only the matter of the old Portuguese woman and the rasher of bacon. The prosecutor asked for Manuela to be tortured to make her confess.

Alone, only 22 years old, before the court of canon lawyers and a bishop, Manuela answered the charges defiantly. She had probably worked out that the accusations came from the servants, given that they were almost all about food preparation. She defended herself well, denying absolutely that she had eaten less during Advent or that she did not eat pork. She had explanations for her acts. Sometimes on Saturdays they ate food left over from the day before, which did not require reheating. If she occasionally salted the meat it was to stop it going bad.

A week later, on 15 March 1649, Manuela, still energetically taking her fate into her own hands, asked to be heard again. She said she remembered having killed a capon that she had then hung up and left dripping blood while she attended to an urgent dispatch of tobacco. The capon dripped blood but it was not because she was obeying the Jewish dietary laws which require the blood to be drained.

As she sat and thought in her solitary cell, Manuela knew that the weak point in her defence was her husband Thomas. What was he saying? She had reached the conclusion that the inquisitors were not likely to trust the evidence of a few spiteful servants. So she told the court that she had beaten one girl, Ginesa de Castañeda, for lying and not, as the prosecutor had said, because she had basted a partridge with lard. In the end, Manuela had thrown Ginesa out of the house because the servant was having an affair with Luis Gómez, Thomas's brother. Manuela handed the court a set of notes she had written – she was evidently fully literate – for her defence lawyer. Her defence was based on denying the good faith of Ginesa de Castañeda and another servant, María Rodríguez, whom Manuela had accused of stealing tobacco from the shop. The defence lawyer asked the court to question these women. Had they stolen and fornicated and sworn vengeance when Manuela dismissed them? Manuela also named as a possible hostile witness Diego de Céspedes, whom she suspected had denounced her because she had resisted his attempts at seduction.

The inquisitors, however, were up to Manuela's tricks, and noted soberly on the documents that they had no reason not to believe what the servant Ginesa had said. Manuela had made the right guess: it was indeed Ginesa who had given the prosecutor evidence against her, though Manuela was never told this. The inquisitors questioned María Rodríguez also, but concluded that they saw no reason to doubt her evidence, since Manuela and Thomas had not dismissed her for stealing. Again, Manuela was sent back to her cell to think long and hard. This time the Inquisition, probably overwhelmed with other cases, left her for three months.

When she was brought up again, the court reminded her that the prosecutor had many individual testimonies against her. Did she not want to confess first, for this would give the court a reason to treat her with mercy? No? Then the evidence, which was still mostly about the dietary habits of the household, was read out. Manuela denied the accusations flatly. If she cut the fat off the meat, it was to keep it for other purposes, she claimed. Yes, she had eaten meat on a fast day, but she had a dispensation. She changed the bed and table linen on Christian holy days and not to honour the Jewish Sabbath. Once she salted a carcass that a friend had given her, but this was to preserve it and not as part of the Jewish dietary laws.

The Inquisition was very suspicious but was obviously in a quandary. So, not being subject to any requirement to release prisoners after a certain time, it sent Manuela back to a cell for another month.

The inquisitors were not totally convinced of the value of the testimony. Perhaps also they had some feelings of humanity. They discussed whether to torture Manuela or merely to show her the instruments. But, in the meantime, Manuela had made an error. Three days later, the Prosecutor fulminated against her. She had committed one of the gravest offences of disrespect to the court. She had tried to communicate with her husband to tell him to deny the accusations. Unfortunately she had been detected and now the court was sure she was hiding a lot.

Answering the charge of collusion with her husband, Manuela confessed only that she had exchanged a word or two with another prisoner, but she had not received any written notes. However, the woman was weakening. The next day she said she remembered communicating with Thomas through other prisoners by a system of tapping on the cell wall. The court sensed that Manuela was on the point of surrender.

On 3 September 1649, the Prosecutor presented more evidence, including one testimony which probably came from Thomas's brother Luis, who confirmed everything that the servants had said about Manuela's observance of the Jewish dietary laws. More importantly, this witness confirmed what the inquisitors probably already knew: that Manuela was the dominant half of the couple.

Three days later, Manuela confessed that she abstained from blood. She asked for more time but the inquisitors, realizing that she used her time to think up what she hoped were convincing half-truths, told her she could have only until that afternoon. Then Manuela told the court what she hoped would satisfy the inquisitors.

When they had left Guadalajara, she said, they had stopped in Madrid before continuing south to take up the tobacco concession in Ciudad Real. In the capital they had spent the night with Manuela's grandmother Isabel Núñez, who taught her the main points of the Law of Moses. Shortly after settling down in Ciudad Real, she had told Thomas what her grandmother had taught her. However, Manuela took one step forward and one back in her admissions. The inquisitors were disappointed when Manuela told them that she had not really believed what her grandmother had told her. They in turn did not believe her. She was trying to wriggle out of her guilt (*andaba buscando subterfugios*), they noted.

However, the next evening, at eight, the hopes of the Chief Inquisitor, Don Gonzalo Brabo Grajera, were raised when the gaoler came to tell him in his private apartments that Manuela wanted to see him. It was too late to assemble the court but Don Gonzalo did not want to risk

Manuela changing her mind overnight. After all, his task was to save her immortal soul now that she might be ready to make a full confession. Manuela was brought in. The inquisitor invited her to speak. She said that, as had been given in evidence, it was her habit to sweep out the house on Friday afternoons, putting clean linen on the table and the bed 'to observe the Law of Moses'.

At last she had confessed, but when Don Gonzalo asked her why she had committed the further sin of denying her offence, she said that she had repented but directly to God. She had not confessed her Judaizing to a priest, so she did not feel it necessary to confess to the court. Claiming private confessions to the Almighty and setting aside the Church was not likely to impress the inquisitor, though he could see that Manuela was giving in little by little.

In further interrogations on 27 September and 8 October 1649, Manuela said nothing more. Now the Prosecutor read out the testimonies of spies in the prison. The Inquisition employed such people to watch through holes in the doors and the ceilings of cells. The gaoler had put a spy in the cell next to Manuela, and her messages, conveyed by tapping, had been betrayed. Now the inquisitors knew for certain that Manuela had communicated with her husband. This itself was an offence, but what had they said to each other?

Thomas had assumed that Manuela would confess her Judaizing at once. In his statement he admitted that at first he had threatened her if she said anything, but now he loved her so much 'he wanted her to live more than anything else in the world' (*más la quería viva que cuantas cosas había en el mundo*). He had told her this through an intermediary. Manuela asked this person to find out if Thomas had betrayed her. He had, and Manuela told the messenger to tell her husband that she was more of a woman than he was a man (*más mujer era ella que él hombre*). After all, she had said nothing to the court about him. Now, said she, still according to the intermediary, she could 'lighten her conscience' and tell everything. In such a way did the Inquisition destroy the intimacy and mutual trust of husband and wife.

From this anonymous evidence of conversations held through a third person, the inquisitors learned that Thomas's grandmother, Francisca del Campo, and his mother, María Núñez, who was also in prison, were Judaizers. Of course, no modern court would accept this sort of evidence, consisting of reported conversations repeated by spies. The Inquisition, however, knew that Manuela was guilty of Judaizing. The Prosecutor had no need to prove it to a jury. All that was needed was to present the proofs in such a way that Manuela could not deny them.

There was no reason to suspect that the court or the prosecutor wanted to invent a case, nor did the witnesses have any reason to lie. The very ingenuousness of their reports of words which they heard badly and could not understand suggests this. Thomas, for example, was heard by six separate witnesses to say that some olives from Córdoba had disagreed with him. Was this a coded message? Manuela spoke of 'the post travelling' (*corría la posta*). Was this a message or perhaps merely a line from a popular song?

The court was still not really content with the prosecutor's case. Manuela spent five more months in her cell, this time presumably prevented from communicating with anyone. What did she think as she ruminated on her story? Perhaps, if the court showed so much concern about innocent acts such as avoiding pork and blood, or cleaning the house on Friday afternoons, it really was sinful to perform them. Could a few instructions from her grandmother and, years earlier, from an old Portuguese woman, have had such an influence on her that she endured months of arrest, separation from her husband and the ruin of their business? The judges of the Inquisition probably thought the same. There was more to Manuela's life than she had admitted. Since proof of her guilt was at least partially established, perhaps they ought to put her to torture, both to confess her own culpability – confession *in caput proprium* – and to name her accomplices – confession *in caput alienum*.

On 3 March 1650, as Manuela entered the second year of her imprisonment, she was taken down to the torture chamber. The town executioner, whose job included torturing suspects, was called. Was Manuela shivering with fear or had she buoyed herself up to resist the worst? Unless she had learned the nature of judicial torture from somebody who had suffered it, she had little idea of what awaited her.

The Inquisition regulations were particularly exact here, and inquisitors followed them meticulously. Before entering the torture chamber she was exhorted to tell the truth and again as she was stripped: 'she should tell the truth and not see herself in such travail'.

The torturer and his assistants were accustomed to their job. They may have taken sexual advantage of women whom they tortured to make them confess in criminal cases. Here, however, in the presence of the inquisitors, the torturer had to behave with circumspection. Although the victims were told that any permanent disability was their own fault, the inquisitors were concerned that no such injury be caused.

It would of course be easy to accuse the inquisitors of sadism. At the time, and not only in Spain, people enjoyed the sight of the physical punishment of a criminal. Yet the whole atmosphere conveyed by the secretarial record of an Inquisition torture session communicates formality, impassivity and distance. Apart from the cries of the victim, the only emotion manifest is the increasing shakiness of the secretary's writing.

When the Holy Office decided to use torture to force a suspect to confess, it seems to have been indifferent to the sex of the culprit. However, if a woman was menstruating, the torture was postponed. On 1 September 1656, for example, when Gonzalo Báez de Paiba's wife Catalina was taken down to the torture chamber, the doctor, who was required to be present, confirmed that Catalina had her period. The scene is moving. Catalina had been tortured before. Now, accompanied by the doctor, the secretary and the inquisitors, as she descended the stairs it was not fear of torture that disturbed her but shame that men would see her condition. She was the only woman there.

It is indeed strange, considering how many women passed through Inquisition gaols, that no matron was employed for their care. Women like Catalina de Paiba and Manuela de Almeida were absolutely alone, with no female companion with whom to discuss intimate matters, or to talk of their husbands or children. Furthermore, these women, whom perhaps even their husbands never saw naked, were stripped completely for torture. If this were not enough, Catalina's anguish, knowing that her underwear was stained with her blood, carries across the centuries in the prose of the secretary:

> And Catalina de Paiba said: 'Sir, no, for the love of God do not torture me . . . a woman of my class should not be stripped naked twice . . . by the wounds of God,' which she said with many tears.[11]

The torture session normally lasted an hour, though if the inquisitors thought the victim was about to confess they might extend it. The usual torture in the seventeenth and eighteenth centuries was to tie the victim to a bench and tighten cords round parts of his body by means of a special wheel, the *mancuerda*. Here in more detail is the matter of fact description of the torture procedure explained by the Toledo court to the *Suprema* in a report of 5 February 1654:

> In this court the torture consisted of seating the criminal, for the cords to be tied, on a narrow bench fixed against the wall, securing him by the chest against the wall with a thick rope tied to an iron ring in the wall. His feet were tied to a beam under the bench. His

arms were tied and his body secured with different knots. Then the *mancuerda* was turned as many times as considered necessary.[12]

This was the beginning. If the prisoner were a man of some physical strength, he might be able to resist sufficiently for the torturer not to be able to twist the cords to their maximum. Nevertheless, the documents make no reference to physical resistance or struggles in the torture chamber. Then the victim was strapped to the rack. Here is a description, taken from the same report:

> In appropriate cases the torture was continued and the prisoner was taken to the rack. His head was down and secured by a wide iron ring. They proceeded to tie the cords around his legs, feet and thighs. Then the twists which were considered necessary were given to his thighs and shins.

That is to say, as well as the atrocious pain that the accused was made to suffer, they lay head-down. Was this possibly to try to prevent fainting? The rack was clearly a more practical way of carrying out the torture, as no movement of the head or body was possible.

The report from the Toledo court to the *Suprema* continued:

> This form of torture was used until 1648 when, during a visit by Don Gonzalo Brabo Grajera, the torture of Simón de Fonseca Peña was proposed [this presumably means that the appropriate moment to torture this suspect came during the Inquisitor's visit]. So a professional torturer from another town was summoned and by order of Don Gonzalo the form of torture was changed. The victim was made to sit at the top of the rack and his feet were tied to the first step [the rack or *potro* seems to have been in the form of a ladder]. His body was tied to the wall to two rings and a rope. His arms and legs were tied underneath. Completely secured in this way, loops were placed around his big toes and tightened as appropriate with a wheel called the *trampazo*.

Clearly, the new method could pull off the victim's big toes. This happened to María Carlos, whose trial record in 1675 in Murcia shows that she had to be carried out of the torture chamber with one big toe ripped off by the inefficiency of the torturer. Other permanent disabilities were not uncommon, usually as a result of over-tightening the cords. Medical assistance was available to treat the open wounds caused by the cords and to set fractures for which the official report blamed the torturer's clumsiness. The Holy Office was not interested in the death of sinners, especially before confession, but rather in their repentance. Nor did the Inquisition want the penitents to appear at the *auto de fe* showing obvious signs of torture. Even so, reconciliations with the Church or burnings in effigy of people who had died in prison were common enough. While probably most of these were deaths from natural causes, death as a result of torture cannot be always ruled out. The Inquisition itself admitted this in the cases of the deaths of Gabriel Perea in Llerena in 1680 and Antonio Rodríguez in Cuenca in 1660.[13]

Torture was used mostly for those accused of Judaizing, a crime which was hard to prove. It was also necessary to disentangle a complicated network of Judaizers – a *complicidad* – that is, a whole community of suspected observers of the Law of Moses. These were people whose crime was, in effect, deceit, a life in the shadows, a crime which they could not excuse by saying that they did not know it was such. The purpose of the Inquisition was to elicit confessions, so torture was used in most cases. In the second half of the seventeenth century three out of four Judaizers investigated by the Holy Office suffered the torturer's cords.[14]

As one reads the trial transcripts, one sees that the arrested Judaizers tended to refuse to betray their accomplices, as they were called. They endured the cruellest of torture before betraying the names of their Judaizing relatives and friends, and gave an example of unparalleled courage and integrity. If a victim refused to confess under torture, he might save himself and all the others in his group. Certainly, many were unable to withstand torture, or they suspected that the others had not been able to endure it and had betrayed them. If such were the case, there was no point in refusing to speak, because the Inquisition knew the truth, and to refuse to mention the names of others was to invite conviction and burning at the stake as a *negativo*. The Inquisition used secrecy, loneliness, anxiety and torture to undermine the strength of mind of the most resolute. These men and women, small and big businessmen, even major financiers, were very different in class from the murderers and other violent criminals whom civil justice regularly tortured to extract confessions. Judaizers were tortured to force them to incriminate their spouses, parents and children, even if the guilt of the latter had already been established. Confession was more important than family love or loyalty. In the second half of the seventeenth century, and again in the twenties and thirties of the eighteenth, there were many examples of such heroic behaviour by Judaizers immured in the dungeons of the Holy Office of the Inquisition.

On 3 March 1650, then, Manuela de Almeida was taken down to the torture chamber and stripped. As each garment was removed by the torturer's assistant, the inquisitors urged her to confess. As she was tied to the rack, the secretary wrote that she screamed for Jesus and the Virgin Mary to help her, that she was innocent. As they tightened the cords around her limbs, however, she began to confess, screaming, 'I have been a Jew and Moor [*sic*] all my life!'. At the first twist of the *mancuerda*, she accused her mother-in-law, María Núñez, and Jorge López, her sister-in-law's husband. The torture procedure was slow. Every time the *mancuerda* was given a turn, the torturer was sent out of the room, for it was none of his business to know what Manuela might confess, and summoned back when the inquisitors decided the young woman should be tortured further. Manuela was hysterical with pain and nervous tension. She could stand no more, so the inquisitors decided that, as she had begun to mention names, it would be best to give her a rest. Perhaps, alone again in her cell, the mere fear of further torture would impel her to tell all that she was still concealing.

On 9 March they took her up to the court room again. She listened to the Prosecutor as he read out yet another set of testimonies. In spite of what she had suffered, Manuela remained obstinate, denying all she could. Yes, it was true that her mother Beatriz del Campo used to light a candle on Friday evenings, the eve of the Jewish Sabbath, but Manuela could not say why. Yes, her brother Juan was also an observer of the Law of Moses.

Sometimes there came a point when the inquisitors despaired of extracting any more information from a suspect. They had enough admissions by now to impose the full penalty on Manuela. The inquisitors were apprehensive for the prisoner's health. On 14 May, Manuela asked to be heard and told the court that she had ceased to menstruate and that her eyes were continuously watering. Three days later the doctor examined her and recommended bleeding.

Never hurried, on 28 July 1650 the inquisitors decided that Manuela should appear at a public *auto de fe*, clad in the shameful yellow sanbenito. She would make a solemn abjuration of her sin. Any goods that she still owned would be confiscated and she would stay in the penitential prison for 2 years.

This was quite a mild punishment. That was the view of the Prosecutor who, basing himself on Manuela's obstinacy – itself a sin – appealed against the sentence. A month later, the *Suprema* increased it to perpetual imprisonment. In practice, this probably made little difference. Lack of room usually meant that after a year or two of regular attendance at Mass and other services, frequent confession and catechization, prisoners like Manuela were set free, though this young woman was forbidden, as all convicted heretics were, to wear fine cloth and precious stones.

Juana de la Peña

The widow of Manuel Cortizos, Luisa Ferro, had a close friend, an elegant lady like herself, Serafina de Almeida. Serafina was charitable and sometimes visited a poor Portuguese woman called Mencia de la Peña, giving her money to pray and fast for the soul of Manuel Cortizos. When Mencia's daughter Juana was to be married, Serafina sent Mencia two hundred silver reals to pay for the bridal gown, a jet necklace and red silk stockings for the bride. Shortly afterwards, Juana de la Peña was arrested by the Holy Office. The case of this young married woman of 24 is one of the most typical of its kind.[15] She suffered three sessions in the torture chamber, and many of the other elements in her case are also emblematic of the fate of Judaizers under the rod of the Inquisition.

The Inquisition's filing system was so efficient that Juana's name was found mentioned in evidence given as long as nine years earlier, on 6 May 1651, in the Cuenca court, by twelve-year-old Escolástica Gómez, who had testified against a Portuguese widow called Mencia de Apena, the Portuguese form of the surname De la Peña. This widow, Juana's mother, lived in Madrid, in the Calle Jardines with two sons and two daughters. One of the daughters had told Escolástica that the family observed the Law of Moses and that they used a code to refer to the days on which the festivals of the Jewish calendar fell. The code was the words '*Hoy voy yo*', meaning 'I'm coming (or going) today'. As Escolástica stood before the judges, perhaps innocently confident or trembling with fear, they asked her how Mencia and her children spoke to each other on this subject. Once, Escolástica replied, Mencia had been talking to her neighbour Doña Gracia and Gracia's daughters Felipa and Isabel. The latter asked Mencia's daughters, one of whom was Juana de la Peña, 'if they were going' (*si iban*), to which they answered that they were.

This was very thin evidence indeed, but Escolástica was a valid witness to crypto-Jewish practices, for on 25 May and 2 June 1651 she was called back and revealed some details of her own family, who had been searched for by Inquisition agents during the roundup of Portuguese noted by Jerónimo de Barrionuevo in his diary. They abandoned their home. Escolástica remembered that their flight had been financed by a certain Joseph Rodríguez. The court instructed the secretary to note carefully Escolástica's vivid description of this man, who was short and fat, with turned up moustaches and 'when he walks it's as if his whole belly sways'. They sheltered in an inn and, probably thinking they were safer in a busy place, spent the day in the main meeting-place of Madrid, the Puerta del Sol, where Escolástica, her mother, her cousins and a nephew, an apprentice barber, were arrested.

Escolástica told the inquisitors that she had seen her family fast regularly to mark the Jewish festivals. In particular she said that the family used to be given a silver real by Doña Antonia Blandón, wife of one of the great financiers of the time, as a reward for imploring divine intervention for some sick person.

The inquisitors listened carefully to what she said about Juana de la Peña. The latter was married to Julián Vázquez. In July 1660 he was about to take over the tobacco concession in Toledo. Up till then the couple had lived in Madrid, where they had a shop selling tobacco and jewellery. Answering the inquisitors' questions about her family, Juana said that both sets of her grandparents were from Portugal. Asked whether any member of her family had ever been punished by the Inquisition, she was unable to deny that her brother Francisco had had to do penance. He had appeared wearing the sanbenito at an *auto de fe* and had later died while serving his sentence in the penitential prison. She claimed to know nothing about her husband's family. They had been married for nine years, that is to say she had been wed at the age of fifteen. Five children had been born, of whom four were living, aged between one and a half and six. One may imagine the anguish of this young mother worrying who was caring for her children, since she knew that her husband was also in gaol.

When Juana said she knew hardly anything her family or her husband's, the court knew she was lying and doing so to protect their relatives, about whose secret Jewish practices the Inquisition had collected a lot of evidence. The inquisitors asked Juana to give an account of her life up to then. She told them that at the age of three her parents had taken her from Pastrana, where she had been born, to Madrid.

Juana then was given the first formal admonition to tell the truth. Did she know or suspect why she had been arrested? When she shook her head, the inquisitors formally told her that the Holy Office did not arrest people without cause. The formal part of the interrogation was over. Juana signed the record of the session, elegantly writing 'Doña Juana de la Peña', with a little flourish. Her confidence would not last long.

She remained silent as she received the second and third formal warnings to tell the truth, on 21 and 27 July 1660, despite the advice of her defender. This man was formally appointed and handed a sheet reminding him of his grave responsibilities. If he advised his client wrongly, his goods might be forfeit. All he could really do, however, was advise his client to make an immediate and full confession. He had no right to interrogate witnesses, nor even to know who they were. He might, however, help his client to write out a list of enemies whose testimony the court was obliged to ignore.

As Juana refused to confess her sin of Judaizing, the prosecutor demanded 'that this criminal [*reo*] should be made to suffer torture'. This was a formality at this stage, for the court would give Juana many more opportunities to confess before calling on the public executioner to bind her to the rack. But when Juana heard the prosecutor's request, she valiantly cried out that they should torture her then if they had to, get it over with and let her go home to her children. Either she was hoping that the court had very little proof of her Judaizing or she had resolved to endure the torture.

On 23 July 1661, the prosecutor revealed his first set of witnesses. These were Escolástica and a previous witness who had observed Juana and her mother doing nothing in the house on Saturday, dressed in their best clothes. Juana denied it all. The second set of witnesses included one who claimed that Juana and Julián had said that the Law of Jesus was in error, that the only God was the Holy One of Israel, and that sacred images were made out of bits of wood or painted on paper.

Juana said it was all lies. A few weeks later, as she continued to deny the charges, the court decided on torture. On 3 October 1661, at 9.15 in the morning – these precise details and every word spoken, every cry of agony uttered, were faithfully noted down by the secretary – this young wife and mother was stripped by the executioner.

The torture began. The file contains all the details of Juana's screams and the urgings of the Inquisitors. Finally, she gave in. She confessed that her aunt Violante Rodríguez had taught her the Law of Moses, to fast for 24 hours when it was necessary, to observe Saturday as the Sabbath, changing her clothes and cleaning the house on the Friday, that Jesus was not divine and that confessors could not absolve sinners. Juana, sitting on a stool, her clothes clasped to her body, sobbing, finished her confession by telling the inquisitors that she had told all this to her cousins Felipa and Isabel and other people.

The inquisitors suspected that Juana had more to say. Perhaps, in the long hours alone in her cell, Juana had calculated that her aunt, her

cousins Felipa and Isabel and others were the witnesses who had testified against her. They had almost certainly confessed so, by mentioning
them, she was not placing them in more danger than they were already.
The public executioner was recalled. Juana was placed on the rack
and the cords were tightened around sensitive parts of her body. No,
she screamed, she had no more to say. Finally the torturer went too far
and Juana fainted. She had undergone nearly two hours of torture. The
limit was one hour, but the short interval, when it seemed as though
Juana was going to confess, sufficed to allow a second session. She was
taken to hospital. The inquisitors followed. As soon as Juana regained
consciousness she was to sign her confirmation of what she had
confessed already.

Juana recovered slowly. The next hearing was on 10 November. What
more, asked the inquisitors, did Juana know about her aunt Violante
Rodríguez? Juana was still strong and defiant despite her atrocious
sufferings. She tried to protect her aunt as much as possible. Years ago,
said Juana, Violante had gone to Flanders with her brother Manuel de
Amezquita. Still, the fact that the inquisitors asked about her suggested
that perhaps she was also in prison here in Toledo. Perhaps she was
resisting the inquisitors' questions also. Now the inquisitors asked
a strange question. In what part of the house had Violante taught Juana
the Law of Moses? Juana answered that it had been in the main room
on the first floor. Who else had been present? Nobody. What had her
aunt taught Juana while she lived with her between the ages of ten and
fifteen? Sometimes Violante had taught her to fast, but without proper
explanations. Under the patient prodding of the inquisitors, Juana
mentioned that there were three fasts every year.

Juana was far from making a complete confession. The inquisitors
moved on to another matter. Was she telling the truth when she
claimed that her mother Mencia de la Peña was dead? Other witnesses
had claimed that Mencia was living in Burgos in the north of Spain
with a cousin. But Juana said that Mencia had not answered her letters
and that she had heard nothing from her in two months. She thought
she was dead. Had she done anything, asked the inquisitors, to find out
whether her mother was in fact dead? Yes, said Juana, she had asked the
muleteers who came from Burgos regularly. This was not very convincing and the inquisitors suspected that Juana was hiding something
important. Who were these muleteers? How did Juana know they came
from Burgos? Why did she not send a letter through the post? She had
nobody to go to the post for her, she said, having already said that it
was when she went to the post to ask if a letter had arrived that she

asked if anybody knew if a mule train had arrived from Burgos. 'She did go to the post', an inquisitor wrote in the margin of the document as he read it later, 'so she has been lying'. Did she or did she not go to the post? Juana said that she had gone once. She had nothing else to say. Why had she not written a letter to Burgos to find out if her mother had died?

The inquisitors' suspicion that Juana was hiding the truth to protect her relatives, especially her husband, grew when Juana refused to ratify her confession under torture. She denied that her mother had told her to observe the Law of Moses and she refused to involve her brothers and sister.

The inquisitors accepted that an accused would lie and conceal the truth, but defying the court by refusing to confirm what one had already admitted was galling. So on 23 November 1651 the Prosecutor attacked Juana. Obviously she was lying. Not only was she an impenitent revoker of her own confession but also directly an encourager, helper and concealer of heresy, a Judaizer and observer of the Law of Moses. Her sin affected a whole set of people who had confessed. Actually, Juana could hardly be a helper of people who had already confessed their sin. This did not matter; it was her intention that counted and Juana's was to revoke her confession on the unacceptable pretext that she had misunderstood the questions. The Prosecutor hissed that she was shielding people she knew to be Judaizers. He asked for the severest punishment.

Still in hopes of finding out the ramifications of Judaism in Juana's family, the court voted for further torture. Since Juana had already endured two sessions, the court was obliged by its regulations to consult the *Suprema*. The fastest messenger left Toledo for Madrid on 29 November, and by 10 December the *Suprema* had given its consent. On 16 February, with astonishing valour, Juana endured another session on the rack. She confessed nothing, so on 9 March 1662 the Prosecutor was forced to bring more witnesses statements to the court.

According to one of these, in 1651 when Juana was only thirteen and already engaged, presumably to Julián Vázquez, he slept with her every night in the house where she lived with her mother. The secretary's notes of these statements are confused, especially because the names of the witnesses could not be revealed. Phrases are used such as 'a very close person', meaning a close relative, or 'someone who lives close by'. It is clear, however, that the Prosecutor was using the evidence to try to establish that the family were concerned to marry Juana to another crypto-Jew.

The witness who said that the fiancés slept together was probably Julián himself. Juana, who had suffered cruelly to try to protect him, must have realized that he had already given her away. Alone with Juana, in bed and promised to each other – did they consider the act of sexual intercourse as a Jewish marriage? – they had told each other they were observers of the Law of Moses.

Julián had fallen ill, and lay for 4 months in bed in Mencia's house. Juana denied that she and Julián had spoken of the Law of Moses until they married and moved to the jewellery shop in the Puerta de Moros in Madrid, but she confessed that they did talk about Judaism sometimes when Mencia, her mother, visited them. Juana's denials were now directed towards protecting Mencia who, she claimed, had gone to Burgos. Why, asked the court, had she gone there? A witness, surely Julián, had said that Mencia was trying to escape the Inquisition. He said that he wrote to Mencia, not in Burgos but further north, on the route to France, addressing the letter to 'Doña Aldonza de Vitoria'. As emerged later, Mencia had never gone to Burgos.

The Prosecutor brought out more statements from anonymous witnesses. Most of these were probably members of Juana's family who talked about the shop in the Puerta de Moros where they assembled to observe 'the fasts of the Great Day and Queen Esther'. This was all, but, in a remark which throws light on the lack of privacy in seventeenth-century life, the witness had added, '[F]rom the street door, looking in, most of the house could be seen, and since the Puerta de Moros was such a public place they did not dare give people the chance to see . . . '[16]

Now at last Juana began to confess. The court noted her long silences and hesitations, marked on the sheet by the word '*ojo*' meaning 'note this'. She confessed and implicated her husband. She admitted that she had observed the festivals of the Jewish calendar by fasting in the company of her mother and her siblings. Asked why she had endured torture and not confessed earlier, she said she feared Julián would kill her, but now she realized that it was her husband who had given evidence against her. As for her mother, she confessed that Mencia had gone to Bayonne and that the stories of her journey to Burgos, her disappearance and rumoured death were all false. She had lied to protect Julián, her husband, who had sent money to Mencia in Pamplona, presumably to pay somebody to take her over the frontier. Juana still denied knowing how much money he had sent and insisted that Mencia had not told her she was going to Bayonne.

On the next day, 10 March, Juana ratified her confession. She was told that her admissions would be used against her sister and her two brothers, her mother and others. In the formula used by the Holy Office, Juana certified that she named her 'accomplices' in the crime of heresy, 'not out of hatred but to lighten her conscience'.

The case was now complete and ready for sentence. Juana de la Peña, who had already endured months of imprisonment and cruel torture, would be punished as a heretic, apostate and Judaizer. She had been sacrilegious – presumably because she had fulfilled her Christian obligations of confession and communion while she was Judaizing – negative, and a false penitent when she had confessed only under torture and then revoked her confessions. The Inquisition had been forced into certain procedures, by which the court meant using torture. This, in the court's view, was Juana's fault, for it was her own obstinacy that had forced the inquisitors to summon the public executioner to bring the grim tools of his trade.

As a punishment for revoking her first confession the *Suprema* added public shaming. Juana appeared at an *auto de fe* in the Toledo church of St Peter Martyr on Tuesday 11 April 1662. The following day she was paraded, mounted on a donkey, bare to the waist, around the busiest streets of this town, as the public executioner punished her already tortured body with one hundred lashes.

The psychological collapse produced by months of solitary imprisonment, separation from her husband and children and the long day at the *auto de fe*, the emotion of that ceremony and the pain and shame of being treated like a common thief probably destroyed the resolute courage that this brave woman had displayed in gaol. Less than a year after entering the penitential prison to serve her life sentence, on 9 April 1663, the sanbenitos were formally removed from Juana de la Peña and her husband Julián Vázquez. Their Catholic behaviour must have been exemplary.

8

The Inquisition and the Crisis of the Second Half of the Seventeenth Century

Political and natural disasters

Though Spain recognized the independence of the Dutch United Provinces in 1648, she did not find the peace she needed. Rebellions had to be suppressed in Catalonia and Italy, and England had to be fought in the Caribbean. In 1656 and 1657, the British destroyed Spanish fleets off Cadiz and Santa Cruz de Teneriffe. Spain was blockaded. Portuguese independence from Spain was assured at the battle of Elvas. It was impossible to go on fighting a losing battle. Spain had to reach an agreement with her enemies. The Treaty of the Pyrenees of 7 May 1659 deprived Spain of what remained of her Habsburg inheritance. As Spanish power in Europe collapsed, Philip IV died on 17 September 1665, to be succeeded by his physically and mentally degenerate son, Charles II.[1]

Natural disasters were regular aspects of seventeenth-century life. Spain was swept by epidemics: influenza decimated Málaga in 1674, and plagues left Cartagena, Murcia and most of Andalusia desolate between 1676 and 1680. The earthquake of 9 October 1680 caused widespread destruction in Málaga. Crops rotted, prices inflated and thousands died of hunger.

Vigour of the Inquisition at the century's end

The weakening of Spain did not lead to a decline in the Inquisition's activity. On the contrary, the statistics show a marked rise in the number of *autos de fe* between 1670 and 1690. In many courts the figures reached those previously achieved only in the early years of the

Holy Office two hundred years before.[2] There were 89 trials of Judaizers in Toledo between 1680 and 1700,[3] but the real increase was seen in the delegated court in Madrid. In the last two decades of the century 205 Judaizers were tried in the capital.[4]

In Málaga, which was suffering so many natural disasters, the years between 1668 and 1678 saw mass roundups, in which more than 500 people were arrested. Málaga was a bustling seaport, open to international currents of opinion. Judaizers passed through it on their way to freedom overseas.[5] The evidence from one large trial stated that up to one hundred Judaizers met to pray regularly in a field where they thought they were safe. As a result, 79 appeared at an *auto de fe* in 1672; six died at the stake and others held out till the last moment, when their courage failed them and they asked for mercy and to make a full confession.

The city suffered the loss of many enterprising families. From then onwards, few would trust their merchandise or extend credit to Portuguese merchants for fear of the Holy Office confiscating their goods and seizing the funds of their debtors.

The Inquisition's hand was felt particularly heavily in Palma de Mallorca, where 212 Judaizers were reconciled in four large *autos de fe* in 1679. Nevertheless, secret Judaism was not destroyed. The remaining Marranos planned to flee to Leghorn in 1687 aboard an English merchant ship. Their attempt ended in disaster. Over the next three years the court was swamped with a large number of cases of Judaizers who had already been reconciled once. In 1691, 93 men and women appeared at four more *autos*, and 36 of them died at the stake. A contemporary work by the Jesuit Father Garau, though violently hostile to the victims, gives much useful historical information about the trials and the *autos de fe* on Majorca.[6] Garau explains that there were only three obstinate Jews: Rafael Valls and Caterina and Rafael Benet Tarongí, who were brother and sister. They died proclaiming that they were Jews. Given the immense pressure to which the victims were subjected to make them confess and save their eternal souls, even if not their earthly bodies, it is amazing that anybody could resist, before a crowd estimated at thirty thousand, and accept death without even the aid of the executioner's garrotte.

For Father Garau, of course, the undeniable valour of these three *negativos* could be explained by the presence of the Devil within them. This could clearly be seen, explained the Jesuit, by the expressions of fear and rage on their faces, and their struggles against their bonds, while those who had confessed and saved their souls sat tranquilly through the *auto de fe*. Like some of the preachers at *autos de fe*, Father Garau, directing his barbs perhaps at other secret Jews who might read his book, accuses them of being not only bad Christians but also bad Jews, as though they had even the slightest chance of obeying the demands of Judaism more than minimally. He writes that some of the victims claimed to be rabbis, though by this is to be understood not formally qualified teachers of Jewish law but spiritual leaders who knew somewhat more of their religion than the vague ideas possessed by most of the descendants of the fifteenth-century converts. One of these would have been the *negativo* Rafael Valls, of whose agonizing death Garau gives a particularly nauseating description. During his trials, Valls had compared the planned flight from Majorca to Leghorn to the rescue of Shadrach, Meshach and Abednego from the fiery furnace in the Book of Daniel. For the Jesuit, the failure of the escape attempt and the capture and trial of most of the Judaizers allowed them to save their souls.

The violence of the Inquisition displayed in these *autos de fe* reveals a level of fear and hatred unparalleled since the early decades of the Holy Office in Spain. Secret Judaism on Majorca was wiped out, though the descendants of the reconciled victims, known as *chuetas*, have remained identifiable until today.[7]

The great general *auto de fe* of 30 June 1680

118 victims appeared at this giant spectacle in Madrid, the last of these costly public acts. Its image has been preserved in Francisco Rizzi's canvas in the Prado. Its purpose was for the king to demonstrate his religious zeal by honouring the act with his presence and by taking the oath to support the efforts of the Holy Office, which was always uttered by the highest secular official present.

For the *auto de fe* to be sufficiently grandiose to merit the royal presence, prisoners were brought to Madrid from Inquisition gaols all over the country. They are portrayed in Rizzi's painting, sitting on four rows of raked seats on the right as one looks towards the royal box, actors in a solemn drama, when, before the hushed crowd, Church and State demonstrated their unity in the struggle against heresy.

Next came the sermon, after which the penitents were brought one by one from their places to hear their sentences. The first to stand before the Inquisition secretaries were those who claimed to be sorcerers and witches, pretended priests, bigamists and suchlike. With number 11, María Ruiz, known as 'La Esmeralda', the secretary began to read out the sentences for Judaizing. María abjured *de vehementis*; she was strongly suspected but full proof was lacking. She was sentenced to some years of exile from Madrid and Toledo. The next man was less fortunate. This was Manuel Díaz Sardo, if that was his real name, for he used several aliases in his life as a swindler who had already been condemned to ten years in the galleys by the criminal court. Now he learned that, if he survived the galleys, he would be immured in the Inquisition's penitential prison for the rest of his life. The next man was a Portuguese from Mogadoiro, who sold spices in the street. He received two hundred lashes for being *vario y revocante*, that is changing and then denying his confession. Next came an entire family named Núñez Márquez, all Portuguese. There was Pedro, who sold cloth, his brother Jerónimo, a doctor, Leonor, widow of Rodrigo de Silva and Angela, widow of Francisco Correa, with her daughter Blanca. All received sentences of imprisonment.

Altogether, at that *auto* 56 Judaizers were reconciled in person, 22 fugitives were burnt in effigy and the bones of another eight were taken to the stake in wooden boxes. Eighteen Judaizers were burnt to death. This supreme penalty was inflicted on only one non-Judaizer. The was Luis Fernández, alias Mustafa, a Christian who had adopted Islam and who refused to renege.[8]

For these Judaizers, whether they had confessed and abjured, or whether they obstinately refused to confess or proclaimed their Judaism impenitently, the *auto de fe* came after months or often years of resistance, doubts and anxiety. The *auto* meant that the inquisitors had finished with them, that there would be no more interrogations when they would stand before the court and try to answer questions about events which might have happened years earlier or which they may not even have understood properly. These men and women would emerge from their dark, solitary cells into the bright light of the Madrid summer day. They would look around, anxiously searching for parents, brothers and sisters, spouses and children. Surrounded as they were by familiars of the Inquisition, they would not be able to talk to their relatives. Nor did they know what to expect, unless they had observed another *auto de fe* or they had been found guilty of Judaizing for the second time. In the latter case, the *auto de fe* was the anteroom of death. Those who were going to be reconciled with the Church did not know their penance – was it imprisonment only, or public shame and whipping as well? – while those who were to die were informed of their fate a day earlier. This, the Inquisition hoped, would give them time to repent and save their souls.

Did the victims know that they were to play a part in a drama, to contribute to a ritual, perfect in its tiniest degree? The great *auto de fe* of

1680 was announced a month in advance. Even in the solitary cells of the Inquisition prison some rumours may have penetrated about the ritualized ceremony in which the Judaizers were to be important protagonists.

The stage built for the *auto* of 1680 occupied 1,500 square metres of the Plaza Mayor. It was 3.6 metres high, the height of two tall men.[9] It was even larger than the stage built for the great *auto* held in Córdoba in 1655, which was 1.155 square metres in area and two metres high:

> The day after the *Auto* was announced, bids were invited for making the dais, and the lowest bid was taken, as is customary. I must describe the stage so that readers may get a clear idea of the drama which was played on it. This city has a very capacious square, known as the *Corredera*, because bulls are fought in it and spectacles are provided for the public as the rulers of nations have done throughout the ages for public enjoyment.

In these words Dr Nicolás Martínez, medical officer of the Córdoba court, described the preparations for the great *auto de fe* of 3 May 1655.[10] The spectators had a good view of the penitents. While before the *auto* the procedures of the Inquisition had been concealed by a thick veil of secrecy, now, in the *theatre*, the victims and their emotions, hatred and rancour or, more probably, shame, depression and terror, were exposed to the full light of day. The spectators could see the altar, with the green cross of the Holy Office, the plinths for the preacher and for the secretaries who read out the sentences.

Everything was regulated down to the smallest detail, as in the bullfight today. And indeed, the victims had to play their role as do the bulls, to accept their penance well and to behave as expected. They might repent even at the last minute, just as the bull who has refused to play his part and fight may turn against the matador at the end. Only the negative victim refused to play his part, like the bull who will not fight. Even so, all the victims, penitent and impenitent alike, acted like protagonists in a classical tragedy. The *auto de fe*, however, was a literal act of faith performed by the Church, the civil authorities and the spectators. It exalted the triumph of Spanish Catholicism and sought to redress the insult with which heresy had offended the Divinity.

The *auto de fe* was also a major public ceremony, where places were reserved according to the social rank of the spectators. It affirmed established power and demonstrated the rightness and good order of Spanish society, with Crown and Church united at its apex. In the presence of

Aquellos polbos.

2 Number 23 of the series 'Los Caprichos' by Francisco Goya (1746–1828).
The title refers to the saying *'Aquellos polvos traen estos lodos'* ('That dust
brings that mud') meaning 'You are suffering the consequences.' *I thank
Professor H.P. Salomon for drawing my attention to this saying.*

condemned heretics, the spectators, consumed with morbid curiosity at the sight of the victims in their mitres and yellow penitential tunics, experienced a form of catharsis. When the long day was over, they went home, purged of any doubts they might have had, aware that Christian truth had been reinforced and that the unity of civil society and the Church had been confirmed.

From the early hours of the morning, the Inquisition officials had begun to prepare the penitents. They were given food, though one wonders if their anxiety allowed them to eat. Over their heads went the sanbenitos, tunics of coarse yellow linen on which was painted a St Andrew's Cross with a double, single or half crosspiece according to the severity of the offence. The victims probably did not know the significance of the different forms of the cross, but they would soon understand the meaning of the flames painted on some of their fellows' *sanbenitos*. People who had escaped the stake by the skin of their teeth wore robes with the flames painted upside down (*de fuego revuelto*), while those who were to be burnt at the stake wore robes painted right way up with flames and devils. Each one wore a mitre on his head, also painted with devils and flames. Every victim, except those who were to be cast out and burnt, carried a candle which would be lit after they had abjured and when they were absolved and received back into the Church. Then all were placed in order, first those who had been absolved with a warning (*ad cautelam*), then those who would abjure though the court had only suspicions of their heresy (either *de levis* or *de vehementis*), then the reconciled and lastly those who were to be 'relaxed to the secular arm'. The rear was brought up by the life-sized effigies of fugitives and the boxes of bones of the dead. These would be burnt and the ashes scattered, so that nothing would remain of the memory of these heretics who were now in Hell. As each victim took his place in the procession, a familiar stood on either side, exhorting him, particularly the negative ones for whom this was the last chance to save their souls, to repent of the fearful sin of heresy.

During the first few hours of the *auto de fe*, which in hot summer days often lasted from early morning until after dark, the penitents had little to do: assemble, put on their sanbenitos and mitres and walk in procession between the familiars to the place, usually a church, where the *auto* was to be held. Then, called one by one to hear their sentences, they were to say nothing until the moment of abjuration. Everything was ritual, ceremony, spectacle, indeed theatre, as is clear from the many reports sent up from the local courts to the *Suprema*. These reports reflected the Inquisition's desire that everything should go well, that nothing should minimize the prestige of the Holy Office in its role as Spain's guardian against heterodoxy. The penitents played the part of silent objects here. For this reason the gaoler had prepared gags for condemned victims who might cry out their loyalty to Judaism and disturb the solemnity of the moment. There was certainly no fear on the part of the Inquisition that the spectators would sympathize with the victims. On the contrary, the military escorts which were present occasionally had to protect them from assault by the excited crowd. Any interruption to the order and dignity of the ritual would affect the prestige of the Holy Office.

Even though the burning at the stake of a *negativo* was a failure on the part of the court and the friars who had ceaselessly tried to persuade him to confess and abjure his sin, it nevertheless represented the triumph of Good over Evil. If, at the last moment, the friars who stood by the victim until the smoke and flames forced them away convinced themselves that they had noticed a spark of repentance, and if they could summon the executioner to garrotte the wretch before the flames reached him, this would also prove the triumph of Truth.

A high point in the *auto de fe* was the sermon preached by a eminent religious orator. One of the best-known examples, because it was rebutted in a famous essay by Rabbi David Nieto, Haham or spiritual leader of the Spanish and Portuguese community in London, was that of the Archbishop of Cranganore, Diogo da Anunciação Justiniano Alvares, preached at an *auto de fe* in the Plaza del Rocío in Lisbon on 6 September 1705. The archbishop turned to face the Judaizers whom he described as the 'wretched relics of Judaism' (*desgraçadas reliquias do Judaismo*), and told them that not even real Jews respected them: 'You are the detested laughing stock of the Jews, because you are so ignorant that you do not know how to observe the very law in which you live.' Some crypto-Jews did indeed confuse Judaism and Christianity. As has been seen, some Marranos may have thought that a symbiotic Christian–Jewish religion was possible. That the Marranos were ignorant of normative Judaism was evident. However, if the archbishop thought he knew enough about Jewish communities to be able to state that the Jews despised the Marranos (it was exactly the opposite case – Marranos who were martyred for their faith were thought of with the highest respect), his knowledge was certainly insufficient for him to avoid the crass error of declaring that day in September to be Purim, the anniversary of the events described in the Book of Esther, which always falls in the winter.[11]

These sermons usually stressed aspects of Christianity which the reconciled Judaizers would hear constantly in the months or years of catechization that would follow the *auto de fe*. Much stress was laid on the christological messages in the Old Testament, the superseding of the Old by the New Testament, the loss of the Land of Israel, the Temple in Jerusalem and national liberty as punishment for the crime of deicide.

It seems unlikely, however, that the prisoners in the great Madrid *auto de fe* that hot day in June 1680, tired, thirsty, in despair, intensely anxious and many of them with little education, could have understood the complicated phraseology and the rhetoric of Friar Tomás Navarro, the royal preacher, whose sermon, considering the number of pages it occupies in José del Olmo's account of the day, must have lasted at least an hour if not more. No matter; the sermon was part of the ritual of the *auto de fe*. As Friar Tomás explained, in a wave of confidence which displayed all the self-assuredness typical of the Inquisition, 'The holy court of the Faith on earth resembles in all ways the divine court on high, for both act with the same justification.' If this did not convince the guilty of their fault, the solemn rites of the *auto de fe* would ensure that they would be persuaded by the end of the day. After the sermon, as each name was called, the culprit came down from his place, stood in front of the secretary and heard his sentence read without specifying the particular Judaizing acts that he had committed, for fear of a hostile reaction from the spectators, or perhaps in some cases imitation.

The punishment of the Judaizers almost always included confiscation of their property, if any remained after it had been sold at auction to pay for their maintenance in prison. Few of the reconciled Judaizers escaped the Penitential prison. Except in very mild cases or when the Judaizer was only an adolescent, prison was for life (*perpetua*) and frequently without chance of remission (*irremisible*). Flogging was frequently imposed and, even if the penitent was excused because of age or physical condition, the public shaming that accompanied it was always carried out. The victim was paraded half-naked the next day on donkeyback through the most crowded streets of the town, to the jeering of the mob. Thereafter, the reconciled Judaizers would have to attend Mass regularly in a group, as well as see to their own livelihoods, dressed in the humiliating sanbenito so that their shame would be reflected in everybody's sneering glance. The internal exile that was frequently part of the sentence might come as a relief after prison, though it would be a heavy blow for those who had commercial interests in the towns from which they were now expelled. Reconciled Judaizers were also unable to follow certain professions or hold particular posts, wear jewels or fine cloth, or ride on horseback. They were not robbers, bigamists or prostitutes, but the Judaizers were treated as if they were common criminals.

As the long hot day on the stage of the *auto de fe* drew to an end, the abjuration was read. As dusk fell and those condemned to the stake were taken off to their deaths, the reconciled Judaizers were told to kneel around the altar to renounce their error. Penitent and shriven, the Judaizers recited the following:

I, XYZ, an inhabitant of C, here present before Your Lordships, as Inquisitors into the sin of heresy by apostolic and ordinary authority, with the sign of the Cross and the four Holy Gospels before me, recognising the true Catholic and Apostolic Faith, abjure, detest and anathemize all sorts of heresy and apostasy which rise up against the Holy Catholic Faith and the evangelical Law of Christ our Redeemer and Saviour, and against the Apostolic See and the Roman Church, especially that heresy into which I as an evil person have fallen and have confessed before Your Lordships, which has been read here publicly to me and of which I have been accused; and I abjure and promise to keep and observe that holy faith which the Holy Mother Church of Rome holds, keeps and teaches, and that I shall always be obedient to our Lord the Pope and his successors who canonically follow him in the Holy Apostolic See, and to his decisions, and I accept that all those who act contrary to this Holy Catholic Faith are worthy to be condemned, and I promise never to have anything to do with them and to persecute them as far as I am able, and I shall reveal any heresy of which I hear and notify any Inquisitor and prelate of the Holy Catholic Church, wherever I am. And I swear and promise that I shall humbly receive with all my strength and power any penances that are or may be imposed on me, and shall comply with them in all respects without resistance. I want, consent and declare my agreement, that if I at any time, may God forbid, go against anything of the aforementioned ... that in that case I should be taken and held as relapsed and impenitent, and I submit myself to the correction and severity of the Holy Canons, so that all punishments and penalties contained in them shall be imposed on me as on anyone guilty of heresy, and from now on I consent that they be imposed on me and that I should suffer them if ever anything is proved against me for having committed what I have abjured, and I ask the secretary here present to give it to me as a statement, and those present to be the witnesses.

Since many of the Judaizers were illiterate, the secretary read the abjuration aloud and the reconciled victim repeated it. It is not clear if it was read for each one. If so, the reading would have taken a very long time. Despite the solemnity of the occasion, the presence of so many civil and Church dignitaries and others of high standing, of several companies of soldiers to maintain order, the crowd could not be forced to keep silent for so many hours. At the great *auto de fe* of 1680, the reading of the sentences alone lasted until nine in the evening.[12] An individual repetition of the long abjuration for each penitent would have been impossible. However, the document was read individually to each one the next day.

Now the *auto de fe* reached its apotheosis. In the candle-lit darkness, the penitents were kneeling around the altar. They listened as the inquisitor, robed as for Pontifical High Mass, wearing his mitre, asked the questions of the Articles of Faith, beginning with: 'Do you believe that God is One in essence and three in person, all-powerful, without beginning, middle or end?' and ending: 'Do you believe that at the end of the world He will come to judge the good and the evil, and He will grant glory to the good and lasting punishment to the evil?' To each question they replied in chorus 'Yes, I believe' (*Sí, creo*).

Exhausted by the long day but intensely relieved to learn that they would not lose their lives, that there was hope, that the Inquisition had shown mercy toward their sins, by that moment the Judaizers had probably abandoned all vestige of their Jewish awareness, and were wondering how they could have separated themselves from society in that way. It would be difficult to be a part of it again, but far from impossible. They would listen with fervour to the exorcism '*Exorcizo Te, Immunde Spiritus...!*' At that moment the choir began to sing the Psalm *Miserere Mei*, while the officers of the Inquisition struck the shoulders of the penitents lightly and symbolically with canes. Then the note changed. The inquisitor began to sing the hymn 'Veni, Creator Spiritus' and the Green Cross, symbol of the Holy Office, which until then had been covered with a black cloth, was unveiled. Then, after a triumphant *Te Deum*, came the supreme moment: the absolution of the penitents. When this was done the soldiers fired their muskets, the band played joyful music and the candles carried by the reconciled penitents were lit. It was a moment of supreme exaltation, as sin was erased and the guilty were now readmitted to the Church and Spanish society.

The condemned

For the Judaizers who were to go to the stake, things were very different. They had received 24 hours' notice of their fate, so that the friars could alternate, not leaving them a moment alone, persuading them to accept Christian truth and save their souls if not their mortal bodies. The Holy Office used a formula, which an inquisitor read to each condemned person in the cell:

> Brother (or sister), your case has been examined by very learned persons, and your crimes are so grave and so evil, that for their just punishment and as an example to others it has been decided that tomorrow you shall die. Be warned and prepare yourself: here are two friars for you to do what is appropriate.

What would be the atmosphere in the cell of a man or woman now condemned to die horribly, under constant persuasion from a friar skilled in his office? Could the victim, stunned, perhaps not even able to control the natural movements of his body, concentrate on what the friar was whispering in his ear? In most cases, the friar told the authorities that the condemned person had shown signs of repentance, which justified instructing the executioner to garrotte him before the torch was applied to the faggots. At least the death would be quicker than by asphyxiation or worse when the flames took hold of the victim's clothes.

After the sentences were read at the *auto de fe*, the condemned, mounted on donkeys, accompanied by soldiers and usually by a mob which insulted them, were taken off to the place used for burnings (the *quemadero*).

Jewish martyrs

Some victims, far from denying or confessing their Judaism penitently, boasted of it. They glorified in what the inquisitors and the spectators at the *auto de fe* considered a sin, one which not only was an offence to the deeply felt values of the Hispanic world of the time but also a self-condemnation to eternal perdition.

Some New Christians emigrated to Spanish America, perhaps hoping to be free to practise Judaism there. One of them was Francisco Maldonado da Silva, a doctor who lived in Tucumán, in the north of present-day Argentina, the son of a Judaizer reconciled in 1605. Arrested himself in 1626, Maldonado da Silva spent thirteen years in prison. But he refused even to swear an oath by Jesus Christ or the Cross, insisting that he would do so only by the God of Israel. He rejected all efforts to persuade him of the truth of Christianity. He ate no meat, fasted often and circumcised himself using a knife and scissors. He allowed his beard to grow long and called himself Eli the Nazirite. Challenging the discipline of the Inquisition prison, he tried to speak to other prisoners whenever possible and even composed treatises against the Inquisition, using any materials he could find. At last the Inquisition despaired of persuading him to return to Catholicism, and decided he should appear at an *auto de fe* and be burnt at the stake in Lima on 23 January 1639. Here, 61 Judaizers appeared, ten were burnt and the bones of a further two were hurled into the flames. As Maldonado da Silva awaited death, a strong wind began to blow. He cried out, according to reports, 'The God of Israel has decreed this, to see me face to face from the sky'.[13]

In a description of this *auto de fe*, one author speaks about two rabbis who 'taught apostasy and the dead Law to many'. These were Manuel Bautista Pérez, a slave merchant, in partnership with Sebastián Duarte, his brother-in-law. Pérez owned a silver mine and a luxurious mansion.[14] He was strictly observant of the Law of Moses and the leader of the Portuguese New Christians in Lima, who called him '*el capitán grande*'.[15] Both men died at the stake. At the same *auto de fe* the tortured body of Diego López de Fonseca, a Lima merchant, was carried to the stake where he died impenitent, faithful to Judaism.[16]

Possibly the most fiercely pursued of all the crypto-Jewish families was that of Núñez Bernal, three of whose members were burnt at the stake in 1655.[17] Manuel Núñez Bernal, born at Almeida (Portugal) in 1612, called himself secretly Abraham. Setting himself up in business in Ecija, near Seville, he married Leonor Báez, a New Christian, who bore him five children whom he brought up as Jews. The Inquisition uncovered what it considered a source of 'infection' in this Andalusian town, so that at the *auto de fe* of Córdoba of 3 May 1655 a large number of Judaizers appeared. The *auto* was public and general, that is everybody was free to come and watch, and it was held in the public square, the Corredera, and required a wooden dais and stands as well as the hiring of soldiers to maintain order and protect the victims from the mob. The promise of entertainment on a fine spring day brought hundreds of people from all over Andalusia. Three bigamists, four witches and a renegade Berber woman were quickly dealt with. Then came 36 women and 42 men condemned for Judaizing. Two had died in gaol and eighteen were burnt in effigy because they had managed to escape the round up. These included Manuel Núñez Bernal's cashier and personal manservant. This suggests that, if the servants and employees managed to get away, the master and mistress could have done so as well but preferred perhaps to meet their fate as martyrs. Five Judaizers were relaxed to the secular arm to be burnt, including Elena Méndez, relapsed and impenitent, the wife of Francisco Rodríguez de Almeida, who was reconciled at the same *auto* with his daughter María, while his other daughter, Blanca, perished in the flames.

The last to be relaxed was Manuel Núñez Bernal, who was described by Dr Vargas, the court doctor, as

> Such an obstinate Jew that, though grave and saintly friars sought to persuade him all night in his cell and all day on the dais, even though their words would have melted bronze and softened coral reefs . . . weary of his perversity they retired baffled.[18]

At these spectacular *autos de fe*, aristocrats competed for the honour of acting as familiars, who would accompany the impenitent victims, trying to persuade them to save their souls. In the case of Núñez Bernal,

> The Most Excellent Marquess of Los Vélez approached him and, with a crucifix in his hand and much Christian zeal in his heart, begged him by the entrails of Christ to accept His holy law. This edified and moved everybody to tears, but only rendered the unfortunate wretch more obstinate. He saw him, heard him but went on to the stake, where he was burnt alive. The flames took possession of his body as they will his soul, to burn in the eternal flames of Hell.[19]

Even at the final moment, Manuel Núñez Bernal refused the chance of a quick death at the hands of the executioner, preferring to be burnt alive. One hopes that he lost consciousness before the flames touched his flesh. Did his Judaism matter more to him than to his wife and son, who both survived the *auto*? Leonor Báez was sentenced to prison, after receiving two hundred lashes as she rode on an ass through the busy streets. Jorge, their 13-year-old son, was imprisoned and intensively catechized during the next four years so that he would forget everything his parents had taught him about their religion.

When the notice of this *auto de fe* reached the Spanish and Portuguese Jewish community in Amsterdam, they held a service of mourning, at which the sermon was preached by the famous rabbi Aboab da Fonseca. The Jewish poets of the community collaborated in, composing a volume of *Eulogies Earnestly Dedicated to the Blessed Memory of Abraham Núñez Bernal, Who Was Burned Alive in Cordoba on 3 May 1655, Sanctifying the Name of his Creator*.

Two months earlier, Abraham's nephew, Marcos or Isaac de Almeida Bernal, was executed also. He had spent five long years in the Inquisition gaol at Valladolid in Castile, refusing to abandon Judaism. Not only did he refuse to admit that he had sinned and to ask for absolution, as his spiritual advisers continued to beg him to do all the way to the *quemadero*, but, since they feared he might cry out his loyalty to Judaism, they gagged him. As they asked him if he was ready to confess his sin, he shook his head. Once however, when they thought he had nodded agreement, they removed his gag. But they had made a mistake and, despite his terrible and imminent fate, Marcos summoned up strength to cry out his faith in the God of his ancestors, and accused the friars of idolatry in that they bowed down to images and statues. The soldiers and familiars struggled to protect Marcos from the rage of the mob. When they reached the stakes, it began to drizzle, which the authorities judged to be a divine favour, because it would give them more time to persuade the victim to save his soul. But Marcos continued to shout his defiance, so soot and tar were brought to encourage the wood to burn and, as the flames rose, the Jewish account of Marcos's martyrdom describes him as singing psalms.[20]

Jerónimo Melo

Not all these valiant victims of the Inquisition enjoyed posthumous fame. How did the brothers Rafael and Jerónimo Melo, 48 and 42 years old respectively, live their Judaism? Rafael, who owned a candlemaking business, died before he could appear at the *auto de fe* held at Murcia on 30 November 1724. His brother was sentenced to the stake. Jerónimo watched Rafael's effigy paraded, ridiculed and finally thrown, together with his disinterred bones, into the flames. Was it complete rejection of society or his strong convictions which impelled Jerónimo to turn away from the persuasive tongues of the friars who exhorted him to ask for mercy and confess his sin, so that his soul would go to Heaven? The Inquisition saw that Jerónimo Melo was obstinate and morally strong, so they gagged him during the *auto de fe* and on the way to the *quemadero*, watching him closely for any sign of repentance, until the flames and smoke drove the confessors away.[21]

Diego López Duro

One of the most famous examples of obstinacy or heroic constancy, depending on the point of view of the observer, was that of Diego López Duro, 26 years old, in business in Constantina, not far from Seville. He was arrested in 1698. At an *auto* on 20 December 1699, he received a relatively mild punishment, except for the hundred lashes he endured as he rode on donkeyback through the city. He would have to stay for a year in the penitential prison wearing the tunic of shame, the sanbenito, and of course lose all his property. One day in 1700, as he heard Mass together with the other penitents, in Santa Ana Church, full of inhabitants of the Triana district of Seville, he stood up and shouted at the preacher who was saying that the Law of Moses was dead and invalid. 'You lie! You lie! Long live the Law of Moses!' The Inquisition familiars quickly moved in to protect him against the anger of the congregation as the other penitents shrank from him in fear. Diego was taken at once to a cell. Here he remained obstinate, practising what he could of Judaism. Two teams with three skilled friars attended him in shifts from three in the afternoon on Friday 26 October 1703 until dawn on the Sunday, when the *auto de fe* was to be held, trying to 'direct his soul along the road to salvation'. Did Diego sleep at all during those 40 hours? Did he perhaps think that God had saved his life at his first trial so that he might proclaim Judaism in front of everybody in Church, even if he died for it?[22] The Inquisition had no alternative but to condemn him to the stake, hoping that at the last moment he would ask for mercy and return to the Catholic flock. Almost three years after entering gaol for the second time, Diego López Duro was taken to the place of execution. Tranquil amid the shouting of the crowd and the persuasive words of the accompanying friars, Diego ended his life. His memory was preserved in the form of a mural by Lucas Valdés called *The Ordeal of Diego López Duro* in the Sevillian church of La Magdalena, built at the end of the seventeenth century on the site of San Pablo el Real where many *autos* took place.[23]

Diego López De Castro

In Toledo, on 28 October 1723, Diego López de Castro, who added the surnames Paz, Coronel y Quirós to his patronymic, a 51-year-old business representative, born in Betanzos in Galicia, died at the stake. During his imprisonment, a spy had been placed in his cell. He reported to the inquisitors that Diego changed his shirt and underwear on Friday nights and that this Jew – seeing his persistence, he can hardly be called a secret Jew – refused to eat forbidden food included in the prison rations, such as rabbit, eels, blood sausage, hares and bacon.[24] Condemned to die, Diego resisted the efforts of those who strove to make him repent. He died '*negativo, convicto, revocante y pertinaz*' (negative, convicted, revoking earlier confessions and obstinate). As in other cases, a gag had been prepared in case he proclaimed his Jewish convictions and caused a riot, but as the donkey plodded towards the *quemadero* with him on its back he said nothing.[25] Was he reciting psalms or perhaps the *Shema*, the Jewish confession of faith?

Leonor Margarita de Yuste

Hers is perhaps the most moving example of Marrano martyrdom that can be found. On 7 April 1720, twelve people appeared at an *auto de fe* in Madrid, including three crypto-Jewish women. Two of them, Leonor Diaz and Luisa del Valle, had been reconciled at an earlier trial and had relapsed. Just before the flames were lit they asked to confess their sins. They were killed mercifully by the executioner's garrotte and their bodies then burnt. The third woman, however, Leonor Margarita de Yuste, a humble 22-year-old seamstress of Madrid, refused to repent. Perhaps because she was unbalanced, or perhaps she wanted to die quickly, the young woman threw herself into the fire. The Inquisition did not care for this sort of heroics, so its officials immediately confiscated a ballad on the event which was already in press the following day.[26]

Repentance *in extremis*

One could, provided one was not a relapsed Judaizer, save one's life at the last moment by asking for mercy and making a full confession. María Feliciana Hurtado de Mendoza Pimentel, for example, who belonged to a substantial group of Madrid Judaizers at the beginning of the eighteenth century, had refused to betray her fellow Judaizers during her long interrogations. On 24 February 1723, however, as she heard her sentence of burning read at the *auto de fe* – though she had already known her fate for at least 24 hours – she whispered to the friars who accompanied her that she wished to confess. One of the inquisitors took her to the sacristy of the church of St Peter Martyr in Toledo where the *auto* was taking place, and listened to her confession. When the inquisitors deliberated, they decided that her confession was sufficient to save her from death, and sent her back to her cell. On 28 October 1723, María Feliciana appeared at another *auto de fe*, where she heard the Inquisition secretary read out her sentence of prison for life wearing the sanbenito, and public shame with two hundred lashes, 'as a very late confessant' (*por muy tarda confitente*). Medical reasons adduced by the doctor, however, impelled the court to excuse her this punishment.

Fernando de Castro

The case of Fernando de Castro, condemned to die at the same *auto de fe* as María Feliciana, was similar. He learned his fate at about 10 or 11 the previous night. After that, unable to withstand the terror he felt either at the idea of death or the Hell to which he might go if Christianity were true, he could no longer resist. At 7 next morning, as the sanbenito with the painted flames was slipped over his head, he asked to make his confession. He wept as he admitted the Judaism that he and his companions had practised, and said that he had not slept for three nights. What would be the thoughts of this man, left alone in his cell, as he heard the steps of the other prisoners leaving for the *auto de fe*? Guilt? Shame? Relief? On 1 July 1725, Fernando de Castro appeared at another *auto de fe*. However, despite his previous collapse, he was now condemned again to be burnt as impenitent and *revocante*. He had probably revoked his confession. Perhaps he had gathered his moral strength to proclaim his Judaism in a way which was particularly provocative to the Holy Office, which saw his earlier collapse as a sign of divine mercy.

The stake was reserved for the impenitent and the relapsed. The insolent, defiant, late or insufficient confessants received the lash, delivered during the shameful parade on an ass's back around the streets of the town. There is no report of the hospitalization of any of the victims, who received in some cases two hundred lashes, which suggests that the aim of the punishment was not to cause serious physical damage but to humiliate. Those punished do not seem to have lost consciousness nor to have suffered wounds which were slow to heal. One may, however, imagine the state of mind of a mature married woman, naked to the waist, uncomfortably mounted on a donkey, forced, by a fork in which her neck is resting, to sit upright, surrounded by the mob jeering at her, just as Goya conveys the scene in Number 24 of *Los Caprichos*, entitled 'There was no alternative' (*No hubo remedio*). Actually, Goya shows each of the constables with a stick in his hand, but they are not striking the victim, nor does the public executioner, who usually administered the punishment, appear in the drawing. Shame was evidently the principal purpose of this ritual, which took the victim through the main streets of a town where he or she was well known, surrounded by a jeering mob, screaming insults and even throwing rotten vegetables or worse.

This was not the end of the hideous experience of arrest, imprisonment, isolation, separation from one's family, anxiety and terror, interrogation, possible torture, unbearable anticipation of the sentence and perhaps psychological collapse, sense of guilt for having Judaized or perhaps having betrayed one's accomplices and usually close family, dread at learning that people were to be burnt at the stake and shame at having to appear in public clad in the sanbenito and to be humiliatingly paraded around the streets. Almost always the penance imposed included a period of reclusion in the penitential prison, which in theory

3 Number 24 of the series 'Los Caprichos' by Francisco Goya (1746–1828). The title *'Nohubo remedio'* ('There was no alternative') refers to the decision to impose the sentence of public ridicule to which the victim is being subjected.

was not commutable. What this meant was that the Inquisition decided when one was ready to be released. The penitential prison was usually a rooming-house, bought or rented by the Inquisition. When there were a lot of prisoners, they were crowded together with their families in conditions more unsanitary than those of the secret cells. In Murcia in 1726, for instance, a contagious illness killed six or seven prisoners a day.

While one stayed in the penitential prison, however, one had to maintain oneself, so the prisoners, whose property had been confiscated and sold, were allowed to try to earn their living while wearing the shameful sanbenito. Occasionally they might be able to take some cheap goods on credit and sell them.[27]

The conditions of life for prisoners undergoing penance were very difficult, especially for those who had previously enjoyed middle-class standards. Some had been wealthy. María Guiomar Arias, for example, who appeared at the *auto de fe* in Toledo on 19 March 1721, was the wife of Francisco de Miranda, a rich businessman and general collector of the *millones* tax. Both had been arrested in the great roundup of Madrid Jews. He appeared at the *auto de fe* in Toledo on 18 May 1721. Both were sentenced to life imprisonment and two hundred lashes, she at the age of 50 and he at 55. She was reduced to begging the Holy Office to return enough of the money taken from her husband to enable them to live. The Inquisition gave them the pittance of 4 reals a day.[28]

Consequently, among the correspondence between the local courts and the *Suprema*, letters often appear from prisoners asking to be freed. On 16 September, 1702, for example, Manuel Rodríguez Moreira wrote from Toledo to the *Suprema* asking for a pardon and to be given some decent clothes, as his were in tatters. On 29 March the following year he appealed again, explained that he was suffering from continual fevers. The *Suprema* wrote to the Toledo Inquisitors, who in their turn consulted the clergy who were overseeing the spiritual reeducation of the prisoner. They were happy to say that 'he complies humbly with his obligations and attends Church frequently. He suffers from attacks ...'[29] There is no record of the result of Manuel Rodríguez Moreira's appeal. We can but hope that it was favourable and he was released.

Another confessed Judaizer, Manuel de Robles, complained on 17 March 1702 about conditions in the Toledo penitential prison. The Inquisitors answered the *Suprema*'s enquiry saying that Robles was indeed showing signs of true penitence. Nevertheless they added, perhaps somewhat stung by the implied criticism, 'And as for the lack of facilities, this is the general complaint of all the prisoners. Our opinion is that he should serve his sentence ... ' Despite this advice, the *Suprema* decided, 'The Council's view is that what is left of his life sentence may be commuted.'[30]

It would seem from these examples, if they are typical, that generally the Inquisition responded favourably to appeals for the commutation of sentences. The prisoners had experienced the weight of the Inquisition's hand. If now they were indeed complying with the demands of the Church, why keep them in gaol any longer, especially as the space was probably needed for others? Besides, in the unsatisfactory conditions of the penitential prison other undesirable situations could arise, as when, on 19 April 1701, the Toledo court wrote to the *Suprema* as follows:

> Having heard from the gaoler of the Penitential prison that Manuel de Andrade and Isabel del Castillo, who are serving the sentences imposed on them, are not living morally and are giving cause for scandal, we have decided that they should be transferred to separate prisons.

However, the Inquisition seemed concerned that they might come together again, so they recommended that Manuel de Andrade should be transferred to the jurisdiction of another Inquisition court to serve his sentence. Manuel was duly sent to Cuenca.[31]

Amid the squalor of their lives, even the comfort of love was denied to Manuel and Isabel. Perhaps in the end they were united, but such information is not available. Did the comfortably off among them ever manage to rebuild their finances despite internal exile, which was frequently imposed, or was their ruin permanent? Certainly the Holy Office did not need to burn heretics in order to ruin whole families morally, physically and economically.

The big fish fell into the net one after the other. As the Spanish Crown reduced its foreign obligations, the bankers of the second half of the seventeenth century – Sebastián Cortizos, Simón de Fonseca Piña and Diego Felipe de Montesinos, who farmed the tax on salt and the *alcabala* or excise tax – were no longer needed. Montesinos left for Amsterdam, but his sons continued to manage the Spanish branch of his firm.[32] By the last decade of the century almost the only important crypto-Jew in Spain was Francisco Báez Eminente, who managed the *almojarifazgos* or customs duty collections for Castile and Andalusia, and was one of the purveyors of supplies to the army and the navy. Monsieur Lantéry, a French merchant living in Cadiz, recalled how all these responsibilities were in the hands of Don Francisco Báez Eminente, 'because they are associated with the customs . . . '[33]

One day in 1677, a friar was quarrelling with Don Francisco about some cloth. Raising his voice he offensively called him a Jew. Lantéry comments: 'Perhaps he was happy to be called what he really was in his heart of hearts. because those who are called that word are rather proud to be called Jews.'[34] It was a strange comment. Lantéry, the foreigner in Spain, must have known how dangerous it was to reveal what was in one's innermost thoughts. Still, he must have had his reasons for writing the words.

Actually, the great financiers and *asentistas* were out of Spain and Portugal by now, though they often acted as representatives, even diplomatic ones, of Spain and Portugal. One of the most interesting families were the Curiels, who had been called Nunes da Costa in Portugal. This family occupied important roles in diplomacy, yet several of its members were imprisoned and underwent torture at the hands of the Inquisition, while Duarte Nunes de Costa himself played an important part in the life of the Spanish and Portuguese Jewish community of Amsterdam.[35]

Two Portuguese Marranos, Antonio Alvarez Machado and Isaac Pereira, supplied military stores to William of Orange in his campaign against James II in 1688, while the first Jew to receive a knighthood for his services was the ex-Marrano Sir Solomon de Medina (1650–1730). The best-known of these purveyors in England was perhaps Joseph Cortissos (1656–1742), a descendant of the famous Manuel Cortizos, as the name was spelt in Spain. Joseph Cortissos supplied goods and food to English armies during the War of the Spanish Succession of 1700–1714. He lost a fortune and spent the rest of his life trying to recover what he had spent in the service of his adopted country, which, nevertheless, had given him freedom to live in it according to his conscience.[36]

That these men were Jews did not prevent Nunes da Costa serving Portugal nor Isaac Nunes (Manuel) de Belmonte, later Baron de Belmonte, serving Spain.[37]

The Curiel or Nunes da Costa family figures also in the history of the efforts by the Portuguese King João IV (1640–1656) to retain the financial support of the New Christians for his newly independent state. An important part was played in this by the Jesuit Father Antonio Vieira, who was convinced that the health of the Portuguese economy required the return to Portugal of the New Christians and that consequently the harsh stance of the Inquisition towards them needed to be modified. However, despite Vieira and the support of the king, the Portuguese parliament remained hostile towards the New Christians. Vieira suggested that the Jewish merchants who lived abroad should be allowed to return. It was essential, wrote Vieira, that the Inquisition be prevented from seizing the goods of these merchants because confiscations made people wary of taking business risks in general. On 10 March 1649, Vieira and others succeeded in creating a great trading company, what would now be called a holding, the Companhia Geral do Brasil.[38] The Companhia would employ a fleet of 36 galleys to protect Portuguese shipping against Spain and Holland.[39] Portuguese New Christians financed a fleet which raised the blockade of Bahía. One of them was Duarte da Silva (1596–1688), who owned one of the best-known business houses in Lisbon. His imprisonment in December 1647 led to a serious collapse of Portuguese credit on the international markets.[40] He was tortured and had to abjure *de vehementis*. To try to compensate him for his suffering, he was given privileges and honour by the Portuguese authorities, who sent him to England with his brother Francisco in 1662 as part of the mission to discuss the marriage of the Princess Catherine da Braganza and Charles II.

As in Spain, the Holy Office was too powerful in Portugal for new ideas to be introduced. Nobody could cherish any hopes after the deaths at the stake, on 15 December 1647, of Isaac de Castro Tartas, brought from Brazil to Lisbon to face the Inquisition, and on 1 December 1652, of Manuel Fernandes Vila Real, a distinguished supporter of the Braganza monarchy, and a diplomatic representative of his country in Paris, arrested on a visit to Lisbon and denounced for Judaizing. Among other crimes, he had celebrated Passover with the Marranos of Rouen.

On 11 June 1670, the Portuguese New Christians, always under suspicion, were blamed for the theft and desecration of some religious objects from a convent. A number of New Christian merchants were arrested. An offer was made of a sum sufficient to equip an army of five thousand men, but Inquisition fanaticism proved stronger than *raison politique*. Any concession, it was feared, would encourage the return and the 'infection' of Portugal by Jews who lived openly as such abroad.[41] Far from appreciating the vision of Father Vieira, Portuguese society reinforced the rules which excluded people of New Christian descent from public employment and the legal and medical professions. The arguments used in Portugal in the late seventeenth century were like those used in Spain fifty years earlier. During the rule of Olivares, it was the Portuguese Church and Inquisition which were particularly hostile to any tolerance towards the New Christians. At the end of the century, public opinion prevented the ideas of Vieira from coming to full fruition. On 2 May 1674 the New Christians in Portugal asked the Pope for another general pardon. The Portuguese parliament, however, objected to the proposal and to any reform in the procedures of the

Inquisition. Nevertheless, the Holy See was not at all happy with things as they were. The Inquisition in Portugal had recently burnt two nuns, who were probably innocent, while the New Christian merchants had offered half-a-million cruzados to Catholic Poland to help in the struggle against the encroaching Ottoman empire. As a result, on 16 October 1674, the Holy See suspended the Inquisition in Portugal.[42] The suspension, nevertheless, lasted only till 22 August 1681. The lifting of the suspension was followed by eleven years of *autos de fe*, with 988 victims.[43]

Both in Portugal and in Spain, on the eve of the century of the Enlightenment, the Inquisition was still energetically pursuing crypto-Judaism among the descendants of the New Christians of the fifteenth century. Secret Judaism, astonishingly, was still alive and would call forth a still more fierce and bloody response in the first decades of the eighteenth century.

9

'A great deal of Judaism is to be found in Spain'[1]

The economist Francisco Máximo de Moya Torres, who made this statement in a report submitted to King Philip V in 1727, had no hesitation in warning his sovereign of the continued presence of Jews in Spain. The accusations he makes to justify the hunt and eradication of crypto-Judaism had hardly changed in over two centuries:

> [T]hese vile people are hidden, infecting so much ... Their usual life, Sire, is one of profit and usury: their professions are those of doctors, *rentiers*, merchants, confectioners, and all their trades are of idlers; they are clever and astute and take vengeance on Christian blood.[2]

Moya Torres accuses the Judaizers of transferring their capital abroad. He insists that deceit has made them all rich even though the Inquisition confiscated their ancestors' property. They even change their names and marry Old Christians, he claims.

His solution, like the one proposed a century earlier, was to punish the Judaizers severely before expelling them from Spain. Alternatively, they should be physically mutilated so that they could easily be identified and kept under watch.[3]

Moya Torres was not the only anti-Jewish writer in Spain. In 1721 and again in 1731 new editions were issued of the well-known work by Father Torrejoncillo, *Centinela contra judíos puesta en la Iglesia de Dios* ('Sentinel against Jews, stationed in the Church of God'), first published in 1674 and imitated in 1736 by Antonio de Contreras's *Mayor Fiscal contra judíos* ('Principal accuser of the Jews'). These writers insisted that, despite baptism, the supposed moral defects of the Jews were passed on to their descendants, the great majority of whom must by now have become assimilated to the general population. In these anti-Jewish writings, 'Pages, chapters and entire works follow one another, all obsessed by something which does not exist objectively: the Jew.'[4]

Actually, Jews did exist objectively in Spain. Clearly their presence mattered a great deal to some people, even if the anti-Jewish writers exaggerated the prevalence of secret Judaism and assumed that a person descended from somebody punished for Judaizing by the Inquisition was *ipso facto* suspect. The important issue, however, is whether the number of Judaizers detected by the Inquisition in the first half of the eighteenth century was high enough to justify Moya Torres's statement that there was '*muchísimo*' Judaism in Spain.

In one particular activity, the State tobacco monopoly, Philip V prohibited the employment of New Christians if they had undergone Inquisition penance.[5] The occupations of Judaizers listed in the accounts of the larger *autos de fe* in the eighteenth century confirm that administering the tobacco monopoly – at different levels ranging from a simple local tobacco retailer to the director of the monopoly in Aragon or Castile – was the occupation of quite a number of Judaizers. Farming this monopoly was a speculative matter, because the people involved guaranteed to sell certain quantities of tobacco products as well as to collect the tax.[6] Perhaps the marked involvement of Judaizers in the tobacco trade came about because much more of this product was being used. A tobacco container was frequently found among the personal possessions of persons, even women, who were arrested by the Inquisition. A blending industry was developing in Amsterdam, seat of the greatest community of ex-Marranos.[7] Nevertheless, the fact that many Judaizers were in the tobacco trade does not mean that most of them were so engaged, nor that most of the people in that business were Jews or descended from New Christians. Nor, of course, does it mean that they served the State monopoly – the *estanco*, as it is still called – any worse than Old Christians.

The last major campaign in the Inquisition's war against crypto-Judaism began with a wave of arrests in 1715 and subsequent years. For the following twelve years *autos de fe* were held, at a rate of almost one a month, in almost all the cities in Spain where there were Inquisition courts. The phenomenon would continue at a slower rate until the 1740s. The reasons for it were complicated and arose to some extent from a conflict with new Bourbon ideas about the relation between the State and the Inquisition.

Charles II, the last Habsburg monarch of Spain, had died on 1 November 1700 without an heir, though the State Council had decided on the Bourbon Philip of Anjou as the successor. As Philip V of

Spain, the latter made a State entry into Madrid in April 1701. This was followed by a British and Dutch declaration of war in support of the Austrian archduke Charles. The chaos and disorder caused by the War of the Spanish Succession brought about a lull in Inquisition activity in the first fifteen years of the century. In addition, as Philip was fighting, the queen, Marie Louise of Savoy, supported by the powerful Princesse des Ursins, her French finance expert Jean Orry, the French ambassador Amelot and the royal confessor Father Robinet, strove to put order into the chaotic affairs of Spain. Sinecures and appointments made without royal consent were cancelled. Rigid financial control was instituted, especially over property confiscated by the Inquisition, which retained a percentage before it handed the rest to the Treasury.[8]

Already during the previous reign, on 12 May 1693, a proposal had suggested limiting the range of Inquisitorial jurisdiction, because the Holy Office sometimes acted high-handedly over the heads of the royal judges themselves. In the early years of the new century, this problem would loom large.[9]

The suggested reforms, however, were not intended to reduce the power of the Holy Office to attack heresy, only to limit its privileges when they conflicted with those of the king and the State. Here, the key person was Melchor de Macanaz (1670–1760). Between 1709 and 1714 this distinguished statesman and lawyer led a centralizing and regalist reform, designed to reinforce the power of the State over other powerful bodies, particularly the Church, with which Macanaz came into conflict. He was not to be forgiven.[10] Reaching the apogee of his power in November 1713, when he was named *fiscal general* or chief legal officer of the kingdom, Macanaz, the Princesse des Ursins and their advisers strove to assert the independence of Spain from the Holy See and to transfer power to a new class of lawyers and civil servants. Macanaz drew up a document restricting Rome's power over the Spanish Church and the Holy Office, limiting the jurisdiction of the Inquisition, taxing its privileges and immunities, and forcing it to submit to the authority of the Royal Council of Castile.[11] He even proposed verifying the details of deathbed confessions, in order to discipline those priests who induced the dying to bequeath their property to the Church. This proposal was unsuccessful, but it nevertheless added to Macanaz's reputation of impiety, while the 'oppressed Inquisition' became a weapon in the hands of xenophobes in their fight against French influence and against Macanaz.

In a letter to the king of 7 February 1714, Macanaz wrote, in a triumphant tone, that 'the entire ecclesiastical estate, both secular and regular, which, as Your Majesty knows, has more power than Your Majesty himself, has been contained . . . '[12] Macanaz's proposals were condemned by the Inquisition in July 1714. He had advocated abolishing the right of the Church to grant dispensations for marriages between close relatives, giving the king the right to appoint bishops and introducing the taxation of religious orders. There was, nevertheless, no suggestion of touching the Inquisition's obligation to pursue heresy.

On 12 September 1714 Barcelona fell to Philip V. The War of the Spanish Succession came to an end. Queen Marie Louise had died on 14 February 1714, and this unleashed a process which would lead to the fall of Macanaz. The young widower Philip V remarried on 24 December 1714. His bride was Isabel Farnese, niece of Mariana de Neoburg, the widow of the previous king, and a powerful woman of independent mind. Orry, Macanaz and Father Robinet were immediately dismissed, and Cardinal Giudice reoccupied the post of Inquisitor-General from which he had been ejected the previous year as a result of an altercation with the Princesse des Ursins.

Giudice was personally hostile to Macanaz who had prevented him, as a foreigner (he was an Italian), from becoming Archbishop of Toledo. Fearing the worst, Macanaz fled to France.[13] The Inquisition embargoed his property and investigated his genealogy, but could not do what would, in its eyes, have explained Macanaz's campaign against it: prove that he was of New Christian descent.[14] Had the Holy Office's investigations revealed a conviction for heresy in Macanaz's family within the last two or three generations, he could have been accused of having occupied his great office illegally. The enquiry, however, was probably instigated in the hope of accusing Macanaz of Judaizing. But nothing could be found against him and, some twenty years later, he would write a major defence of the Inquisition.[15]

Had the Inquisition not supported the cause of Philip V during the War of Succession, perhaps the Bourbon king would not have defended it against the French advisers and Macanaz. But the Holy Office had encouraged the faithful to report any priests who had advised them to rebel against the king. Consequently, once the war was over and Philip V was securely on his throne, he continued to grant the Inquisition the autonomy it had always enjoyed.[16] What is more, on 28 March 1715, Philip V publicly retracted his support of Macanaz's proposals to reform the Inquisition. In a letter circulated to the various Inquisition courts, he wrote that he had been 'sinisterly influenced and advised . . . but now, properly informed . . . he intended to give total support to the Inquisition.'[17]

There was, consequently, no foundation for the statements made in 1718 by an Inquisition prisoner and witness, Antonio Rodríguez Carrasco, before the Toledo court. According to him, a Judaizing woman, María de Tudela, had said that Macanaz was a Jew who had fled to Leghorn.[18] María de Tudela, who repeated what she had heard in the Judaizing circles in which she had lived before her arrest, said that if the Holy Office arrested the well-known Dr Zapata for Judaizing, the king would release him just as he had Macanaz. Furthermore, María de Tudela said that another Judaizing family, the Carrillos, were close friends of the Princesse des Ursins. Yet there was no smoke without fire here, and it does seem as though the marked expansion in the Inquisition's persecution of secret Jews from 1715 onwards reflected a serious recrudescence of the phenomenon of crypto-Judaism, due possibly to the weakness of the Holy Office in the first fifteen years of the century.

The Inquisition at the start of the eighteenth century

Despite the chaos caused by the war, Inquisition activity against secret Judaism had continued. There were still trials for Judaizing. Approximately 441 victims appeared at sixty *autos de fe* between 1700 and 1715.[19] Penances were relatively mild, save for some burnings at Valladolid where in the years 1700 to 1706 there were many arrests and seven *autos de fe*. The latter were the consequence of arrests made before the war, probably of Portuguese passing through Spain on the way to France.[20] The total number of those convicted by this very energetic court between 1699 and 1704 is 147, including ten who were burnt at the stake. It would appear, nonetheless, that the severity of this court had no equal in any other Spanish Inquisition court until the 1720s. In Toledo, for example, the years 1706 to 1715 produced minimal figures,[21] among other reasons because of the chaotic political situation.[22] In Seville, *autos de fe* in 1702, 1703 and 1715 produced fifty victims.[23] A study of the Holy Office in Valencia shows the dire financial position of that court during the war years.[24] In Granada, usually a very active court, while there were 39 *autos de fe* between 1680 and 1700, there were only 17 over the following twenty years, and most of these after 1715 when there was a wave of arrests of Judaizers.[25]

It may have been true that the reduction in Inquisition activity between 1705 and 1715 reflected the rise in power of the Princesse des Ursins, Macanaz and the modernizing French advisers. Yet there is no reason to think that the political atmosphere hindered the arrest and trial of Judaizers. The post-1715 heightening of the Inquisition campaign can probably be explained by the economic recovery which came with the end of the war, and by a reaction against the danger represented by the Macanaz regalist tendency. The important Portuguese New Christians who had previously supplied funds and material to Spanish armies had been eliminated by the Holy Office. Their descendants, such as Joseph Cortissos, were now living outside Spain and serving England and Austria.[26] There was, consequently, no longer any protection in high places for Judaizers.

The Inquisition girds its loins

During the years when Cardinal Giudice (1715–1717), José de Molines (1717), and Juan de Camargo (1717–1733) were Inquisitors-General, orders were regularly issued to the district courts instructing them to put their archives in order and set to work to deal with a wave of crypto-Judaism inundating the country.

The evidence given by witnesses and prisoners, particularly in the series of trials held in Toledo between 1718 and 1721, suggests that the most important and wealthy of the Judaizers of the capital, Francisco de Miranda, had earlier been negotiating the right of Jews to live openly in the Calle Mayor and the Calle de Atocha, two of Madrid's important commercial streets, and in some ports.[27] Here 'openly' must be understood as meaning without being troubled by the Inquisition, as in France where the *marchands portugais nouveaux-chrétiens* were not officially living as Jews but where their behaviour was an open secret.[28]

The Toledo court began to make arrests, detaining on 19 July 1716 Antonio Rodríguez, the 51-year-old manager of the royal gunpowder factory at Tembleque. Accused of Judaizing, he denied the offence for three years. Threatened with torture, in 1719 he made a complete confession. His physical condition excused him the years in the galleys to which the court sentenced him.[29]

He confessed that he had observed the Law of Moses for sixteen years. Before his wife Isabel had died, she had told him that he should marry her niece, 'according to the rite of the Jews who marry the nearest relative of the dead wife'. Jewish law does indeed permit marriage of uncle and niece, but Christian law did not, so Rodríguez and numerous other Judaizers who married their nieces claimed that it was their cousins that they wanted to marry. For this a dispensation was granted by the Church, though at quite a high cost. One day in 1714, said Rodríguez, he went to see Francisco de Torres, an important tax farmer and owner of a wholesale grocery in Madrid. Torres offered to help Rodríguez. It was difficult to obtain the dispensation because the Church was in conflict with the authorities over the question of its rights and privileges. In another case, Francisco de Torres even told his wife's brother Juan de Ribera that he could marry the widow María Luis without obtaining a dissolution of his marriage. Juan de Ribera insisted that he was sexually impotent with his virgin wife, but he would not be if he married a widow. Actually it probably would not have been difficult, though perhaps expensive, to obtain a dissolution of his marriage if it had not been consummated. Torres, however, claimed that, as polygamy was permitted in the Bible, though prohibited by rabbinical decree and unknown since the Middle Ages among western Jews, Juan de Ribera could marry María Luis 'according to the Law of Moses'. That was what the couple did, asking Melchor, the firstborn son of Francisco de Torres, to bless them in the name of the patriarchs Abraham, Isaac and Jacob, a rite unknown in Jewish marriage. In yet another case, Torres forged a dispensation for two first cousins, Francisco de Lara and Francisca Alvarez, to marry.[30]

Antonio Rodríguez had first met Torres at the house of Francisco de Miranda, the richest of the Madrid Judaizers and someone whom the others tried to protect, refusing to mention his name in their confessions to the Inquisition court. Rodríguez suspected that the Inquisition was after him. He had heard that questions had been asked about whether it was true that he had followed Jewish customs in washing his dead wife's body, dressing her in a white shroud and burying her in virgin earth. He defended himself before the court by saying at first that it was his wife, not he, who had been the Judaizer. He did not know the Jewish customs about burial and Torres had had to explain to him what to do for his dead wife. During his conversations with Torres, however, the latter had told him that mere ignorance would not save him from the Inquisition and that he had better flee. Rodríguez refused to believe that he was in any danger. He could not afford the costly journey and he did not want to lose his profitable post in Tembleque.

The likelihood is that Antonio Rodríguez was only on the margins of the crypto-Jewish group. He had learnt that Torres was a leading Judaizer from his nephew Rodrigo de la Peña, who was tried in Logroño in 1717. Rodrigo was married to María de Tudela, whose loquacity was responsible for hundreds of arrests all over Spain.

María de Tudela

María de Tudela's endless chatter about the Judaizers of her time was used as evidence against a large number of people. She was the daughter of Luisa del Valle, who was burnt at the stake on 7 April 1720. María had lived in Madrid and was familiar with what the Inquisition called the *'complicidad judaizante'* of the capital. She certainly knew that Francisco de Torres, one of the leading Judaizers, had only recently been reconciled with the Church and that the trial of Francisco de Miranda had been stopped for lack of evidence because the Judaizers had not given this important and wealthy man away.[31]

A certain Antonio Rodríguez Carrasco (not the Antonio Rodríguez who managed the saltpetre monopoly) offered himself voluntarily as a prosecution witness at one of the trials.[32] This man had been in the criminal gaol accused of murder, but claimed to be a Judaizer because he felt safer in the better conditions of the Inquisition prison. The Inquisition had exercised its privileges and had him transferred to its own gaol. He gave his evidence in several long sessions between 30 April and 19 July 1718. He may be the Antonio Rodríguez Carrasco sentenced on 31 July 1718 for bigamy.[33] He was certainly a very deceitful person. When he saw María de Tudela, whom the Inquisition had allowed for medical reasons to walk up and down the corridors of the prison, he lied to her, telling her that he was a circumcised Jew. Why he did this is not too clear. Perhaps he hoped for clemency from the Inquisition court, which was usually very harsh on bigamists, by deceiving María and extracting all the information she had about the Judaizing families, and then repeating the details to the court. The man was probably in the habit of promising marriage to every woman he met, if it profited him in some way. When later, as Francisco de Torres tried to suggest that María's dozens of pages of testimony, transmitted through Rodríguez Carrasco, were not to be trusted, he told the court that María had discovered that her husband had died in prison in Logroño and that she was hoping to marry the feigned Judaizer Rodríguez Carrasco.[34]

Yet even if this was true, the details of what María told Rodríguez Carrasco were confirmed by later investigations and other witnesses' statements. It did not matter that there was probably a background of hidden personal rancour here. María de Tudela had been brought up as a Judaizer, as was so often the case in that shadowy world of shadows and secrets, by her aunt, Leonor del Valle, who had managed to flee to Bayonne. María and her mother had looked after the pregnant niece and second wife of the Antonio Rodríguez who had the gunpowder interest in Tembleque and who was her husband's uncle. But when the woman gave birth, they put the baby into an orphanage. All this story was told to the court by the gaoler, who had heard it from María herself. When Antonio Rodríguez and his niece and second wife were

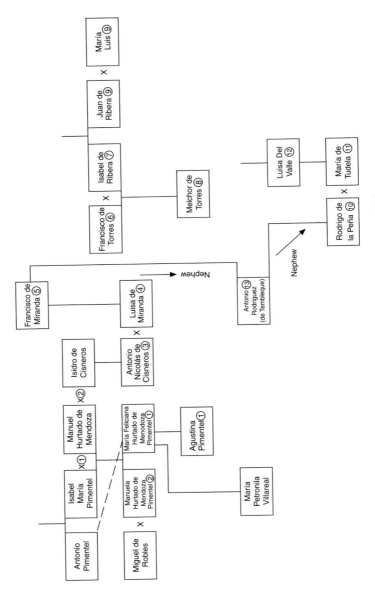

4 Judaizers in eighteenth-century Madrid

Notes to Illustration 4

1. Agustina was the daughter of María Felicina Hurtado Mendoza de Pimentel, who appeared at the *auto* of 28 October 1723, and of her uncle Antonio Pimentel, married 'according to the Law of Moses'. Agustina, in love with Melchor de Torres, appeared at the *auto de fe* of 19 March 1721.
2. Appeared at the *auto de fe* of 17 March 1721.
3. Appeared at the *auto de fe* of 21 February 1721.
4. Trial suspended because of her madness.
5. Appeared at the *auto de fe* of 18 May 1721.
6. Appeared at the *auto de fe* of 19 March 1721.
7. Died 16 August 1720, and reconciled in effigy.
8. In love with Agustina Pimentel. The decision in his case has been lost.
9. Appeared at the *auto de fe* of 22 December 1721.
10. Reconciled at an *auto de fe* in Logroño in 1716.
11. Reconciled at an *auto de fe* in Logroño in 1717.
12. Relaxed 17 April 1720.
13. Appeared at the *auto de fe* of 19 March 1721. Relaxed as recidivist on 12 March 1724.

arrested, they implicated and indirectly caused the condemnation and death at the stake of Luisa del Valle, María's mother, presumably because they thought that Luisa had behaved wrongly over the baby. There was also enmity between María and Francisco de Torres. She told the bigamist Antonio Rodríguez Carrasco that Torres had threatened to betray all the Judaizers, and that he was 'a vile man'. Was it possible that the abundance of information given by María de Tudela as she chattered to the smooth-tongued Antonio Rodríguez Carrasco, information that he repeated in successive hearings to the court, was a reflection of some deep desire for vengeance? That, at least, was alleged by Torres's wife, Isabel de Ribera, when she gave evidence at her husband's trial.

The conflict arose possibly out of some older family history, for María de Tudela and Torres were descended from the same family. This seems to have been the normal state of affairs. Indeed, the 80 or so Judaizers implicated in Inquisition trials at this time in Cuenca were almost all related in some way, and this was probably true for most of the 1400 Judaizers condemned in Spain in this period.[35]

Francisco de Torres was in deep trouble, because he had been reconciled to the Church once before. Now the court was learning that he had not confessed all he knew, that he had been a *confitente diminuto* (insufficient confessant), itself a grave sin. Consequently, charged a second time, Torres confessed fully, giving profuse information about the Judaizing practices of his group, and escaped the stake. His wife, Isabel de Ribera, also made a full confession, particularly because she was outraged, or so she said, by the atmosphere of illicit sexual relations surrounding another person in the group, María Feliciana Hurtado de Mendoza Pimentel.[36]

María Feliciana had the reputation of being loose. Her 17-year-old daughter Agustina was the result of a sexual liaison with her uncle by marriage.[37] Francisco de Torres and Isabel de Ribera suspected that María Feliciana had administered a love philtre to their son, Melchor de Torres, to make him fall in love, against their plans for him, with Agustina. Melchor was reported by people to be silent and melancholy, and at his trial insisted that he had no religion at all. But he certainly was in love with Agustina, probably without the need for a love philtre. María Feliciana was disliked also by the rich and influential Francisco de Miranda, because the latter's daughter, Luisa, had married María Feliciana's half-brother Antonio Cisneros, against her parents' wishes. All this ill-feeling explains perhaps why Torres gave evidence so willingly against María Feliciana and her family.

Still according to Torres's evidence, when the Judaizing community learned that María de Tudela had 'spilt the beans' *(descubierto toda la empanada)*, Francisco de Miranda managed to pass a message to Torres telling him to deny everything as he had during his previous arrest. It was also rumoured that the gaoler had given Torres a drug that time to help him withstand torture. It was probably the gaoler who informed Torres and Miranda that María de Tudela was chattering ceaselessly to the bigamist Antonio Rodríguez Carrasco about the Judaizers.

When Francisco de Torres was indicted for the second time, faced now with the stake, he was in no mood to protect anyone. He even told the court that the gaoler had enjoyed María Feliciana's sexual favours and that Miranda's wife was having an affair with another Judaizer.

Thus it seems that María de Tudela's uncontrolled tongue, together with the hatred of Torres and his wife for some of the other Judaizers, brought about the destruction of the crypto-Jewish families of early eighteenth-century Madrid. The collapse can be followed in the Cuenca and Toledo trial documents, the only ones preserved, and in many references in other series of Inquisition papers. Were it possible to examine trials in other courts, such as Seville and Murcia, mostly destroyed during wars and revolutions in the nineteenth-century, a similar process, including often people related to the Jews of Cuenca and Madrid, could probably be observed.

María de Tudela mentioned the names of Judaizing families all over Spain, which spurred the other courts into activity.[38] On 28 May 1718, the Supreme Inquisition Council dispatched the following circular:

> The gentlemen of his Majesty's Council of the . . . Inquisition, having taken note of . . . the general evidence of crimes of Judaism sent by the Inquisition court of Madrid, the scrutiny of records carried out in the Córdoba and Cuenca courts, the trials of Francisco de Torres and his family and Rodrigo de la Peña, who were previously reconciled in the courts of Madrid and Logroño, and the trial in the Madrid Inquisition of Francisco de Miranda which was suspended . . . noticing that Francisco de Miranda and his son-in-law Antonio Nicolás de Cisneros are wary and that something should be done at once, said that they should order and they ordered.[39]

Three days later the orders for arrest were issued:

> With these [letters] we are sending you copies of the vote and decision of the Council, having examined various charges . . . and

witnesses' statements received in this court about Judaizing offences, for you to arrest those offenders who live in your district . . . advising the Council . . . of the result of your activity.[40]

The *autos de fe* of the eighteenth-century

Once recovered from the chaos caused by war, the Inquisition set to work with speed and efficiency. Soon the prisons of the various courts of the Holy Office overflowed with prisoners. The 170-odd names that Antonio Rodríguez Carrasco mentioned as having been quoted to him as Judaizers by María de Tudela were read over to him, as was the Inquisition custom, and he was told that his statements would be used against them.[41] In the *autos de fe* which followed these revelations, many more people would appear. Most of the autos took place in the six or seven years after María de Tudela's tireless gossiping betrayed so many Judaizers. Here is a list of *autos de fe* based on the accounts published by the bookseller Serrete and on various other sources.[42]

Date	Place	Burnt	Effigy	Reconc.
14.2.00	Córdoba	1		
25.9.00	Toledo			2
?. ?.01	Toledo			6
19.3.01	Valladolid[43]	5		41
2.9.01	Santiago	1		
9.9.01	Toledo			4
23.10.01	Valladolid			21
5.3.02	Seville			21
12.11.02	Toledo			2
21.12.02	Valladolid	2		28[44]
18.3.03	Toledo	1		3
22.4.03	Granada			
28.10.03	Seville[45]			15
21.12.03	Valladolid			15
14.12.04	Valladolid	2		25
22.11.05	Toledo			1
21.12.05	Valladolid	1		19
28.11.06	Valladolid	2		17
27.1.09	Granada			
15.6.10	Murcia			10
20.7.10	Valladolid[46]			
25.9.11	Toledo			1
15.12.15	Seville			14
24.4.18	Córdoba			4

Date	Place	Burnt	Effigy	Reconc.
?.?.17	Logroño			2
14.11.17	Granada			
20.12.17	Granada			
24.4.18	Córdoba			4
29.9.18	Murcia	2	3	
12.2.19	Granada			
? ?.19	Logroño			1
7.4.20	Madrid	3	3	6
25.7.20	Seville	1		5
21.12.20	Granada	4		
22.12.20	Cuenca		2	11
19.3.21	Toledo			15
20.4.21	Córdoba	2		25
18.5.21	Madrid	5	5	9
23.11.21	Cuenca	1	5	26
30.11.21	Granada	12	8	37
14.12.21	Seville		7	31
22.2.22	Madrid			11
24.2.22	Seville			11
8.3.22	Valladolid	2	1	4
15.3.22	Toledo	1	11	21
12.4.22	Córdoba	4		34
17.5.22	Murcia	1		35
30.5.22	Granada			48
29.6.22	Cuenca			18
5.7.22	Seville	4	3	21
24.8.22	Valladolid			7
18.10.22	Saragossa	1		9
18.10.22	Murcia			27
25.10.22	Toledo			12
22.11.22	Cuenca		3	11
30.11.22	Llerena			17
30.11.22	Seville	4		39
31.1.23	Granada	12		42
31.1.23	Barcelona			4
21.2.23	Cuenca			1
24.2.23	Valencia	2	1	6
24.2.23	Toledo	1	2	3
9.5.23	Cuenca			1
13.5.23	Murcia	1		17
6.6.23	Seville	2		30
6.6.23	Valladolid			2
6.6.23	Saragossa			1
13.6.23	Córdoba	5	2	15
20.6.23	Granada			31
26.7.23	Llerena	1		9

Date	Place	Burnt	Effigy	Reconc.
10.8.23	Seville			5
24.10.23	Granada			23[47]
24.10.23	Valladolid			
28.10.23	Toledo	1		5
19.12.23	Granada			
20. 2.24	Madrid	3	6	11
12.3.24	Valladolid	4		1
2.4.24	Valencia			5
23.4.24	Córdoba	4	4	18
11.6.24	Seville	1		32
25.6.24	Granada	5	16	17
2.7.24	Córdoba			6
23.7.24	Cuenca		1	1
2.8.24	Valladolid			
30.11.24	Murcia	2	1	5
21.12.24	Seville			8
14.1.25	Cuenca	2	6	2
4.2.25	Llerena			4
4.3.25	Cuenca			1
5.3.25	Valladolid			
13.5.25	Granada		7	13
1.7.25	Toledo	1		6
8.7.25	Valladolid			5
24.8.25	Granada			9
26.8.25	Llerena			10
9.9.25	Barcelona			1
21.10.25	Murcia			5
30.11.25	Seville	3		8
16.12.25	Granada	1		9
31.3.26	Valladolid		1	
31.3.26	Murcia			6
12.5.26	Córdoba		2	7
18.8.26	Granada			7
1.9.26	Barcelona		1	
26.1.27	Valladolid		1	16
18.5.27	Granada	2	8	
18.5.27	Valladolid	2	1	22[48]
9.5.28	Seville			1
15.5.28	Córdoba			5
12.6.29	Valladolid			
3.5.30	Córdoba	1	10	4
14.5.30	Llerena			2
24.9.30	Valladolid	2		
4.3.31	Granada		1	
4.3.31	Córdoba		4	2
16.5.32	Granada			

Date	Place	Burnt	Effigy	Reconc.
20.3.38	Toledo	1		11
14.11.34	Granada			
21.12.38	Toledo			1
22.11.39	Valladolid			
21.12.40	Valladolid	1	4	20
22.2.41	Valladolid			
23.9.42	Valladolid			
23.6.43	Valladolid			12
13.6.45	Valladolid	1		3
5.12.45	Córdoba			1
11.1.56	Toledo			1
24.11.59	Granada			
8.5.68	Valladolid			

The totals are 123 victims burnt at the stake, 129 burnt in effigy and 1,240 reconciled with various penances imposed, a grand total of 1,492. These figures are certainly less than the real ones. Assuming that, as in Valladolid and Granada, there were many *autos de fe* in other towns which are mentioned only in the internal correspondence of the Holy Office and not listed in the published sources, at least a third more *autos de fe* than have been identified actually took place, and the number of victims may have been as many as two thousand.

The sources may well indicate that the Inquisition was less active during the War of the Spanish Succession of 1700–1713 and during the rule of Macanaz and the French advisers, which lasted until Philip V's marriage to Isabel Farnese in December 1714. However, the reaction of the Holy Office after the fall of Macanaz in 1715 was ferocious. The famous nineteenth-century Catholic historian, Marcelino Menéndez y Pelayo, who is concerned to attenuate the reputed harshness of the Inquisition, claims that the figures given by the first historian of the Inquisition, Llorente, who had been Secretary of the Holy Office, of 54 *autos* with 981 victims in this period, are false.[49] Actually, on the same page that Menéndez y Pelayo quotes, Llorente writes that the reign of Philip V (1700–1746) witnessed 782 *autos de fe* in Spanish Inquisition courts, not counting those in Portugal or South and Central America. This figure seems disproportionate. Nevertheless, many more *autos de fe* might appear as researchers plough through the masses of correspondence between the courts and the *Suprema*, especially the so-called *autillos* which were held in the courtroom itself and where perhaps a single offender was reconciled to the Church. Llorente's global figures of 1,564 burnt in person, 782 in effigy and 11,730 reconciled, do indeed seem extreme, perhaps because they include not just the Judaizers but also the blasphemers, bigamists, fornicators, priests who took advantage of the confessional to abuse women sexually, sodomites, necromancers, sorcerers and the others who came under the Inquisition's jurisdiction. However, the people sentenced to die at the stake that are listed in the printed accounts of *autos de fe* were always negative or relapsed Judaizers, so that the figure of 1,564 that Llorente gives for these still seems high compared with the 123 found in the printed accounts. All the same, Llorente gives exact figures, so that he was either over-stating intentionally or he had the true data in front of him. The fact that so many courts appear moribund, at least from about 1724 onwards, while de Prado Moura's investigation of one – Valladolid – reveals remarkable energy, suggests that courts like those of Barcelona, Saragossa, Logroño or Santiago de Compostela, which rarely appear in the printed sources, must have been more active than is suggested by the information found up till now. It may well be, then, that the impression received by Francisco Moya Torres, that 'a great deal of Judaism is still to be found in Spain', was not so wide of the mark.

Opinions of an inquisitor

Certainly, reconciled Judaizers were sufficiently numerous for a former Inquisitor of Seville, Francisco Pérez de Prado, Bishop of Teruel and future (1746) Inquisitor-General, to publish a book specifically directed to them.[50]

In his book the bishop speaks directly to the reconciled Judaizers of Seville, using the knowledge he has acquired of their lives, particularly of the way in which they transmit Judaism to their children, whom he compares in their innocence to Adam and Eve before the Fall.[51] Once the child's curiosity is awakened, writes the bishop, he is told that he will be burned at the stake if he reveals anything. Pérez de Prado writes, with a certain blindness if not hypocrisy, that this intense secrecy proves the diabolical nature of Judaism, which produces children who are crafty, fearful and cowardly.

The bishop also attacks another characteristic of the Spanish and Portuguese Jews, even when they are living in safety abroad: their pretensions to noble descent:

> Hardly have your children reached an age of discretion, old enough to keep a secret, when you take them apart and, pretending you are going to reveal a great mystery, you tell them that they should know

they are descendants of the ancient and distinguished patriarch Abraham, and thus of very high lineage. You impel them to despise everybody who is not of their descent, and even in private you refer to yourselves as Basques [*vizcaínos*].[52]

Pérez de Prado points out that, if Jews are descendants of Abraham, so are Christians, at least in the spiritual sense, and he sneers at the pretensions to noble descent of the Spanish Judaizers: 'If the experience I have of many of you, and what I have read of others, counts for anything, very few of you know who your great-great-grandfather was.'[53]

The inquisitor did not really understand the issue. Spanish Jews had a tradition that their presence in Spain dated from the Roman period, on the basis of verse 20 of the biblical Book of Obadiah – 'And the captives of Jerusalem who are in Sepharad'. The ancient Aramaic translation and the Hebrew commentary by the twelfth-century Spanish exegete Abraham Ibn Ezra, interpreted 'Sepharad' as Spain. Ibn Ezra also explains that the exiles to which Obadiah refers were those brought from Jerusalem to Roman Spain after Titus had conquered the Jewish capital in the year 73.

The Spanish Jews assumed that they were descended from these exiles, who were the aristocracy of Jerusalem. In the trial of Diego de la Mota in 1721 and 1722, the marriage of his brother Enrique to a woman who ran a spice shop was opposed by the parents because 'the parents of this confessant [Diego] say that they are very noble and descended from kings, while the woman descends from shoemakers'.[54] In Cuenca, Josepha Díaz explained that 'it was very honourable to descend from the tribe of Judah and they would not cease for any reason to state their origin.'[55]

In Madrid some Judaizers insisted that they were from the tribe of Levi. In the small London community of Marranos whom Cromwell permitted in 1656 to live openly as Jews, a visitor noticed, when he visited their synagogue on 2 April 1662, that each bore the insignia of his tribe.[56] In reality, the visitor may have misunderstood, or perhaps his informant garnished the truth a little, for no Jew knew his tribe except those of Levi because their particular role in the synagogue service passed down from father to son.

If, as Pérez de Prado wrote, the crypto-Jews did not know the details of their ancestors, this reflects the difficult history of the New Christians, whose ancestors had changed their surnames when they were baptized, as well as frequently afterwards, not only because surnames of brothers and of fathers and sons were not always the same, but also in efforts to put the Inquisition off the track. In any case, if Judaizers, interrogated by the court, could not tell the inquisitors the name of their great-great-grandfather, why did the inquisitors always ask them that question? Actually, the claim to noble descent was a tradition and quite innocent. What it really meant was that those New Christians who had wanted to preserve their Jewish consciousness had practised endogamy. Endogamous Jewish descent was often part of the confession of Judaizing that the accused almost always denied at the first court hearing and gradually confessed as the months and years passed.

The bishop also attacks the Judaizers for not being real Jews. He was aware of the insistence on the part of Sephardi rabbis outside the Peninsula that Marrano men arriving in Amsterdam, Leghorn or London should be circumcised, and interprets this correctly as meaning that the rabbis recognised the ex-Marranos as Jews despite the absence of circumcision. But for the bishop this was false. How could the rabbis accept a person as a Jew if he had been baptized? Perhaps it is unfair to accuse Pérez de Prado of not understanding that a Jew is one who is born of a Jewish mother. The absence of circumcision and the fact of involuntary baptism is irrelevant to this. The bishop saw the baptism of infants and the absence of circumcision as attempts of the Judaizers to be Christians and Jews at the same time. In his own words, it was 'having God at your convenience'.[57] Without apparently realising the irony in his words, his view is that if the Judaizers want to be Jews they should leave Spain. But this was forbidden. To be captured as a fugitive, that is leaving Spain to go and Judaize elsewhere, was a *prima facie* proof of guilt. Many Judaizers were punished after having been captured on their way to the French frontier, and a common restriction on reconciled Judaizers was that they should not approach frontiers or ports.

These were the considered views of an inquisitor. But how did the Judaizers see themselves and their Judaism?

Endogamy

If the Madrid and Cuenca families punished by the Inquisition in the early eighteenth-century are examined, a close pattern of relationship emerges. The thread could be picked up anywhere. For example, Manuela Hurtado de Mendoza Pimentel, María Feliciana's sister, was married to Miguel de Robles, who in his youth had been the bookkeeper of his later wife's uncle. Robles had been born in Bayonne and, as will be seen, knew a lot more about Judaism than many of the group. He played an important part in the lives of the forty or so Judaizers who comprised the Madrid section of what the Holy Office called the Great Judaizing Complicity revealed by María de Tudela.

Robles farmed the *millones* tax in Ceuta and the tobacco monopoly in Toledo. He managed to get away at the time of the great roundup of Judaizers, reached Saragossa and then managed to inform his wife, Manuela, that he was safe, probably in Bayonne. She appeared at an *auto de fe* on 19 March 1721. A woman of 47, born in the seaport of Cadiz, she was sentenced not only to life imprisonment and the sanbenito and the loss of all her property, but also to flogging through the crowded streets of Toledo, because she had refused to talk and had 'obliged' the Inquisition to torture her.

Her sister, María Feliciana, has made an appearance already. Agustina, her daughter, 24 years old, had a bad heart and was pardoned the two hundred lashes to which she was sentenced as a late confessant. In the torture chamber Agustina had fainted and the doctors had warned the inquisitors that she would die if further tortured.

Manuela and María Feliciana had a half-brother, Antonio Nicolás de Cisneros. He appeared at the *auto de fe* of 22 February 1722 in Madrid. His punishment was harsh, not only life imprisonment preceded by flogging, but five years in the galleys for being a late confessant, and a blasphemer who had 'insulted Jesus Christ and Our Lady by word and deed'. This last offence referred to a series of physical attacks on holy images and statues. Antonio was married to Luisa, daughter of Francisco de Miranda. Her trial was suspended because she went mad.[58] What tragedy did the Spanish word for madness (*locura*) conceal? Did Luisa's personality disintegrate because of the cruel fate of her parents and husband?

To return to Francisco de Torres, his brother-in-law took as his second and probably illegal wife the widow María Luis, whose family was from Cuenca. María's sister-in-law was Rosa Rodríguez, who was related to Rodrigo de la Peña, married in his turn to María de Tudela and related through her to Torres. Thus the Judaizers of Madrid were related to those of Cuenca where up to eighty persons were punished in *autos* on 22 December 1720, including Juan de Ribera who went to the galleys as a bigamist, and on 23 November 1721 when the recidivist Judaizer Catalina Pinedo was burnt at the stake. Since she was very penitent (*muy arrepentida*) one may assume she was garrotted first. Another *auto de fe*, on 29 June 1722, punished eighteen Judaizers, and another, on 22 November 1722, fourteen more, including Dr Antonio de Céspedes, his mother and sister, who had escaped and whose effigies were burnt. Eight further were punished on 23 July 1724, six of them at the stake.

They had been reconciled relatively recently but obviously had not taken the danger seriously enough and had begun to practise Judaism again. One final *auto* in Cuenca, on 14 January 1725, dealt with ten Judaizers, two of whom were burnt at the stake, a mother and her daughter, both previously reconciled, while the son escaped with five years in the galleys. These were all surnamed López Laguna. Were they related to Daniel Israel López Laguna (1653–1730), author of a metrical translation of the Psalms published in London in 1720?[59] These *autos de fe* destroyed the four large families of Judaizers in the little city of Cuenca, most of them occupied in the tobacco monopoly, or collectors of rents, clothmakers and some shop assistants and seamstresses.

Cuenca stands on top of a mountain, between two rivers. There was little space. The houses had up to twelve storeys and were built close against each other. It was impossible to keep one's daily life private. The neighbours knew what one was eating or, more importantly, what one did not eat. The Judaism of these families must have been an open secret. It was perhaps because of this that they were over-confident, and this caused their downfall when the Inquisition court arrested them *en masse* in the summer of 1718. The 98 Judaizers punished by the Inquisition represented one in seventy of the population of Cuenca, which in 1719 was 6,532.[60]

It may well be that among Old Christians, as well as among New Christians of the same social class, the level of endogamy was high, especially if they lived in a small town. Nevertheless, the importance of endogamy in the preservation and transmission of secret Judaism cannot be overstated. In the pre-Expulsion period the converts married among themselves if they wanted to preserve their Jewish religious heritage, at a time when many married into Old Christian families. Among the Judaizers, the important consideration was that one should marry another descendant of New Christians. One of the witnesses in the trial of Juana de la Peña – probably her mother Mencia – gave the evidence which allowed the prosecutor to allege that

> one day, when the person named by the witness was alone with the close relative of the accused, she said to him that her close family had told and advised her that she could make good marriages of any of her family [daughters is meant] with that person and his family, because they were observers of the Law of Moses. That is why she had organized the marriage of the accused with this person, who had replied that what she had been told was true.[61]

In other words, the conditions for arranging the marriage of Juana to Julián Vázquez had been that the young man was a descendant of New Christians and an observer of Jewish law.

The Inquisition took careful note of the details of the Judaizers' endogamous practices. In the trial of Ventura Luis in Cuenca, the Inquisitors noted precisely that 'the Judaizers could only marry someone who followed the same Law'.[62] Ventura's father Gabriel, according to María de Tudela, chattering away to Antonio Rodríguez Carrasco, had asked María if she knew a 'good Jewish lad' (*un buen mozo judío*) to marry his daughter.[63] Gabriel Luis had already tried to marry Ventura off to a relative of his in Murcia, a silversmith who was one of the Melo family, who were cruelly punished by the Inquisition.[64]

Marrying out of the group was severely disparaged. When, for example, Diego de la Mota married an Old Christian, his parents refused to speak to him.[65] His sister María said that the wedding had been against his parents' will, because his wife, María Serrana, was not of the same Law. 'Now', said Diego's mother to him, according to his sister, '"You will eat forbidden fat, blood and other things", giving him to understand that having married a woman not of his religion he would no longer observe the regulations of the Law of Moses.'[66]

The trials do not reveal whether any particular Jewish formula was employed to effect the marriage. What did Rodrigo de la Peña mean when he alleged that Flor de Ribera, the sister-in-law of Francisco de Torres, had married Joseph de Molina 'in the Jewish way' (*a usanza de judíos*)?[67] It may be that the 'Jewish way' was no more than what the father of María Luis did before she married her first husband. He took her aside, made her kneel, put his hand on her head, prayed silently and then said 'Go with the blessing of God, for you go married'. (*Vaya con la bendición de Dios, que ya va casada*).[68] While this does not constitute a Jewish marriage, it does suggest that the Catholic rites were thought unnecessary, although of course they had to be performed.

It was only with endogamous marriage that the Judaizers could establish the minimum circumstances to preserve the religious traditions and integrity of the group. It was because of intense endogamy that Francisco de Torres, giving evidence at the trial of María Feliciana Hurtado de Mendoza Pimentel, could say that the Hurtado de Mendoza, Pimentel, Miranda and Carrillo families were Jews 'like all their ancestors.'[69] Only because of endogamy could the Cuenca Judaizers Antonio Rodríguez 'pig's foot' and his wife María Fernández say of the Law of Moses, 'It is the one followed by all our ancestors.'[70]

In what, then, did being an 'observer of the Law of Moses' consist? What beliefs, rites and ceremonies were still held and performed by the descendants of the converts of more than two hundred years earlier, after up to eight generations of ostensible Catholic lives and clandestine Jewish existence?

10

'Which he did in obedience to the Law of Moses'

The Jewish practice of the Marranos

Though the Judaizers had rejected the principles of Christianity, their religious mindset was far from Jewish. To what extent can their Jewish knowledge and practice be calculated?

The question is not easy to answer, because the information available about the secret Jews' religious behaviour comes almost entirely from evidence given before Inquisition courts. Testimony is scarce, always tending to conceal the truth and very likely no more than a weak reflection of a rich religious life. Understandably, a contemporary author states that

> the rites and traditions that the Judaizers of the previous century practised were already very impoverished, as is obvious, and those of this epoch [the eighteenth-century] were equally or more so ... all this has little meaning and the tradition is maintained only as a family legacy.[1]

Among the early generations of converts, deep-rooted customs such as wearing clean clothes on Saturday may well have continued through inertia and family habit. Abstaining from prohibited foods may have reflected personal distaste more than religious observance. Yet other manifestations of Jewish life must have indicated that those who practised them were living intentional Jewish lives. By the eighteenth-century, however, positive Jewish actions must have been a matter not of personal preference or inertia but of deep conviction. Such manifestations, regularly mentioned in Inquisition evidence,[2] included fasting.

Fasts: The great fast of September

The Judaizers recognized that the Great Fast of September – *Yom Kippur* or the Day of Atonement – was more important than the other Jewish holy days. On the Great Fast, said Isabel de Ribera to the court, one did not use tobacco, nor sleep nor trim the wicks of oil lamps.

In reality, with the exception of *Yom Kippur,* fasting is not the way the Jewish festivals are observed. It was for other reasons that the Judaizers fasted on festivals, while some fasted as often as two days per week. The widow Mencia de la Peña, for instance, told the court in 1639 that her husband taught her to fast on Mondays and Thursdays.[3]

At the suppers which preceded and followed the fasts, the Judaizers abstained from meat. No reason for this has been found in the confessions, but it was probably imitated from the Christian rule of not eating meat on fast days. Perhaps they considered it inappropriate to eat meat which had not been not Jewishly slaughtered, on a holy day. Whatever the reason, much evidence describes these meals as consisting of fish, fruit and dessert. Isabel de Paz, for example, confessed to having fasted in company with others, in 1718 and 1720, when the suppers had been of chickpeas, fried fish and fruit.[4]

In 1711, on the eve of *Yom Kippur,* the most solemn of the holy days, the Madrid Judaizers met in Francisco de Torres's house.[5] Of the guests, within ten years Luisa del Valle, María de Ribera and Isabel de Morales would be burnt at the stake; Juan de Ribera, Gaspar Carrillo and Antonio Nicolás de Cisneros would go to the galleys, Luisa de Miranda would go mad, Francisco de Torres, Francisco de Miranda and his wife María Guiomar Arias would be publicly flogged, shamed and imprisoned, while Isabel de Molina would die in prison and be burnt in effigy.

Torres spent lavishly so that his family and friends might receive the great day appropriately. He hired three long tables, with new tablecloths and napkins, and bought a 180-ounce silver candelabrum with ten sconces.

As the ceremony began, they all washed their hands. Then Francisco de Miranda told Torres that he needed salt 'to give the blessing' (*para echar la bendición*). When Torres replied that he had never seen such a ceremony,

> Miranda told him to bring finely milled and very white salt, which he did. Miranda took a silver salt-cellar and put it on the table and, sitting on a chair, with the index finger and thumb of his right hand

he took salt from the salt-cellar and put it on the tongue of each of the above-mentioned people who knelt before him. Then he performed a rite which was to cover them with the scarlet cloak he was wearing and rest his hand on their heads and pronounce the blessing: 'May this fast be counted by the Lord as pardon for your sins'. He did this for each one present. Although it was not for Miranda to give the blessing or the salt but for the witness [Torres], since he was master of the house, the latter gave him permission and the privilege to do so.[6]

In reality, the description of Francisco de Miranda blessing the others and delicately taking a pinch of salt from a silver salt-cellar and placing it on their tongues suggests the image of the Catholic priest distributing the sacred wafer to the faithful. The syncretic aspect of Marrano religion is very evident here.

A Portuguese description of this fast recounts that on the eve of the day they bathed, put on clean clothes, cut their nails and prayed for the dead. Then they dined on fried fish, a dessert and fruit, having made a contribution to the poor. The next day, they met to pray. The trial documents include the prayer

> Powerful and Great Lord
> Creator of the universe
> To You I confess
> That I am a great sinner
> Amen your Great Name[7]

Later the women stood with their heads covered and, covering their eyes with one hand, said

> Lord of the Heavens, Sabaoth, have pity on us, succour us, succour us, free us from our enemies and the Inquisition.[8]

Some of the words and phrases – 'Creator of the Universe' and 'Sabaoth' – echo the Jewish liturgy, but there are also Christian incorporations such as 'I confess I am a great sinner'. A notable difference in Lisbon, commented on by the Inquisition as typical of the observance of the Great Fast, was the reading of a chapter of Ezra.[9] This book is about the return of the Israelite captives from Babylon followed by the rebuilding of the Temple. The symbolism is evident, for the Crypto-Jews lived in exile, as it were, from their own religion.

Tabernacles

When a witness referred to a 'fast which is observed holding sticks in one's hands', which took place in September or October 1709, he may have been referring to the Passover, where Jews sometimes hold walking sticks as if ready for the Exodus from Egypt, or to Tabernacles, a festival whose liturgy is marked by a rabbinical interpretation of Leviticus 23:40, which prescribes the waving of the 'four species': willows, palm branches, myrtle and the fruit of the citron. According to the confession of Rodrigo de la Peña, Tabernacles was still being observed at the beginning of the eighteenth century.[10] In addition, a mysterious episode was recounted by Teodora González, a servant of Francisco de Torres.

Something had impressed itself on Teodora's memory, though she could not put a precise date to it. At the time, Teodora slept with another servant woman in a room under the empty attics. One night the two women were woken by the strange noises and footsteps above their heads, and hugged each other in terror. Teodora specifically mentioned a sound which she described as being like taffeta being dragged along the whitewashed walls of the staircase and over the floor above. The two women had thought they heard tiles being pulled away and thrown down into the yard beneath. When next morning Teodora told her mistress what she had heard during the night, she dismissed her fears saying that Teodora had probably heard a dog or a vagabond down in the patio. However, to explain that the noise of tiles falling had come from below and not from above could have been a way of diverting Teodora's attention from the real cause of the noise.

Usually, by dint of patient and insistent questioning, the Inquisition managed to extract memories of scenes and events which the witnesses were hiding or had genuinely forgotten. In this case however, nobody offered an explanation.

The noise of the tiles falling should, however, have stimulated the memory of the Inquisitors, since in earlier centuries New Christians who wished to continue to observe their faith used to break a tile in order to obey the biblical command to live for one week in a booth open to the sky and covered only by cut foliage.[11] If what Teodora had really heard was Torres pulling tiles off the roof to try to observe the commandment, at least symbolically, could the 'taffeta' have been branches that he was pulling up the stairs and over the attic floor to put over the hole he had made in the roof in order to try to obey the commandment to live in a temporary structure?

Supplicatory fasting

The Judaizers fasted not only on the holy days of the festivals but also, in the words of the young Escolástica Gómez, 'for the dead, the sick, and good fortune'.[12] Some Judaizers may have owned Rabbi Menasseh ben Israel's digest of Jewish law, the *Thesouro dos Dinim*, which explained that fasting was a form of personal supplication.[13] The wealthy gave charity to the poor so that the latter might fast on their behalf. This suggests an imitation of the customs of the surrounding Christian society. For example, Escolástica explained that Antonio Blandón, a wealthy financier, paid her and other women a real per fast.[14] Two poor and elderly women, Isabel de Aragón and Mariana Pacheco, received regular alms from the prosperous Madrid businessmen Francisco de Torres and Francisco de Miranda 'to recommend them to God', that is to say that, whatever the motive, the form in which it was expressed was Christian.

On fast days the secret Jews obeyed the biblical and rabbinical laws for festivals. They abstained from household tasks such as sweeping, scrubbing, cooking or sewing. Yet it was difficult to conceal one's habits in the cramped conditions in which most households lived, with doors and windows open and neighbours walking in and out. Isabel de Paz and her parents, for instance, cooked stew on *Yom Kippur* 1720, but 'it was to dissimulate, because we lived in a tenement house'.[15]

Fasting had come to occupy the place of the joy which characterizes most Jewish festivals. A clear example of this is the way the crypto-Jews observed *Purim,* which recalls the events recounted in the biblical Book of Esther. This day is normally very festive, though it is preceded by a fast. Among the secret Jews, the atmosphere was predominantly sad and characterized by some practices imitated from the surrounding Christian world, such as in this description taken from the trial of Dr Diego López Zapata in 1725:

> [H]e kept the solemn fast of Esther, in which eight people took part, five men and three women, and among them one who was known as the Wise Man ['el Sabio'], who recited the prayers. When this was over, the men sat at the table with their hats on, and the women on the floor for greater penitence, and the Wise Man broke off eight pieces of bread, blessed them, sprinkled them with salt and ashes and covered them with a cloth. He also blessed the wine but without covering it. The bread was shared between the eight of them. The five men ate it at the table with a tablecloth, and the women on the

floor. They abstained from the wine as an additional penance. Hanging from the ceiling over the table was a tinplate lamp with seven wicks covered with another sheet of tinplate, which made the lights dim and gloomy. After eating they prayed again. The next day the same people met again. They ate salted fish with scales, fruit and vegetables. At both meals they first washed their hands and faces. After praying, sitting on the floor, and after the meal, they stripped the upper part of their bodies and gave each other 24 lashes. He received them from the Wise Man. The women modestly covered their nakedness with a veil. They continued with other rites, ceremonies and prayers, and sent one of their number to see if the star had appeared yet. When he came back with the news that it had, they gave thanks to Omnipotent God for having given them strength to keep that fast.[16]

What was the purpose of these fasts, when not even the most ascetic Jewish traditions required them? They must have reflected the profound sense of sin which animated the secret Jews. Perhaps penitential fasting assuaged the feeling of guilt that the Judaizers must have experienced when they worshipped, as Catholics, in a way which they knew was, in the Jewish sense, idolatrous. Thus the mere fact of declaring their Jewishness to each other was profoundly meaningful. It was an act of self-identification which defined them as fundamentally different from those around them, affecting their entire lives and exposing them to the gravest dangers. To state one's Jewishness (often noted in the confession simply as '*declararse*') meant separating oneself from the essential values of Spanish culture, and yet at the same time it demanded ceaseless dissimulation. The consequent psychological tensions created a need for catharsis which fasting could perhaps in part satisfy.

In 1714, the Marranos of Madrid celebrated Passover, which fell in Holy Week.[17] Here, the mental world of the secret Jews, brought up as Catholics and aware of the emotions surrounding Passion Week, conflicted with their celebration of the liberation of the Jewish People in order to serve God according to Jewish law.

Any culture, even a religious one, absorbs characteristics of a stronger surrounding culture. But in Spain there was an additional factor: the Judaism of the Marranos was secret and dangerous, while their Catholicism was open, official, obligatory and universal. Furthermore, they had been Catholics for eight or so generations. When asked to do so by the Inquisition court, they could all recite the Lord's Prayer, the *Ave Maria* and the *Salve Regina*, and they could explain, more or less accurately depending on the level of their religious education, the doctrinal principles of Christianity. They lived in a country where it was inconceivable to be anything else but Catholic. Daily language and discourse, the mental universe and even the physical landscape were replete with Catholic imagery. There were Catholic pictures on the walls of their houses. They recited the *Angelus* and in the torture chamber they called on Jesus and the Virgin to succour them. Time of day was given by church bells, the date by the religious calendar. They had to make an exceptional effort to think in a way that was not Catholic. Probably, the emphasis that the crypto-Jews placed on penitence imitated what they observed daily and shared with their neighbours. When Judaizers said that their confessors had advised them to fast, this might even be true, but had they fasted because their confessor had told them to or because they wanted to observe a Jewish festival in that way?

Anti-Christian Acts

The very ubiquity of the images of Jesus, the Virgin Mary and the Saints explains words – and actions also – that were used to heighten the awareness of their Judaism and clarify that the crypto-Jews could not be Christians and Jews at the same time. The notorious case of the Patient Christ, which ended with an *auto de fe* in 1632, has been mentioned already in Chapter 4. In the eighteenth-century also, some Judaizers testified before the Inquisition court that they had been witnesses to abuse of Catholic sacred objects. On 22 May 1718, for example, the servant Manuela Carrera said among other accusations that, when Francisco de Torres was with her employers they laughed and made rude remarks pointing at a picture of the Crucifixion.[18]

So it appears that Torres and this family, required by custom to have Christian religious pictures on the walls, made an effort – in this case quite innocent though vulgar – to recognize that, 'They had to leave the Law of Our Lord Jesus Christ because one could not have two Gods.'[19] Juana de la Peña's mother and aunt had told her 'that she should not believe in Jesus Christ or his images, or those of the Saints, because they were made out of a piece of wood and painted on a piece of paper.'

Similarly, in Cuenca, Miguel Luis had told his daughter María when she was sixteen, '"So you still believe in that piece of wood? In God! In God alone!" And then her father had taught her that she should believe only in God in Heaven . . .'[20]

In Francisco de Torres's house the Judaizers held a regular gathering, which Rodrigo de la Peña described for the Inquisition court, when 'The men ate separately and the women sat on the dais . . . '

It is these details like the custom, inherited from Moorish times, of the women sitting on the floor on a small raised platform, which bear witness to the honesty of the statements. They spoke of Christians as of idol-worshippers who prayed to gods made of wood. The Messiah had not yet come; there were no saints, nor was there any mystery or sacrament in the Mass,

> because the body and blood of Christ could not be present in the Host and the chalice, even though they were consecrated. There was only bread and wine. Christ was a good man, conceived like every-one else. He was a magician . . . He performed miracles.[21]

On other occasion, Torres had said

> that the Law of Grace was nonsense and that the only way to be saved was by observing the Law of Moses. That the miracles of Jesus Christ were performed by magic, that he had been a liar and that the Virgin had followed the error of her son by believing his apparent miracles.[22]

Someone else had said that the Virgin could not have been a virgin and that Jesus was – using an expression inherited from their Portuguese ancestors – *O filho do ferreiro* (the blacksmith's son), conceived when Joseph was away. It is not clear who said this, but it could have been Antonio Nicolás de Cisneros, for this man was sent to the galleys for five years as a 'blasphemer, insulting in word and deed to Jesus Christ and Our Lady'.[23]

What were these insults 'in deed'? One day in 1714, as he spoke to the group of Madrid Judaizers, Miguel de Robles had taken a little figure of Jesus from his pocket, saying 'This is the liar who says that he is the true Messiah and because he is not we are dragged through the mud because of him'.

María Guiomar Arias, wife of Francisco de Miranda, had taken some wisps of straw, lit them at the brazier and whipped the little figure with them. Her daughter Luisa did the same with esparto grass that she pulled out of a mat, and everybody followed them in the performance of an act which must have had a highly symbolic value for them. Francisco de Miranda explained to the court that they committed this act, seen by the Inquisition as appalling sacrilege, in the belief that Jesus was not the Messiah and that the figure had no spiritual value.

Why did the secret Jews behave in this way, so at variance with the general Jewish attitude to Christianity, which is one of respectful distance? Of course they did not think that by physically attacking the images they were harming Jesus. After all, everything that they said shows that the point of these actions was to underline the materiality of the images and their lack of spiritual value. The words 'It is just a piece of wood' echo back and forth from the case of the Patient Christ in the 1620s to the group around Torres and Miranda in eighteenth-century Madrid.

In the Middle Ages, when accusations of ill-treating images and the Host were current in Europe, the explanation was that the Jews knew perfectly well that the images were divine and that the Host was the body of Christ. That was why they tried to harm them. In the eighteenth-century, however, the summary by the Inquisition court notes the acts and the words of the Judaizers, but simply for what they were: insults to sacred objects that baptized Catholics ought not to commit. The court probably recognized what was happening, for the Judaizers did not destroy the images in order to impose a contrary religious vision on anyone else. To burn or whip a statue of Jesus reinforced the statements that the Judaizers made to each other in their private meetings. It was a way of defending themselves against the pervasive influence of their Christian surroundings. Indeed, if the description of the acts is scruti-nized, nothing appears which might be considered a rite, with a visible effect, or even any sort of symbolic ceremony. Unlike in the case of the Patient Christ eighty years earlier, the eighteenth-century Judaizers did not feel they had to confess that the statue bled or spoke, and the court probably would not have believed them if they had. The purpose of burning and whipping the figurines of Jesus, and of saying that he was not divine and that his mother could not have been a virgin – acts and words that the Inquisition naturally saw as blasphemous and sacrile-gious – must have been purely educational, with the aim of awakening and encouraging the non-Christian awareness of the less-educated people present at the meetings. After all, few of the Judaizers were learned. In the complete Catholic context in which they lived some – particularly the women who were usually illiterate and did not take part in the profounder discussions of the men – had to be convinced that they could not be Jewish and Christian at the same time, and that to be Jews they had to reject certain beliefs that were fundamental in their upbringing and which they saw as undisputed fact. Indeed there certainly were people who thought they could believe in the two faiths simultaneously. Miguel Enríquez, for instance, who was burnt at the stake on 10 May 1682, 'tried to make the Court believe that he had not abandoned the Law of Christ, but that he could be a Jew and a Christian at the same time'; and that the Law of Christ 'did not contradict the Law of Moses in which he believed'.[24]

Messianism

In the statements the Judaizers made to the Inquisition one often finds the opinion that the Law of Moses was the only route to salvation. Francisco de Torres, for instance, said that it was better to live as a Jew than to suffer the torments of Hell.[25] In the meantime, they awaited the coming of the Messiah. María Fernández, the wife of Antonio Rodríguez 'Pie de Gorrino' – was he nicknamed 'Pig's Foot' for some reason to do with his dietary habits? – was taught by her parents, shopkeepers in the Calle de Carreterías, still the main street in Cuenca, that '[u]ntil the Messiah came, his people would not emerge from their captivity.'[26]

The ideas of the Spanish Judaizers about the Messiah were not too clear. Isabel de Ribera believed that if the Great Fast of September fell three times on the Sabbath the Messiah would come. She was awaiting the third time and when that happened, Francisco de Miranda would be the judge and chief of the Jews.[27] *Yom Kippur,* the Day of Atonement, falls on Saturday every now and then, so Isabel de Ribera's statement indicates how confused the messianic ideas of the Judaizers were. Somewhat more reasonably, Diego de la Mota said that his uncle had told him that at the end of the world Moses would come and divide the Red Sea with his staff. The good people, that is those Jews who preserved their religion, would go to the Promised Land.[28] The interesting point is that the Spanish secret Jews associated the coming of the Messiah with their own redemption from captivity, that is their departure for lands where they could worship freely.

In 1665, the notorious false Messiah, Shabbetai Zvi, was acclaimed in Salonika, followed by a wave of messianic fervour all over the Jewish world and particularly among the ex-Marrano communities and to some extent within Spain and Portugal. Even when Shabbetai Zvi apostatized and became a Moslem, some ex-Marranos saw a parallel between his own situation and theirs. This Messiah seemed to justify the apostasy that weighed on the consciences of the Marranos, and they were attracted to Jewish beliefs according to which the Messiah would have to descend to the depths of evil in order to complete the Kabbalistic *tikkun*, that is the rescue of the Holy Sparks, the spiritual lights inherent in Creation, but which Kabbalism taught had been dispersed.[29]

Disbelief

In the ex-Marrano communities, antinomianism, that is the refusal to accept the corpus of rabbinic legislation, was rife.[30] Presumably antinomianism was not absent within the Peninsula either. The Inquisition archives possess the details of the trial of a person with even more extreme views; Melchor de Torres, the 25-year-old son of Francisco de Torres and Isabel de Ribera. Melchor's interrogation began on 8 July 1722.

He made extraordinary statements. The record of his trial recalls that

> He said that there is no God nor soul, because the soul is mortal; that there is no Hell nor Devil nor Angels, and a list of nonsense of the same sort. The kind and Christian persuasiveness with which the natural and supernatural arguments were put to him over and over again were of no use. He repeated the same idiocies for over two hours, which caused particular offence and sorrow to the Court and the reverend gentlemen who were judging his heresy. It was obvious that it was useless to persist, so the hearing was suspended and he was told as clearly as possible that he should look to saving his soul, because he would lose his earthly life.[31]

The Inquisitors were used to extracting confessions from the crypto-Jews, but here they had come up against somebody who was neither a Jew nor a Christian. Yet Melchor was evidently a man of powerful intellect and self-confidence, who could not be convinced by priestly persuasion. The court discussed his case and came to the conclusion that he must be feigning madness. They pressed him, but in vain. He would not give in. He believed neither in the law of Jesus Christ nor in that of Moses, but in the *Natural Law,* and he signed his statements with a firm hand. The friars brought him up from his cell and interviewed him every month. On 10 May 1723, ten months after his first interrogation, he was still saying that there was no Heaven, no Hell, no Purgatory, no God, no Virgin, no Jesus Christ. He said the same on 4 June and again on 8 July, adding that he had held those ideas since his adolescence. Session after session, the gaoler brought Melchor up from his cell for the friars to examine him: 28 July, 9 August, 2 September 1723 and again on 5 May 1724.

In desperation to save Melchor's soul and to fulfil the fundamental task of the Inquisition, which was to reconcile heretics, the Inquisitors ordered the doctors to examine him. On 9 May 1724 they issued a report in which they referred to his 'depraved understanding' and his 'mania'. What did his mania or madness consist of ? In an answer which recalls the diagnosis of madness made by Soviet psychiatrists against people who did not accept the political system, the doctors said that Melchor's madness 'can be seen in the nonsense of his views'. They spoke of his 'stupidity and idiocy' and, in the technical medical language of the epoch, insisted that these qualities were to be seen in his temperament and 'phlegmatic complexion'.

Nevertheless, the doctors identified other characteristics in Melchor which contradicted what they called stupidity and mania, with the result that a definite conclusion eluded them. 'Since it is so difficult to know the way his mind works . . . we cannot positively decide that he is stupid or mad, though he shows signs of feigning.'

Understandably, the Inquisitors were somewhat impatient with the doctors and decided to keep Melchor under their eye for three more months. The young man had already been in gaol for six years, but the Inquisition could not burn a madman. What, however, if he were pretending ? The doctors watched Melchor and reported that his day-to-day behaviour was quite normal. On 20 October, however, the gaoler informed the court of a change. The prisoner lost his temper and threw things if he were not addressed as 'Highness' (*Alteza*), and claimed he was the Duke of Savoy. Had Melchor really gone mad, or had he decided that, to save his life, he had better pretend to have lost his reason?

The court decided to bring his father, Francisco de Torres, from Talavera de la Reina where he was living in internal exile earning a poor living as a barber. How must Torres have felt as he contemplated his younger son, still in prison when almost all the other reconciled Judaizers of the Madrid group were free? Was the boy really mad?

Unfortunately, however, the last sheets of Melchor's file are missing and we do not know if the court finally accepted that he was mad and released him. Let us hope that was the case and that he was finally reunited with his lover Agustina, María Feliciana Hurtado de Mendoza Pimentel's sickly daughter. In prison, Melchor had sent Agustina a message scratched on a piece of cooking chocolate, which he left in the yard when he went down to empty his chamber pot. The message read,

My darling,

Although I promised I would marry the orphan girl I did not know what I was doing, but now I confirm my promise to you although my father swore to God that he would marry me to the orphan. Now I have my free will and I have to marry you and not her. I can't talk to you because they are with me ... tell me if you received a carnation that I sent you.[32]

There had been earlier comments that Melchor was always silent in the gatherings of the Judaizing group. When he said that he did not know what he was doing and that he had recovered his free will, it suggests that he had indeed gone through some sort of mental illness and that, paradoxically, he was now completely sane. Perhaps the experience of standing up for his own views before the Inquisition had strengthened his determination to marry the girl he wanted.

Indeed, the new situation in which these young and single men and women found themselves may have made communication between them easier, even in gloomy solitary cells, than it had been while they were under the parental thumb. Within the dismal fate of many crypto-Jews, the love of Melchor de Torres and Agustina Pimentel shines out in hope of a new future.

It was, however, the responsibility of parents to see that their children were, at some time, told of their ancestry and of their Jewish obligations.

Initiation into Judaism

The statements which most Judaizers made, as they stood apprehensively before the Inquisitors, betrayed confusion and uncertainty about their Judaism, and were couched very largely in Christian discourse. The prime reason for this was their situation which, in contrast with universal Jewish practice, was one where no organized form of education could be instituted. All the same, in the life of every Spanish crypto-Jew there had been a moment when he or she had experienced initiation into the Jewish heritage.

Frequently it was the mother or an aunt, sometimes a man in the family, who took the child aside and spoke to him. Mariana Pacheco, for instance, already an old woman when she was arrested, and who died in prison, had been initiated at the age of ten by her mother.[33] Rosa Rodríguez was taught by her mother not to eat rabbits, hares or eels.[34] Rosa's daughter Ventura Luis explained in her turn that at the age of eight or nine her mother Rosa Rodríguez began to instruct and teach her to believe in the great God of Israel, who is the one worshipped by all the descendants of Judea [*sic*], for her mother was one of them and so was Gabriel Luis [her father] and all their ancestors...The religion of the Christians was not as good for a person to be saved because St Anne, St Joachim, Our Lady and St Joseph and all the good people, that is the saints of the old Law, are descendants of the tribe of Judah.[35]

Despite the precision of Ventura and Rosa's statements, their confusion of Judaism and Christianity is manifest.

Women in Spain were very limited in their movements, rarely leaving home except perhaps for shopping, though some ran businesses. The men, however, did get around more. Thus the moment and means of their initiation into Judaism varied more. One day, for example, when Diego Rodríguez 'the Younger' walked into the shop of his uncle, Antonio Rodríguez ('Pig's Foot'), the latter said to him:

'Oh! Nephew! You must keep the Law of Moses properly.' He answered 'Uncle, what is the Law of Moses? Isn't it the law of God that my teacher tells me?' and Antonio Rodríguez 'Pig's Foot' answered 'I mean the Law of God.'

This Antonio Rodríguez, arrested on Christmas Day 1719, was a jeweller and silk merchant who offered loans and accepted cash deposits.[36] He was 56, and well established with two shops in Cuenca. His trial was a long one. He denied all the charges of Judaizing and insisted that those people whom he suspected were witnesses, who were always anonymous and could not be questioned in court, were not to be trusted. In particular, he *tachó*, that is named as a person who was not to be believed, his shop assistant Manuel de Castro, who, he said, stole money. Confidently, 'Pig's Foot' listed for the inquisitors some people who could answer for his fervent Christianity, as well as a list of enemies. The inquisitors, however, had up to five different sets of witnesses of his Judaizing and so, to force him to confess his sin, they ordered a session of torture. Despite 'Pig's Foot's' age – he was 56 – he bore the torture, but faced with the threat of burning he began to confess to the court. He admitted what the Inquisitors already knew, that his father had Judaized and had been reconciled nearly forty years earlier. In 1687, when 'Pig's Foot' was already married to María Fernández, who owned a shop in the Calle Carreterías, Miguel Luis had come from the town of Cifuentes to sell silk. Luis had said to 'Pig's Foot', 'Let's go for a walk.' They strolled down to the island which is a little below the junction of the two rivers which surround the city. Sitting in that deserted spot, Miguel Luis, a mature man at the time, spoke to the young and newly married Rodríguez about the Law of Moses, of the miracles that God had wrought for his People and of how the Messiah had not yet come.[37]

Normally a relative or family friend would explain the Law of Moses to a person, who would then discover that all the rest of the family were Judaizers. However, they might even deny it. Diego de la Mota, for example, said that he was initiated at the age of eleven by his uncle Diego Suárez, but when he told his parents what his uncle had said, they did not reply, at least so Diego told the court. Of course, Diego may have been trying to protect his parents, since the Holy Office already knew through the confessions of his brothers that the family had observed some of the Jewish holy days.[38]

In Julián Vázquez's case, his 'eyes had been opened', as the phrase was, by his friend Pablo Enríquez, described as coming from Leghorn and therefore one who had lived freely as a Jew. Julián said:

> One day [Enríquez] took this confessant [Vázquez] out into the country and told him that as his friend he was sorry for him because he was destined for Perdition by observing Christianity, and the real Law in which they could all be saved was the Law of Moses.[39]

However, the fundamental ignorance about Judaism of almost all of the Judaizers meant that stating to someone that one was a Jew and communicating whatever information one possessed about the requirements of the Jewish religion was bound to be insufficient unless there was some chance of being taught by somebody who really knew about Judaism or a possibility of obtaining relevant reading matter.

Rabbis and books

As has been seen in the case of Francisco de San Antonio, an important part in the teaching of Judaism to the Judaizers was played by Jews from abroad. When Inquisition documents speak of a rabbi, however, it is unlikely that they are referring to a man who merits the title and more probable that they are referring to somebody with a profound knowledge of Jewish history, law and customs, who goes here and there, is responsible for maintaining the particular spirit of the sect and correcting the heterodox deviations that clandestinity often produces; he directs the prayers, the fasts and the major festivals; he is present at them, supervises the communal prayers, watches over the conduct of rites and ceremonies and, finally, gives them watchwords for their conduct.[40]

While initiation into Judaism was necessarily secret, teaching of Jewish practices and maintenance of Jewish consciousness was often the function of the *junta* or meeting where everybody, women included, contributed what they could. Josepha Díaz said that in Cuenca a group met regularly 'in each other's houses in turn, and they always talked about the Law of the Jews ... '.[41]

María Fernández added that 'they used to visit each other ... and .. behaved to each other and spoke among themselves as believers and observers of the Law of Moses, considering it to be the best and most reliable for saving their souls.'[42]

Francisco de Torres confessed that the Madrid group of Judaizers to which he belonged had been meeting regularly for fifteen years in different houses.[43] Torres gave the court details about who had most authority in Jewish matters, who owned books and who communicated with communities of ex-Marranos in other countries.

Miguel de Robles would seem to have been the most important Jewish 'missionary' of the early eighteenth-century, the man who had directed the celebration of Passover in 1714. He managed to get out of the country just ahead of the Inquisition.

Still according to Torres's ample confessions, the Madrid Judaizers met at the house of Francisco de Córdoba, 'which they call the Synagogue'.[44] Torres perhaps exaggerated, given his own delicate situation as a previously insufficient confessant, and said also that Córdoba was the 'major rabbi of Spain' (*principal rabino de España*) and that he had been elected to the honour in 1709, four days before the Great Fast of September. The choice of Córdoba had to be confirmed by the ex-Marrano community in Leghorn, though Torres did not say why. The confirmation came back signed by Abraham de Córdoba, probably a relative of Francisco, and two others. Despite the suspicion aroused by these rather too convenient statements of Torres, the mention of three signatures suggests the minimum number required by a Jewish court. Back in Madrid, everyone present put their right hands on a book which Torres calls 'the Book of the Law' and swore to respect Córdoba's religious authority. From then on he 'preached and taught the Law' though no evidence of this has been found. However, when in 1717 old Isabel de Aragón fell ill, Córdoba and Diego López de Castro, whose religious constancy would take him heroically to the stake, were brought to her bedside as if they were Catholic priests.[45]

Several witnesses testified that Francisco de Córdoba possessed a substantial library. According to the talkative María de Tudela, Córdoba owned 'a big book of the Law, printed in Amsterdam, which they call *Talmud*.[46] It is interesting that María even knew the word *Talmud*, but however large the book to which she referred, it was unlikely to have been the multi-volumed corpus of rabbinic legislation and discussion written largely in Aramaic and which only a specialist can use. Possibly the book was Menasseh ben Israel's *Thesouro dos Dinim*, reprinted in Amsterdam in 1710, a substantial summary of Jewish law, composed in Portuguese as a guide for ex-Marranos. María de Tudela also said that Córdoba had a small book in French from which he prayed. Perhaps she meant that it was a book which had come from Bayonne. Maybe it was the prayer-book that Isabel de Ribera said that Córdoba had shown her husband.[47] Other people had books from which the families prayed every day (*'por donde rezaban los dichos y sus familias todos los días'*).

Francisco de Córdoba's library was probably destroyed, for no Jewish books appear in its inventory.[48] The 'book of the Law' on which the members of the Judaizing group swore to respect Córdoba's authority was probably a Vulgate translation of the Bible. No examples of the 1553 Jewish Bible translation of Ferrara, nor of the Spanish Protestant versions, are mentioned in the documents examined. There are, however, frequent references to translations of the Psalms of David which the Judaizers recited without the *Gloria Patri* at the end. The likelihood is that Córdoba owned two or three Jewish books printed in Spanish or Portuguese in Amsterdam, which his friends managed to destroy before the Inquisition officials found them. Córdoba failed to escape and, at an *auto de fe* held on 18 October 1722, he was reconciled, but imprisoned for life and sentenced to wear the penitential robe and receive two hundred lashes. Only his indifferent health saved him from several years in the galleys.[49]

There were other books which the Judaizers could use to accumulate some ideas about Judaism. For a person with higher education, there were many sources of information in Jewish literature of the Hellenistic period.[50] According to one of the servants, Francisco de Córdoba's library possessed the biblical story of Judith and Holofernes.[51] This book describes the victory of the Israelites over Nebuchadnezzar. The text includes a brief summary of the previous history of the Jewish People from which the Judaizers could have extracted a lesson with reference to their own situation:

> As long as they did not sin against their God, they prospered; for theirs is a god who hates wickedness. But when they left the path he had laid down for them, they suffered heavy losses in many wars and were carried captive to a foreign country.[52]

In the book, Judith places ashes on her head before begging divine aid in her enterprise and prays emotionally for help against the Assyrians, in words which would easily have been seen by the eighteenth-century Spanish Judaizers as reflecting their own situation, surrounded as they were by idolatry and danger. The book would have resonated for the Judaizers who read it, since it is about a woman who obeyed the dietary laws of her religion, whom Holofernes wanted to seduce, but who preserved her chastity, just as the Judaizers saw their obligation to preserve their ancestral religion before the seductions of Christianity. Judith was as much a heroine of her people as Esther was. Esther fasted for three days, while Judith prayed and purified herself for three days also. Christians might read this as foreseeing the three days of Jesus's death and resurrection, but for Jews it underlined the persistence and valour of the women which brought triumph in the end.

Another author who is mentioned as being read by the Judaizers was the Romanized Jew Flavius Josephus, the soldier and historian of the first century of the Christian era. According to Francisco de Torres,

> the book which contained the Law of Moses was written in folio, and it is a volume of more than three hundred pages and is called *Josepho de Bello Gallico* [sic], because although there is another book by the same author it is in quarto and is about the wars of Jerusalem and this other one is about the Law of Moses.[53]

Torres's statement is confusing and it may be that either he or the Inquisition secretary muddled it. Those of Josephus's works which would be useful to describe religious observances would have been *The Antiquities of the Jews* or *Against Apion*, which existed in Spanish translation.[54] Nevertheless, the Portuguese Judaizer Antonio Ribeiro Sanches recalled that he also read Josephus in Portugal at the beginning of the eighteenth-century.[55] Josephus was read also among the crypto-Jews of Majorca.[56]

Most of the seventeenth- and eighteenth-century Spanish Judaizers were probably aware that Judaism had not been fossilized in the Bible, that in later times the Rabbis had developed Jewish practice into a complete way of life, and that there were Jewish communities which lived according to Jewish Law. Even anti-Jewish literature and the sermons preached at *autos de fe* served to give some information about Jewish practice. According to one distinguished historian, 'I am now convinced that converts who wanted to could know much more than we believed previously.'[57]

The statement, nevertheless, can be true only of the learned. For other people, ignorance of Latin and Hebrew, and the sheer difficulty of getting hold of books, as well as extracting the information about how to observe the detailed rabbinic legislation which guides daily life, would have been insuperable. Referring to the absence of Jewish books in the inventories of sequestered property, a historian writes: 'It is not surprising...that their knowledge of Jewish teachings is not very profound and is no more than the oral memory of some rites, fasts, prayers and ceremonies.'[58]

However, the details of what the Judaizers did at significant moments of their lives, as well as in their daily behaviour, does not quite justify this dismissive tone.

The life cycle

Circumcision

To circumcise a baby who could be seen by a servant or another child would be dangerous for Judaizing parents, and it would be a permanent source of danger for the child throughout its life. So circumcised men among the Judaizers became rare. Some Judaizers were, however, circumcised. Miguel de Robles, for instance, had been born and circumcised in Bayonne, which gave him a certain prestige among the Madrid Judaizers. Francisco de Córdoba, elected 'rabbi' of the Madrid Judaizers, was expected to travel to Leghorn to have the operation performed. Nevertheless, the majority were not circumcised. In London, as in the other ex-Marrano communities, the registers of the Spanish and Portuguese community record frequent circumcisions practised on newly-arrived men born in the Iberian peninsula.[59]

In 1632, perhaps in consequence of a feeling of greater freedom during the era of Olivares, Isaac Farque (alias Antonio de Aguilar) came from Amsterdam to perform circumcisions in Madrid.[60] In the eighteenth-century, however, the Inquisition documents rarely show that men were circumcised. One exception was Francisco de Lara, who in

1707 was suffering from urine retention. Manuela Hurtado de Mendoza Pimentel told the court that she went to visit him. Standing anxiously about his bed were his wife, Francisca Alvarez, and his mother-in-law Isabel de Castro. Doctor Diego López Zapata, who was later tried for Judaizing, was examining the patient. Pointing to Manuela, Zapata asked Francisca Alvarez if she could be trusted. Francisca replied that Manuela was 'like all those present', whereupon the doctor said to Lara:

> 'My friend, there's nothing to do here but insert a catheter to try to free the fleshy obstructions ... which are preventing your urine passing.' To this Lara, clasping the doctor's hands, said 'Oh, I'd rather die than put myself into a surgeon's hands! You know the problem. I shall be found out!' To which Zapata replied 'You don't need a surgeon. It can be done by your wife, Doña Francisca.' And Doña Francisca said she would do it though she saw no problem in calling Blas who was the barber and trusted. ... Zapata said, 'Let's not take risks. It would be better if you did it,' and Doña Francisca Alvarez did what was necessary.[61]

Circumcision could be explained away. Luis de Valencia, for example, a 60-year-old Lisbon merchant, said that the condition of his member was 'because he had been with women' – that is, he was suffering from syphilitic lesions. The doctor said that Gabriel de Córdoba, brother of Francisco, lacked his prepuce and that there was a visible scar at the root of the glans.[62] When Gabriel was questioned about this, he said that he had suffered injuries to his member years earlier and the surgeon had had to remove his prepuce. This first trial of Gabriel de Córdoba was suspended on 15 July 1716 for lack of sufficient proofs of his Judaizing. Arrested again, he did not escape and was burnt at the stake in Madrid on 18 May 1721. One may assume that it was for Jewish religious reasons that he had been circumcised.

Quite frequently, medical opinion was that there had been some sort of surgery on the member, but it could not be said for sure that the circumcision had been performed for religious rather than therapeutic reasons. So often did the doctors say that they were not sure that one suspects that the Judaizers may even have practised a merely symbolic operation.

Childbirth and menstruation

No mention in the later Inquisition documents has been found of the custom according to which Jewish women visit the pool of running water or *miqveh* seven days after having finished menstruating and before recommencing sexual relations with their husbands. That this law was no longer observed is indicated by the insistence in the ex-Marrano communities that a married woman newly arrived from Spain or Portugal should visit the *miqveh*. Nevertheless, one example has been found of the requirement that the mother of a boy wait forty days after giving birth before visiting the *miqveh* and having intercourse with her husband. Luisa de Miranda waited forty days before going to Mass.[63] Evidently the law was recalled, but it was applied to another aspect of daily life.

Death

To pass from a rite associated with birth to the survival of Jewish death and burial customs, here there were some rituals which had survived at least eight generations almost unchanged.

When Manuel Márquez Cardoso died in 1705, his family sought to buy a piece of virgin ground in which to bury him. The corpse would lie undisturbed, as Jewish law requires, rather than being disinterred and the bones thrown into a pit, as was usual because graveyards were so full of human remains. His friend Diego López de Castro went to a monastery to ask for a plot.[64] There was nothing particularly suspicious about this, because burial in the grounds of a religious house was a fertile source of revenue for the monks. On another occasion, in 1610, a Judaizer who died in a village in Murcia left six ducats for his family to bury him in virgin ground.[65] The burial was carried out with Catholic rites but the body was wrapped, according to Jewish requirements, in a white shroud. In the case of Manuel Márquez Cardoso, the least suspicious white shroud that could be found was a Dominican habit.

The period of intensive Jewish mourning lasts seven days. Among the crypto-Jews, who added the two days between death and burial, meat was not touched for nine days.[66] The widow or widower abstained from meat for an entire year.[67] This is another example of syncretic practice. The year's mourning is laid down in Jewish law, but mourning does not require even symbolic fasting.

Just as today, it was the custom to care for the mourners during the first seven days. Francisco de Torres explained that it was customary to send food to the widow. He gave an example of a woman who sent fish to Francisca Alvarez when her husband died, as well as pastries, ice water and chocolate.[68] Like the family of the seventeenth-century financier Manuel de Cortizos, wealthy mourners would distribute charity among poor Judaizers in order to attract divine favour for the dead person's soul. In her evidence, María de Tudela used the phrase 'for the benefit of the departed'.[69] When Isabel de Aragón died, the family fasted. María Guiomar Arias said, 'Children, we do this for the soul of the late lamented, so that God may take her into Paradise.'[70]

The language is clearly Christian, but the customs of fasting or performing an act of charity for the benefit of the soul of the departed have their origin in the Bible and in rabbinic teachings, even though the Judaizers coloured them according to the Catholic ambience in which they lived.

Dietary laws

The Judaizers were concerned with the observance of the dietary laws of the Hebrew Bible. Meal times could even be the moment of initiation of the child into its heritage. María Luis confessed to the Inquisition court of Cuenca that once, in 1712, when she went to the town of Atienza to visit the family of Dr Antonio de Céspedes, she was about to eat a rasher of bacon when Angela de Céspedes, the doctor's mother, stopped her, saying, 'You little bitch ! You're not your father's daughter' (*Ah, perra, no correspondes a hija de tu padre!*). Indeed, María was the daughter of Miguel Luis whom we have seen fulfilling the role of a 'missionary' in Cuenca. She should have known that pork was forbidden. The outraged Angela told her how shocked she was to see that

> a woman who was already married and had had many children, should not know her obligation and what was proper for the daughter of Miguel Luis. She should know that she was wrong and have a care to what she did.[71]

Unlike the earlier generations of converts, by this late stage of the history of Judaizing in Spain, the Judaizers could not buy meat from animals which had been slaughtered according to Jewish law. However, it was usual to buy the poultry alive and kill it at home. The Inquisition frequently heard from the servants that in the Judaizing households the birds' throats were cut rather than wrung.

Even though the Judaizers did eat meat from animals not slaughtered according to Jewish law, they took care to observe that law in the preparation of the meat. The servants of the house in the Calle de Atocha in Madrid where Isabel de Castro, her daughter Francisca Alvarez and her son-in-law Francisco de Lara lived, said that their employers insisted on allowing the poultry to hang until all the blood had dripped out.

They also had to remove all the fat carefully from meat[72] (even though this requirement refers to some parts of the internal fat only). Leonor Rodríguez, in Caravaca (Murcia), bought her meat a day before she intended to eat it – not the usual habit in an age without refrigerators – and, in the words of a servant

> Ordered the witness to put the meat into a pot full of water and leave it to soak for about an hour. Before doing this, Leonor Rodríguez cut away the fat... after the soaking she told the witness to wash the meat very well in the same water... and then she told her to salt the meat and put it into a basket hanging from a nail. On the next day she told her to wash it again and put it on to boil.

This is the process known as making the meat *kasher* or fit. As for poultry, Leonor cut the birds' throats and let the blood drain from them.[73]

According to Jewish law, some animals may not be eaten at all. Witnesses frequently told the inquisitors that the Judaizers abstained from fish without scales and fins, such as eels and all kinds of shellfish. They did not eat pork, hares or rabbits. Mencia de la Peña admitted that she avoided such animals and fish 'because they are forbidden by the Law',[74] that is not because she did not like them or because they did not agree with her, a point which the inquisitors were careful to establish.

Sabbath

Jews keep Saturday as the Sabbath. There is an ancient rite of lighting candles or lamps just before the Sabbath, during which no fire may be lit. In 1615, Pedro Enríquez taught his new and adolescent wife Mencia de la Peña to light these lamps, explaining to her that the Judaizers did not use them to light their work.[75] The neighbours must have wondered why a family kept expensive lights burning all night, or cleaned the house thoroughly on Friday, bringing out clean linen. These acts, together with changing personal clothing on the eve of the Sabbath, serving food which had been cooked the day before and not sewing or doing other household chores, were the ones most noticed and commented on before the court by the non-Jewish servants.

Prayer

As has been seen, the ex-Marranos of Bayonne prayed, using the Jewish liturgy in Spanish rather than in the Hebrew they had not yet learnt.

The trials provide some general ideas about Judaizing prayer customs in Madrid as late as the eighteenth-century. Much probably remains buried in the Inquisition documents or never emerged. The servants reported, for example, that the elderly Isabel de Castro would turn towards the corner of the room, clasp her hands and 'raise and lower her head'.[76] While clasping the hands was a Christian stance, the head movements were mentioned by other witnesses of secret Jewish praying. The soldier Fernando de Castro Ciudad Real said that when he was a boy in Bayonne he watched the Portuguese Jews praying three times a time 'lifting and lowering their heads'.[77] The Inquisition was aware that Jews did not kneel to pray, that they faced East and agitated their heads, hands and bodies in intense and rhythmic movements. Diego López de Castro's cook said that he had to take the candle out of the family bedrooms, presumably because the Judaizers would not extinguish it on the Sabbath. The people knelt at the foot of the bed, facing the window and 'acted as if they were praying'.[78] As for Diego López de Castro himself, who observed the dietary laws faithfully even in the Inquisition prison, he was said to walk about 'muttering'. Another Judaizer, exhaustively interrogated, was Gaspar Díaz, a convict in the fortress of Melilla in Morocco, whom the Inquisition assumed had no reason to lie, since he was dying in hospital. He said that he had recited the established prayers with the family of Alonso de Córdoba in his house in Madrid.[79] Diego de la Mota said that once in his childhood he had come across the adults in his family in the yard, with their arms outstretched, looking for the first evening star, 'and he thought they were praying, from the muttering'. From these occasional testimonies it seems that some secret Jews, who perhaps owned a prayer-book in Spanish published abroad, probably in Amsterdam, prayed regularly. Others repeated fragments that they remembered.

Nevertheless, practices rather than prayers are the most important aspect of Judaism. Scrutiny of the list of practices given to the court by Rodrigo de la Peña in the early seventeenth-century may justify the conclusion that the Spanish Judaizers, even at this late stage of their history, strove to observe the principles of Judaism despite the difficult and dangerous conditions of their lives. Here is Rodrigo's statement taken down in reported speech by the Inquisition scribe:

[A]nd they had to keep four Jewish fasts every year: that of Queen Esther, which falls around Lent and lasts three days; that of the Lamb, which falls after Easter; that of Tabernacles in July or August[80] [Rodrigo de la Peña was wrong here. Tabernacles falls in the autumn, soon after the Day of Atonement], and the great day of September ... and at the first and second evening meal they had to avoid meat, except on the second night of the Fast of the Lamb when they ate meat. And the second meal had to be cooked on the previous day. And they were not to eat pork, hares, rabbits nor meat with blood or fat, and the cattle and poultry had to have their throats cut and be hung up so that the blood drained, according to the Law, nor [could they eat] fish without scales. ... On Fridays all the furniture had to be moved, sweeping first. And all the chairs, chests and tables were to be wiped with oil and everything that was to be eaten on the Saturday had to be cooked, the lamps and candelabra had to be cleaned and refilled with oil and new wicks, and that night a lamp was to be lit in every room if the people could afford it. When they went to bed they changed their underwear, and on Saturday they avoided work and did no labour at all, not even combing their hair nor cutting their nails, nor wrote nor touched money, nor bought nor sold, nor might they order anyone else to do any such things. On Saturday they might wash, play instruments, sing and dance, and the holy day ended at nightfall. And they shaved the body and facial hair of the dead and washed their bodies with wine and wrapped them in white shrouds and they did not sew them up tightly nor tie them at the feet and the hands, and they arranged to bury them in virgin earth if possible, and the day of the funeral they ate what others brought them. They did not light fire but other observers [of the Law of Moses] brought food.

Here, perfectly summarized, was the Law of Moses as practised by the Spanish crypto-Jews in their last generation before they disappear from the Inquisition sources. It was the Law in which they hoped to live and in which many of them died.

Conclusions

Religious liberty

It has taken several centuries for nationhood and nationality to be separated from religious belief. Even today, many people find the idea of a multicultural polity hard to accept, because they see a national culture as inseparably identified with a particular value system or religious outlook. Sometimes, opposition to multiculturality reflects a genuinely held opinion which may well respect other cultures but is sure that the values of 'the others' cannot be absorbed into those of the nation. Such an opinion may be honestly held and certainly does not automatically lead to the atrocities of the Nazis. If anything, the Nazi notion of the 'alien' became a mockery of national unity, because they considered even the most assimilated and 'Germanized' Jews, those whose parents or grandparents had accepted baptism – that is the *conversos* of the time, though they did not Judaize – as alien to the German nation and community.

For this reason, and despite the occasional evidence of 'racist' anti-Judaism in Spain, there is no valid analogy between the Spain of the Inquisition and Nazi Germany. Nor can there be a real equivalence between the expulsion of the Jews from Spain, the aim of which was to persuade most of them to accept baptism and be assimilated, and the tensions which exist today in Europe between long-established communities and recent immigrants, for the Jews of Spain were not recent arrivals.

Was the Inquisition 'wrong'?

It is difficult for the historian and the moralist to decide on criteria which could establish whether certain historical actions were 'right' or 'wrong' in an absolute sense. Was the Inquisition 'wrong' because it was based on a principle – the need for religious unity – which we see today as irrelevant? Or, on the other hand, was it wrong even if the absolute and overwhelming imperative of religious unity is accepted? If Spain is compared with England, Protestants were burnt under Mary Tudor in the sixteenth-century, but, while Catholics were considered disloyal under Elizabeth I, they were not burnt at the stake. During the centuries while Catholics in England suffered disabilities, they were fined for not attending Anglican church, but not persecuted for being false Anglicans, which was the case with the *conversos* in Spain who were obliged to be Catholics.

Heresy in England was a matter of open statements, usually made by leading clerics; heresy for the Inquisition lay in the secret behaviour and thoughts of unimportant people. It seems intolerable today that one's personal religious conscience could be investigated in Spain by a court with the backing of the civil power. Nor did the Spanish Judaizers of the seventeenth and eighteenth centuries have any chance of choosing their religion or the alternative of leaving Spain, as for instance French Protestants did when the Edict of Nantes was revoked in 1689 and the Huguenots came to England.

Furthermore, the Inquisition convicted prisoners on evidence that would be either inadmissible or certainly rejected in a modern criminal court. While it may be true that standards of proof were generally less rigorous in pre-modern courts, the Inquisition court was not really concerned with safeguards for the accused. It considered that the guarantees in place were sufficient if the accused were innocent. Certainly, had the defending advocate been allowed to question prosecution witnesses, he would probably have been able to show up inconsistencies and contradictions in memories of many years earlier, such as were used as evidence. A defending advocate would also have been able to illuminate faults in the witnesses' characters to a degree sufficient to create doubt about their testimony in a neutral jury's mind.

The Inquisition, however, was not a court of that nature. The Holy Office did not arrest people for nothing, as it always told the accused when asking them if they knew or surmised why they had been detained. It had proof of the accused's heresy, but wanted to know more. Its role was to persuade the accused, known always as the *reo* – the criminal – to confess and be reconciled with the Church, not to hold a trial with the assumption of innocence, requiring the prosecutor to prove his case without doubt and to compete in rhetoric with a defender of equal status.

All the same, if the witnesses were insufficient or of doubtful value, the court could always give the accused a severe warning; after all, there was no smoke without fire. The prisoner must have done something. The accused could be made to abjure of light suspicions (*abjuración de levis*) or grave suspicions (*abjuración de vehementis*), which had different implications. In Gonzalo Báez de Paiba's first trial, so doubtful was the court about the witnesses that, though the Inquisitors strongly suspected Gonzalo of Judaizing, and, as his later trials showed, the Inquisitors were justified, they allowed his reconciliation with the Church to take place in private, so that Gonzalo was spared the public shame of appearing in the penitent's robe at the *auto de fe*.

Today we cannot easily detach our repulsion at trying someone for a privately expressed religious view from our opinions about the harshness of the Inquisition, for even a complete and immediate confession would still lead to confiscation of one's property, imprisonment for an indefinite period, and an obligation to denounce everybody else who might have been involved, however remotely, in Judaizing. The procedures of the Inquisition were intolerable. Its punishments were excessive, destroying the livings of the victims, breaking up their families, not to speak of the use of torture, and there was hypocrisy in imposing the physical punishments of the town executioner while recommending mercy.

The Inquisition and Spain

What is perhaps most striking about the Inquisition is not its severity or procedures, but the fact that it lasted so much longer in Spain than elsewhere – even Portugal – and that it took a revolution, rather than a self-reform of the Church, to abolish it. The liberal parliamentarians at the Cortes of Cadiz abolished the Inquisition on 22 February 1813, but on 21 July 1814 Fernando VII restored it, not because of Judaizers, but because the Holy Office guaranteed the suppression of heretical thought and shored up the position of the Church and Spanish conservatism. The Inquisition was finally abolished on 15 July 1834. In reality, it symbolized the refusal to allow Liberal ideas to enter Spain, and at the same time reinforced the pernicious doctrines of purity of blood. All had to conform, and Spain continued to be a highly conformist and closed society until well into the twentieth-century. It has always been difficult for many sections of Spanish society to accept that one can be Spanish without being Catholic. The Jews, the leaven of society, disappeared, and their few Judaizing descendants were persecuted into oblivion by the Inquisition, or took their glorious traditions to new fertile ground, where in Holland, Venice and London, Leghorn, Bayonne, the Caribbean and New York, they resurrected Spanish Judaism.

However, the question remains: did the Inquisition create the society which demanded condign punishment for the Judaizing heretics, or did it arise out of that society? And, if so, why?

The rise of the New Christians, often Judaizers, in Spanish society, coincided with the age of expansion, the maritime and commercial triumph of England and Holland, and the beginning of religious and scientific scepticism. Contrary to what is often asserted, the Inquisition did not isolate Spain completely from new currents of thought, nor did it destroy on principle characteristics which favoured economic expansion. The Holy Office had little interest in finance and commerce as such. In the words of J.P. Dedieu, an expert in Inquisition history, 'If certain books were not read, the main reason was that the Spaniards did not want to read them'.[1]

But why did Spaniards not want to read this literature? It was because the world of commerce and finance was well represented in Inquisition trials, so that a whole class of economic behaviour became stigmatized because two-thirds of those who practised it were converts from Judaism and their descendants. Modern economic ideas were seen by the Spanish Catholic world as independent of the divine word and thus suspect. And though the Inquisition was not itself directly responsible for the growth of obsession for 'pure' ancestry, it contributed to it because the Holy Office administered the system of genealogical investigation.

The Marranos themselves

One of the most difficult aspects of discussing the crypto-Jews is their psychology. There is some sort of parallel in the case of Jewish children brought up by Christian families during the Nazi period. Some of these children, especially in ultra-Catholic Poland, as they approach old age, learn about the murder of their parents and millions of other Jews, and are impelled to seek their own roots.

The situation of these Christianized Jews may help to frame an understanding of the Marrano mentality. It has already been suggested that the penitential aspects of Marrano religion arose out of their sense of guilt for not completely obeying Jewish religious law on the one hand and, on the other, for not being faithful to the teachings of the Church. They have very accurately been called 'Souls in Conflict'.[2]

The Hunt for the Hidden Jew: Crypto-Judaism after the Inquisition

The hunt for the hidden Jew, the 'Judaizing heretic' petered out in the middle of the 18th century, following the great energy displayed by the Holy Office of the Spanish Inquisition in prosecuting Judaizers in the 1720s and 1730s. Yet, given that Judaizing seemed to have been crushed many times before but had nevertheless survived and re-emerged a generation later, there does not seem to be a convincing reason for the apparent end of Judaizing in the mid-eighteenth century unless the decline of the importance of the New Christian contribution to the Spanish economy meant that the leading Judaizers had by 1750 departed with their families for London, Amsterdam and other welcoming centres. Possibly also, the spread of more centralising attitudes under the rule of the Bourbon monarchs of 18th century Spain may have meant that the Inquisition's concern was directed to more general threats to its power, such as the drive for greater independence for the State from the Church. In addition, other dangers to the rigid clericalism of Spain, such as Free Thought, Deism and Freemasonry, may have come to seem more threatening than the by now faint remains of secret Jewish practice. Nevertheless, opposition to the presence of Jews in Spain remained strong.

Jews return to Spain: the end of The Inquisition

The arrival in Spain of Jews seems to have come about haphazardly. There is some evidence of Jews entering Spain in the late eighteenth and early nineteenth centuries. For example, in 1781 a certain Jacob Pereira tried to land at Cadiz[1]. He was arrested, but his attempt suggests that others may have succeeded. Nevertheless, the hostility towards Jews in general persisted, so that when in 1797 the Minister of Finance and

Trade, Pedro de Varela, recommended admitting Jews to Spain, his proposal was rejected.[2] Five years later, in 1802, a royal edict specifically insisted on the exclusion of Jews from Spain.[3] This suggests that there was a definite presence of Jews in Spain or that there was pressure to admit them. A number of Moroccan and Gibraltarian Jews had entered Spain seeking baptism and the benefits that this attracted over the seventy years since the Rock had come under British rule, and this suggests that these Jews were in and out of Spain with some regularity.[4]

The new century was, however, to bring about major events which would lead to great changes in Spanish society, among them the Peninsular War of 1808-1813, the Liberal revolutions of the following decades, economic development, Spain's military activity in Morocco, and the rediscovery by Spain of the descendants of the exiles of 1492.

When French forces invaded Spain in early 1808 they abolished the Inquisition. It is likely that there were Jews among the French troops and accompanying civilians, some of whom may have remained in Spain. There are also reports that French soldiers came across what they took to be hidden Jews.[5] The reports are too vague, however, for one to be sure whether they were *marranos* or merely Jews who happened to be living in Spain at the time.

The end of the Holy Office in Spain was confirmed by the patriotic assembly, the *Cortes* of Cadiz, on 22 February,1813, but the fierce reaction to French occupation which had led to the Peninsular War or *Guerra de Independencia* of 1808-1813 brought about the disgrace and exile of many Spanish progressives and Liberals who might have encouraged the admission of Jews, while the wave of extreme reaction after the defeat of Napoleonic forces led to the re-establishment of the Holy Office by the restored king Fernando VII on 21 July 1814. A Liberal rebellion abolished the Inquisition once more on 9 March 1820, only for it to be re-established when that uprising was suppressed. The Inquisition's last victim, in 1826, was Cayetano Ripoll, a Deist schoolteacher. It was not until 15 July 1834, that the Holy Office of the Spanish Inquisition was finally abolished, after nearly 356 years.

In his famous book *The Bible in Spain*, first published in 1842, which describes his travels in Spain between 1836 and 1840, the itinerant Bible-seller and linguist George Borrow narrates how on his travels in Spain he met a Jew named Abarbanel, who gave him a fantastic account of secret Judaism in the Peninsula which would appear to be a reflection of what was believed about the situation in earlier centuries, with *converso* archbishops coming secretly to kiss the hands of learned Jews.[6] Whether this story was actually told to Borrow by Abarbanel or whether he elaborated the account is problematic. It is somewhat of a coincidence that this person should bear the same name as the famous medieval exegete Don Isaac Abarbanel.

Another report, perhaps more reliable, in the London *Jewish Chronicle* of 28 April, 1848, refers to three Jewish families in Madrid, one of whom had been rescued from North African slavery, having been captured while on a pilgrimage from Poland to Jerusalem. There was also a woman whose father and husband had come to Spain with the French, and a widower from Portugal. The visitor was shown a synagogue in a basement, which his host claimed to have been used for generations by secret Jews.

So, up till then there had been only occasional and unreliable reports of the presence of Jews in Spain, but the political and ideological atmosphere was changing. Liberalism spread into Spain from Europe, bringing with it the tentative opinion that the State had nothing to do with people's religion, together with a more robust view of the market economy where prejudice about people's private religious beliefs had no place. In Spain there had been no Jews and thus no ghettos, but Catholicism and the rule of the Church had been consubstantial with Spanishness. Commercial energy and the entrepreneurial spirit, suppressed by the aristocratic and religious culture that had dominated Spain, required, in the Liberal view, the removal of the dead hand of tradition.

Over the next half-century, unsuccessful attempts were made by Ludwig Philippson, editor of the important German Jewish journal, the *Allgemeine Zeitung des Judenthums*, by the *Consistoires* or official governing bodies of the historic ex-*marrano* Spanish and Portuguese Jewish communities in Bordeaux and Bayonne, and by the influential Sir Moses Montefiore of the London community, to persuade Spanish Governments to rescind the 1492 edict of expulsion.[7]

Despite the official prohibition on their entry, by mid-century, Jews had been coming to Spain in small numbers, particularly as a result of Spain's activities in Morocco, where descendants of the expelled Jews of 1492 still spoke Spanish. In 1844, riots in Morocco impelled a significant number of Jews to cross to Gibraltar, and no objection was raised to their crossing over the bay into Spain. The London *Jewish Chronicle* wrote '...the fugitives felt so much at home with the Spaniards, security having been granted to them under the immediate protection of the authorities of that place, that they saw no reason for putting off a wedding, which took place at Algeciras with all their customs and ceremonials.[8] The refugees returned to Morocco the following year. Their temporary presence in Spain and the holding of religious ceremonies had been tolerated, but it is clear that they could not remain, given the restatements of the ban in 1802 and 1816.

In subsequent years, Jews continued to arrive from Morocco, in particular following Spain's 1859 conquest of Tetuán, which would later become the capital of Spanish Morocco. Some Moroccan Jewish refugees remained in Spain, founding the first post-exile community, in Seville.

In 1859 the Paris Rothschilds financed a medical mission in Tetuán. Spanish expansion had revealed the unhappy situation of poor Jews in Morocco. It was the latter's need for succour and protection that brought them to the notice of their wealthy and influential coreligionists in Europe, some of whom were now arriving in Madrid and Barcelona to participate in Spain's economic development, and to run its railways and banks. These European Jews included representatives of major finance houses such as the Rothschilds and the Péreires of Bordeaux, but formed no established community.[9]

The original connections of the Rothschilds with Spain had been made during the Peninsular War when Nathan Mayer Rothschild had facilitated the transfer of bullion to Spain to pay British troops.[10] In 1834-1835, Lionel de Rothschild of the London branch spent several months in Spain trying to organise loans for the depleted Spanish Treasury. He consolidated the floating debt and set up a long-term scheme to increase Government revenues, which would allow the Spanish Government to honour its obligations and thus keep its international credit buoyant. Here, the role of the Rothschilds was not dissimilar to that of the New Christian bankers whom Olivares had favoured two centuries earlier except that the Jewishness of the Rothschilds was well-known. The latter was, however, no longer of concern to Spanish Governments.

Despite the tolerance shown to the presence of individual Jews, however, the edict of expulsion was still in force. But in 1868 a revolution dethroned the Spanish monarchy. In the expectation of a new constitution which would declare the State religiously neutral, Jewish leaders and organisations in London, Paris and the *consistoires* of Bayonne and Bordeaux, sent letters asking for the edict to be revoked. The reply was friendly. Jews might come to Spain and worship freely, but in private. For the reactionaries, whom it was considered unwise to anger, to rescind the edict of 1492 and to declare Spain religiously neutral, was highly provocative, for it would open the gate in their view to the false liberal values of the modern world.

Once the monarchy was restored at the end of 1874, Rothschilds' agents in Madrid, Daniel Weisweiller and Ignaz Bauer, who were both Jews, advised that it was unwise to press matters. After all, a few Jews did live unmolested in Spain. The census of 1877 showed that 406 people in 21 places said that they were Jews, which probably indicated that there were many more who did not want to call attention to themselves.[11]

Attitudes towards Jews were, of course, largely theoretical. Few Spaniards had ever seen a Jew. To attack traditional Spanish views and to condemn the Catholic Monarchs and the Church for the expulsion of 1492 and for the Inquisition was part of the rhetoric of Liberal politicians and thinkers. However, the 'Regenerationist' movement which followed the naval and military disaster of the war against the United States in 1898, suggested that Spain would prosper economically by renewing links with the descendants of the exiles, who lived in the eastern Mediterranean, in places such as Sarajevo, Salonika, Constantinople, Izmir and Jerusalem, preserving their language and the traditions brought centuries before from Spain. A leading thinker and parliamentary deputy, Dr. Angel Pulido, publicised the existence of these 'Spaniards without a Motherland' as he called them, and of communities formed of the descendants of refugees from the Inquisition in London, Amsterdam, New York and many other places.[12] Pulido's efforts to encourage commercial and cultural relations between Spain and the Spanish Jews of the eastern Mediterranean raised awareness of the existence of the Spanish-speaking descendants of the exiles and led in December 1924 to the granting of Spanish citizenship, though not residence, to those who could produce the required supporting documentation.

Even the reformist and anti-clerical Spanish Republic of 1931 did not venture to rescind the edict of expulsion of 1492, though it allowed some refugees from Nazi Germany to come to Spain. There was, of course, no possibility of rescinding the 1492 edict of expulsion during the long rule of General Franco which lasted until November 1975. In the early years of Francoist rule, it was difficult for the few Spanish Jews to maintain any form of Jewish life, although Jews who lived in Spanish Morocco and especially the substantial community of Tangiers, a city occupied during the Second World War by Spanish forces, suffered no exceptional difficulties. In Spain itself, the private practice of Judaism was not interfered with, though individuals who were not able to produce a certificate of baptism frequently encountered difficulties. The Franco Government admitted many Jewish refugees, though not with the generosity that its post-war propaganda proclaimed, yet it was not solicitous even of the relatively few who had acquired Spanish nationality and certainly not of the majority of those who spoke Spanish and were descended from the exiles of 1492. In particular, the sixty thousand Jews of Salonika, were almost all deported and murdered at Auschwitz.[13]

Following the Second Vatican Council of the early 1960s, the Law of Religious Liberty of 28 June 1967 relaxed the regulations which had made Jewish life difficult in Spain. More Jews began to arrive in ever-more prosperous Spain, particularly from the now-independent Morocco and as refugees from extremist regimes in Latin America.[14] Yet it was not until 1992 that the edict of expulsion was finally rescinded, after the new Spanish Constitution had declared that Spain had no official religion.

As for the descendants of the *conversos,* to be suspected of Jewish descent was considered shameful for centuries. Today, however, it is not rare to meet Spaniards who claim Jewish ancestry. Many recount that in their families some attenuated Jewish customs have been practised, often out of habit. People recall that their grandmothers lit candles on the Eve of the Sabbath, or that when poultry used to be slaughtered at home, the birds were not throttled but rather their necks were cut and their blood was carefully drained in the Jewish way. In some families, male children were circumcised. While many of these people are faithful Catholics, others express a desire to become Jewish. It is impossible for them to prove that they are descended from Jews in the female line, which by Jewish law would make them Jewish, so some seek conversion to Judaism. Thus some possible descendants of the *marranos* have become fully Jewish once more.[15]

The Chuetas of Majorca

The Chuetas[16] of Majorca consist of fifteen families whose names are well-known[17]. They are the descendants of the survivors of the four great *Autos de Fe* which took place in the capital, Palma, at the end of the seventeenth century (see Chapter Eight). The isolation of Majorca meant that they did not mix with the general population but lived and kept jewellery shops in one street of Palma: the Calle de Argenterías, 'the Street of the Silver Shops'. Called the 'People of the Street' ('*d'es carrer,* or *de la calle* in Castilian), their well-known ancestry led people to shun them. Consequently, until contemporary times the degree of endogamy among them has been very high, and most bear at least one or frequently both of the fifteen surnames.[18]

The Catholicism of the Chuetas is, however, undoubted. This is a paradox because, from the point of view of Jewish law, which counts as

Jewish a person who is descended from Jews in the female line, the Chuetas, given their high degree of endogamy, are the most likely of the various groups who claim Jewish descent to be acceptable without a formal act of conversion. Nevertheless, despite some attempt to restore them to Judaism and even to encourage some to go and live in Israel, only one, Nicolau Aguiló, did so, in 1977. He adopted the name of Nissim Ben-Avraham and became a rabbi.[19] While religiously Catholic, the Chuetas' Jewish identity remains strong, both among themselves and in the view of others, although in the last two generations, as a result of the opening up of Majorca to economic development and consequent social mobility, the degree of exogamy is much higher.[20]

The USA[21]

Some Hispanics living in the American South West – New Mexico, Texas, Colorado and California – claim to be descended from secret Jews who survived the onslaught of the Inquisition in Spanish colonial times by fleeing to the less populated northern territories of what was then Mexico. Over the last twenty years there has been an increasing amount of journalism and academic investigation on the subject. Opinion is sharply divided about whether the Jewish practices described were learnt relatively recently or are really inherited from crypto-Jewish ancestors. There is some suspicion that their practices, such as circumcision, the lighting of candles on the Eve of the Sabbath, and the avoidance of pork and the rejection which Jewish law demands of the mixture of dairy food and meat, may have been learned from certain Evangelical groups in the nineteenth century or from association with Jews settled in the area. Others consider themselves Jews though their religion is Christian, while yet others are unhappy when they learn of their Jewish ancestry. In any case, for many their identification with Judaism is genealogical and neither religious nor cultural.

In general, long habit has meant that their Jewish practices are kept within the family. This is, however, changing, but any return to normative Judaism, for those crypto-Jews who want to do so, has to be through a formal act of conversion, which offends those crypto-Jews who consider themselves Jewish already.

The Portuguese Marranos

The numbers and customs of several communities of descendants of Portuguese crypto-Jews testify to the persistence of Judaism in the remoter parts of northern and eastern Portugal, despite more than two centuries of Inquisitorial activity. The Enlightenment finally reached Portugal with the accession to power in 1751 of the Marquís of Pombal, who began by forbidding the Holy Office to hold *autos de fe* without the permission of the civil authorities. Nevertheless, on 24 September 1752, 45 Judaizers, of whom three were burnt at the stake, featured in an *auto* in Lisbon. Altogether, between 1751 and 1761, eighteen victims were 'relaxed to the secular arm'. On 2 May 1768, Pombal ordered the destruction of all registers which identified families as New Christian, and on 23 May 1773 he removed all distinctions between Old and New Christians. The Inquisition held its last *auto* in Portugal in 1778.[22] It was finally abolished on 31 March 1821. By this time some Gibraltarian Jews were living in Lisbon, under the protection of the British representative, and in 1813 a congregation was established. Jews from Morocco settled in the Azores and Madeira and others from Gibraltar came to live in the south of the country. The 1826 Constitution, however, allowed only the private practice of religions other than Catholicism. Yet there was religious slaughter of animals and a Jewish cemetery in Lisbon by the second half of the century.[23]

Crypto-Judaism had survived in Portugal, according to an account by a Jew who lived in Lisbon at this time. He recalled two secret Jews coming to a private prayer-meeting in Lisbon in 1819, enquiring after the date for the Day of Atonement and praying on their knees in Catholic style before the open Ark containing the Pentateuchal Scrolls.[24]

The presence of significant numbers of secret Jews in remote regions of northern and eastern Portugal was not unknown,[25] but it did not become a matter of interest to Jewish communities elsewhere until in 1925 a Polish-Jewish mining engineer called Samuel Schwarz published a book about communities of secret Jews whom he had discovered in 1917.[26] According to his account, when Schwarz had announced himself as a Jew they had not believed him or that other Jews existed.[27] One of the old women who preserved Jewish prayers challenged him to recite such a prayer. Unable to do this, he offered to say the *Shema*. On hearing the word *Adonai*, the euphemism for the ineffable name of the Deity, the old woman recognised him as Jewish, because this word still existed among the Portuguese *marranos*.

In Belmonte, the town which Schwarz visited, and many others in far provinces of the north and east, close to where the refugees from Spain had crossed the frontier in 1492, the New Christians had inevitably abandoned much Jewish practice: circumcision, Jewish animal slaughter and the dietary laws had largely disappeared, but they did keep Passover, baking unleavened bread, which they began to eat on the third, rather than the first night of the festival. This was probably a way of deceiving spies, but, long before the twentieth century, it had become a custom rather than a necessary precaution. The Portuguese secret Jews celebrated *Purim*, the festival which recalls the events of the Book of Esther. They lit a memorial candle on the day after *Yom Kippur* and took a holiday in the following week. This was *Sukkot* (Tabernacles), though *Sukkot* itself had been lost. They lit a candle on the Sabbath Eve and retained some prayers which they recited in Portuguese. Schwarz reported that they ate pork, the staple local meat, thought not on the Sabbath and festivals. This bears some resemblance to practices found among the Judaizers of Spain, who avoided meat on those days. Again, like the Spanish Judaizers of earlier centuries, despite eating meat from animals not slaughtered in the Jewish way, they drained the blood according to Jewish requirements.

Nevertheless, the *marranos* were Catholics like everybody else. They attended Church and were married and buried by the priest. Yet, despite their secrecy about their practices, obviously other people did know that some of their customs were different.

Schwarz had discovered the *marranos* of Belmonte in 1917. Since the 1910 revolution Portugal had been a secular republic, and many *marranos* were choosing to marry in civil ceremonies rather than in church. The time seemed ripe for bringing them back to formal and open Judaism. The Lisbon community consulted the Sephardi Chief Rabbi of Palestine, who replied that, if the *marranos*, female ancestry was wholly Jewish, they should be accepted as Jews.[28] The Lisbon community then requested various Jewish bodies to provide help to re-educate them. In January 1926, on behalf of the Anglo-Jewish Association, the diplomatic expert and historian Lucien Wolf visited Belmonte, Guarda, Bragança, Coimbra and Oporto, and discussed the question of the *marranos* with the President and the Prime Minister of the Republic.

Wolf's report[29] attempted to explain why, given the religious liberty available since at least 1910, the *marranos* had not sought to re-enter the normative Jewish world. He put it down to their spiritual exhaustion after so many centuries of inquisitorial persecution and the departure of the most energetic *marranos* for communities abroad. Wolf underlined the decadence of Portuguese marranism while stressing the Jewish consciousness of the *marranos* themselves. He also pointed out that their ancestry was not entirely Jewish. This particular point was important, because it meant that a campaign of what was effectively conversion was required, which had major implications because Judaism does not actively seek converts. Wolf suggested that a Jewish 'mission' should be established in Oporto, much nearer to the places of residence of the *marranos* than Lisbon, and where there was already a small community run by a remarkable man, Captain Arturo Carlos de Barros Basto, a descendant of New Christians through his father, who had had a distinguished career with the Portuguese expeditionary force in the First World War and who had been converted to Judaism in Tangiers in 1920. He was now stationed in Oporto.[30] In this city there was a handful of Polish and Russian Jews. Barros Basto organised a community and encouraged *marranos* to worship with them.While he fulfilled his military duties, Barros Basto edited a magazine – *Ha-Lapid* ('The Torch'), which carried material on Jewish law and history, including a column which the Captain claimed to be derived from Menasseh Ben Yisrael's *Thesouro dos Dinim* ('Treasury of Laws', a work composed by that famous rabbi in Portuguese for the use of *marranos* returning to Judaism in seventeenth century Amsterdam). Barros Basto, who was already moderately competent in Hebrew, also published prayer-books in Portuguese translation. He made long and difficult journeys by car, on horseback and even on foot to remote places wherever he heard that *marranos* were living, and proclaimed to them that the Portuguese Republic of 1910 was secular and that their Judaism need no longer be concealed; they could declare themselves openly as Jews. On 27 May 1927 he organised the first circumcision, bringing a *mohel* or trained Jewish circumciser from abroad to perform the operation on a *marrano* doctor, who in his turn learnt the technique. On 1 August 1927 Captain Barros Basto took over a plot of land in Oporto on which to build a synagogue.

The London Spanish and Portuguese Jews' Congregation set up the Portuguese Marranos Committee, which decided generously to support Barros Basto for five years at a rate of £300 per year. He was also supported by the French *Alliance Universelle Israélite*. With these funds, the Captain created what he rather grandly called a *Yeshibah* – usually an advanced rabbinical college, but here a secondary school with concentration on Hebrew and Jewish subjects – in Oporto, and set himself to train some boys from the *marrano* communities so they they could return and lead them.

Writing on 7 August 1929, to Paul Goodman, secretary of the London Spanish and Portuguese Jews' community and of its Portuguese Marranos Committee, Captain Barros Basto said he had six candidates for what he was now calling the Jewish Theological Institute.[31] He had found a

French Jew who was able to act as prayer leader. This person knew the Sephardi liturgy, on which Barros Basto insisted, for, despite most of the Oporto congregation being Ashkenazim, he thought it important to follow the Portuguese liturgy and pronunciation of Hebrew for the sake of the *marrano* students.

On *Rosh Hashanah* (New Year) 1929 a visitor reported the presence of 25 or 30 worshippers. They used prayer books published in Leghorn, a well-established Portuguese Jewish centre. On 30 June 1929, the foundation stone of the Oporto synagogue was laid, Captain Barros Basto receiving £500 towards the building costs from the French branch of the Rothschilds. Afternoon service (*Minha*) was recited together with an *Ascaba* or memorial prayer for the victims of the Inquisition. The London congregation sent two scrolls of the Pentateuch, which had been used by a now-moribund community in the Caribbean.

Problems, however, soon arose. Although Portuguese Liberals, who were usually anti-clerical, might look favourably on the return to Judaism of the *marranos*, if only because it angered Catholics, in one town, Bragança in 1928 the Jewish community was denounced as an illegal 'Masonic' body. Captain Barros Basto was himself a Freemason, as one might expect from a person of his views in a country where Freemasonry stood for those revolutionary, Liberal and anti-clerical sympathies which the Church saw as a threat. As conservative hostility grew against the extremes of the Republic, so a strong Catholic reaction arose against Barros Basto's efforts. Doctors lost patients, traders were boycotted and employees were dismissed.

Furthermore, there was conflict between the Captain and others about the level of adherence to Jewish law that might be expected from the ex-*marranos*. A rabbi arrived from Salonika, the great centre of Iberian Jews since 1492, and was disappointed at the level of religious observance. He found Barros Basto too authoritarian.[32] Schwarz, based in Belmonte, and the Lisbon community were of the opinion that a very high standard of Jewish observance should be enforced, as had always been the case with crypto-Jews returning to Judaism in London, Amsterdam and other centres. The problem was that the *marranos* continued to practise some form of Christianity. They still asked the Catholic priest to recite prayers at funerals and went to him for marriage. Jewish authorities might well question the Judaism of the Portuguese *marranos*. The Captain's view was different. He thought that there had to be legally-established Jewish communities so that the rights of Jews could be protected by the State against clerical attack. In any case, he disagreed that the *marranos* could become fully-practising Jews overnight. It was hard enough to convince them that that it was no longer dangerous. The richer ones feared ostracism, the poorer ones for their jobs. Both fears were reasonable. If over-heavy demands for rigorous Jewish observance were made, the *marranos* would revert to their centuries-old habits.

By the autumn of 1931, the Oporto *Yeshibah* had fourteen students and four teachers. The relatively high quality education and maintenance were free. Perhaps some parents sent their sons as much for this as for their return to Judaism, especially as Barros Basto did not enquire too closely into his pupils' backgrounds. Like him, they may not have been entirely Jewish by descent.[33] Nevertheless, once formally converted they would be fully Jewish.

Since 1926, Captain Barros Basto had been receiving financial support from the Portuguese Marranos Committee in London. Its secretary, Paul Goodman, visited Portugal in 1931 and produced a pessimistic report.[34] Goodman remarked that the current increase in Portugal in religious freedom was, paradoxically, inclining more and more *marranos* to abandon their own practices. He thought it was now impossible to bring any significant number of them back to Judaism.

However, great publicity was created for the *marranos* by the British historian Cecil Roth's book *The Marranos of Spain*, published in 1932, which included some details of the contemporary Portuguese *marranos*. One of the results was that the millionaire Kadourie family financed the completion of the building of the synagogue in Oporto where as many as fifty people attended services led by *marrano* boys from the *Yeshibah*. In Bragança a community had been established with American aid, using a scroll donated by the historic Sephardic community of Leghorn.

By this time, however, the atmosphere in Portugal had changed. A reaction had set in against the secular Republic. Antonio d'Oliveira Salazar had taken power and would continue as authoritarian ruler of the 'New State' until 1974. Captain Barros Basto, accused of slack supervision of political prisoners in the army prison he commanded in Oporto, was dismissed. But worse was to come.

In 1933 a scandal blew up about homosexual behaviour in the Jewish Theological Institute, the official name for the *Yeshibah*. The Army wanted Barros Basto out, because he was a Leftist, a Freemason and a Jew at a time when Salazar was creating his New State. While the presence of *marrano* officers was accepted, the self-proclaimed 'Apostle to the *marranos*' was embarrassing. The Church accused him of inveigling boys by free tuition and maintenance when they were baptised Catholics. Other Jews who were involved in the *yeshibah*, in particular Leon Cassuto and his son Alfonso, who had fled Nazi Germany, found the Captain difficult and authoritarian.

Police enquiries exonerated Barros Basto from the charge of homosexual actions. Some boys had made accusations, but admitted later that they had done so under pressure. The Army nevertheless court-martialled him. He was declared innocent on 12 June 1937 but the Court concluded that, without being a doctor, he had treated the male member of a recently-circumcised boy. His conduct was judged unbecoming, and he was dismissed from the service.

It was in these unhappy circumstances that the synagogue in Oporto was completed in January 1938. Few people would ever worship in it and even fewer *marranos*. Barros Basto was ruined and the *yeshibah* was closed.

In 1938, what was to be the last pre-Second World War report of the Portuguese Marranos Committee said that about ninety pupils had attended the *yeshibah* since its foundation. Little more was heard about the Portuguese *marranos*.

The Lisbon Jewish community did not want to rock the boat in the political atmosphere of the time, although its leader, Professor Moses Amzalak, was a distinguished university rector and a personal friend of Salazar. It became impossible to continue Jewish activity in the towns – Covilhã, Belmonte and Bragança – where ex-*marrano* communities had been established. To take circumcision as an indication of a firm decision to enter normative Judaism on the part of males, there was a record of twenty-four such operations carried out in the 1920s and 1930s, but pages have been removed from the register, presumably by people who thought it better to cover their tracks. Sometimes, when the boys went home from school, there would be conflicts between what they had learned and the attenuated secret Judaism of their parents. In all, it seems that few of that generation remained normative Jews and it may be that Captain Barros Basto allowed his enthusiasm to get the better of him. All the same, it is worth remembering that even in the free atmosphere of 18th century London and Amsterdam not all ex-*marranos* chose the path of Judaism.[35]

Perhaps too much was expected of twentieth century crypto-Jews. Captain Barros Basto admitted his difficulties in his correspondence with Paul Goodman, preserved in the archives of the London Spanish and Portuguese Jews' Congregation. He was however a man of infinite optimism, who believed that it might take two generations to bring the *marranos* back to Judaism. The task had to be begun, but was his the right way to go about it?

The Portuguese Marranos Committee in London met on 8 February 1950. It concluded that work among the *marranos* could not be continued. The German Jews who had stiffened the Oporto group had now left. On 20 February 1950 the Committee asked Professor Amzalak whether the Lisbon community would take responsibility for the Oporto synagogue and received a positive reply. The last minute of the Committee on 20 November 1957 reported that the synagogue in Oporto had forty members, as well as twelve *marranos* who came for *Yom Kippur*. They needed a prayer leader and a Jewish slaughterer.[36] In the late 1950s, an American visitor to Oporto secured an interview with Barros Basto and was taken to the hardly-used synagogue where the gaunt ex-captain recited the *Shema* before the Ark. He died two years later, on 8 March 1961. As for the *marranos* of the time, the always optimistic Captain told his visitor that even if they did little that was Jewish, he still tried to dissuade them from marrying in church or calling on the priest to recite burial prayers. But the visitor noted that surviving students of the *yeshibah* had married Christian, not *marrano*, women.[37]

Belmonte was, in contrast, exceptional, because due to the invigorating presence of Samuel Schwarz, it survived the disgrace of Barros Basto.[38] In 1992, after one of the young men went to Israel, the *marranos* of Belmonte decided to become fully Jewish. Since then, Portuguese-speaking rabbis have been sent and a synagogue has been opened. There is now (2004) a split caused by the different level of response to demands of Jewish observance made on its members. The synagogue counts 170 members. However, the folklore collectors and commercial interests are confusing the situation and making the display of Judaism into something like exhibitionism. The community of course profits from hosting Jewish tourists but at the same time resents being on show. The future of Judaism among the Portuguese ex-*marranos* remains to be seen.

Notes

Introduction

1 Archivo Histórico Nacional, Madrid, Inquisition Section, Legajo 174, Carpeta 1 (hereinafter AHN, Inq.)

2 For the account of this *auto de fe* see British Library 4071 bb 43: *Relación de las personas, que salieron en el Auto de Fe particular, celebrado el Domingo Quince de Marzo de este año de 1722. En la Iglesia del Convento de San Pedro Martyr, Orden de Predicadores de la Ciudad de Toledo.*

3 *Auto da fe*, in the Portuguese spelling, is the usual rendering in English, but since this book is about Spain the Spanish spelling *auto de fe* is used.

4 Marrano (literally 'pig' but probably originating from an Arabic word meaning 'forbidden') is a term habitually used by Jewish historians though it is not found in the Inquisition literature. Convert (*converso*), New Christian (*cristiano nuevo/cristão Novo*) and Jewish convert (*judeoconverso*) are the terms used by Spanish and Portuguese historians, even when they are referring to the distant descendants of baptised Jews. Not all New Christians, in fact probably only a minority, practised Judaism in secret. Those who did were called *Judaizantes* (Judaizers), a word which underlines the heretical nature of the behaviour which is the subject of this book. Crypto-Jews, from the Jewish point of view, are those who secretly tried to live according to the laws of Judaism, even though their style of life and their religious practices often did not correspond to what Jews did at the time in other countries. (See the essay by Jaime Contreras, 'Conversos y Judaizantes después de 1492: una relación desigual', in *Los judíos de España. Historia de una diáspora (1492–1992)* (Madrid: Trotta, 1993) 60–70.)

5 G. Henningsen, 'La elocuencia de los números', in Angél Alcalá y otros (*et al.*) *Inquisición española y mentalidad inquisicional* (Barcelona: Ariel, 1984, 207–225).

6 David Willemse, *Un 'portugués' entre los castellanos. El primer proceso inquisitorial contra Gonzalo Báez de Paiba 1654–1657,* 2 vols (Paris: Fundação Calouste Gulbenkian, 1974) Introduction, xxiv–xxv.

1   The Extent of *Convivencia*

1 See J. Caro Baroja, *Los judíos en la España moderna y contemporánea*, 3 vols (Madrid: Istmo, 1978) I, pp. 39–40.

2 See E. Ashtor, *Korot Ha-Yehudim bi-Sefarad ha-Muslemit* (Jerusalem 1960–1965), transl. *The Jews of Moslem Spain*, 3 vols (Philadelphia: Jewish Publication Society of America, 1992) I, 159ff. and II, 47ff.

3 See L. Suárez, *Judíos españoles en la Edad Media* (Madrid: Rialp, 1980), and the bibliography appended to it. The most valuable works on the history of the Jews in Spain are: Y. Baer, *Die Juden in Christlichen Spanien* (Berlin, 1929–1936), transl. *History of the Jews in Christian Spain*, 2 vols (Philadelphia, Jewish

Publication Society of America, 1978); Ashtor, *Korot Ha–Yehudim* . . . and translation; and A. Neuman, *The Jews in Spain: Their Social, Political and Cultural Life During the Middle Ages* (Philadelphia, Jewish Publication Society of America, 1944).

4 See Y. Assis, 'The Jews in the Crown of Aragon and its Dominions', in H. Beinart (ed.), *The Sephardi Legacy*, 2 vols (Jerusalem, 1992) I, 318–345.

5 See Baer, (English version) I, 150ff. For a detailed study of the disputations see H. Maccoby, *Judaism on Trial: Jewish–Christian Disputations in the Middle Ages* (London: Associated University Presses, 1982).

6 On the *Siete Partidas* and the Jews see Baer, (English version) I, 116. On Alfonso X and the Jews in general see A. Mackay, 'The Jews in Spain During the Middle Ages', in E. Kedourie (ed.), *Spain and the Jews* (London: Thames & Hudson, 1992) 31–51.

7 See the analysis of the religious and social causes of the 1391 attacks on the Spanish Jews in P. Wolff, 'The 1391 Pogrom in Spain; Social Crisis or Not?', *Past and Present* (1971) no. 50, 4–18. This article was followed by A. Mackay, 'Popular Movements and Pogroms in Fifteenth Century Castile', in *Past and Present* (1972) no. 55, 33–67, which demonstrates the close relationship between the food crisis and attacks against Jews and, in the fourteenth century, against converted Jews.

8 N. Roth, *Conversos, Inquisition and the Expulsion of the Jews from Spain* (Madison: University of Wisconsin Press, 1995) 34, thinks that the destruction of the Jewish communities has been exaggerated. Nevertheless, his views are not shared by the exhaustive sources quoted by J. Blázquez Miguel, *Inquisición y Criptojudaísmo* (Madrid: Kaydeda, 1988) 23–31. See also M.A. Motis Dolader, 'Población, urbanismo y estructura política de las aljamas de Aragón en el siglo XV', in *Hispania* (1996) no. 194, 885–944, who uses tax returns to demonstrate the catastrophic fall in the Jewish population after 1391.

9 See H. Beinart, 'The Conversos and their Fate', in Kedourie, *Spain and the Jews*, 92–122.

10 A. Domínguez Ortiz, 'Los conversos de origen judío después de la Expulsión', in *La clase social de los conversos en Castilla en la edad moderna* (University of Granada, 1991 edn) 181. See also the very interesting analysis of motives and behaviour in J. Edwards, 'The Conversos: A Theological Approach', in *Bulletin of Hispanic Studies* (1985) no. LXII, 39–49.

11 See Maccoby, *Judaism on Trial*, and Baer (English version), II, 173ff.

12 See Baer, (English version) II, 139–150.

13 Domínguez Ortiz, 'Los conversos . . . ', 12.

14 The full text can be found in N. López Martínez, *Los judaizantes castellanos y la Inquisición en tiempo de Isabel la Católica* (Burgos, 1954) 391–404. There is an English translation in D. Gitlitz, 'The Book Called Alborayque', in *Mediterranean Language Review*, (1990–1993) no. 67, 121–144.

15 For *limpieza de sangre* see A. Sicroff, *Les controverses des statuts de 'pureté de sang' en Espagne du XV au XVII siècles* (Paris: Didier, 1960). For a lucid account of the history of converts from Judaism between the events of Toledo in 1449 and the Expulsion of Jews in 1492, see J.M. Monsalvo Antón, *Teoría y evolución de un conflicto social: el antisemitismo en la Corona de Castilla en la Baja Edad Media* (Madrid: Siglo XXI, 1985) chs. XI, XII.

16   See A. Mackay, 'The Hispanic–Converso Predicament', *Transactions of the Royal Historical Society* (1985) no. 35, 159–179.

17   Baer, (English version) II, 307–308, quoting a contemporary chronicle.

18   J. Blázquez Miguel, *El Tribunal de la Inquisición en Murcia* (Murcia, 1986) 11. For an analysis of the perceived adaptation of the Papal Bull to the political needs of the Catholic Monarchs, see R. García Cárcel, *Orígenes de la Inquisición española: el Tribunal de Valencia 1478–1530* (Barcelona: Península, 1985) 49–53.

19   Besides previously cited works, further basic titles about the Inquisition include B. Bennassar, *Inquisición española: poder político y control social* (Paris, 1979: Barcelona: Crítica Grijalbo, 1981); J. Pérez Villanueva and B. Escandell Bonet (eds), *Historia de la Inquisición en España y América*, 2 vols (Madrid: B.A.C. 1984); J. Pérez Villanueva (ed.), *La Inquisición Española: Nueva visión, nuevos horizontes* (Madrid: Siglo XXI, 1980); M. Jiménez Monteserín, *Introducción a la Inquisición española: documentos básicos para el estudio del Santo Oficio* (Madrid: Editora Nacional, 1980); H.C. Lea, *A History of the Inquisition of Spain*, 4 vols. (New York: Macmillan, 1906–7); J.A. Llorente, *Historia crítica de la Inquisición española* (Paris, 1812: 4 vols; Madrid: Hiperión, 1980); J. P. Dedieu, *L'Administration de la Foi: L'Inquisition de Tolède (xvième–xviiième siècles)* (Madrid: Casa de Velázquez, 1989); S. Haliczer, *Inquisition and Society in the Kingdom of Valencia (1478–1834)* (Berkeley and Los Angeles: University of California Press, 1990). See also an annotated bibliography of recent bibliography on the Inquisition by Luis Javier Coronas Vida in A. Domínguez Ortiz, *La clase social de los conversos . . .* , xxxvii–xlii. For a complete bibliography on the Inquisition see E. van der Vekene, *Bibliographica Historiae Sanctae Inquisitionis*, 3 vols, 2nd edn (Vaduz: Topos Verlag, 1982–1992).

20   This question has led to a controversy between leading Jewish and other historians, including Benzion Netanyahu, Norman Roth, Haim Beinart, Yosef Haim Yerushalmi, Henry Kamen and others, about the reality of Crypto–Judaism in the Iberian peninsula before and after the Expulsion of 1492. See H. Beinart, 'The Records of the Inquisition: a Source of Jewish and Converso History', in *Proceedings of the Israel Academy of Sciences and Humanities*, II (Jerusalem, 1968), 211–227; B. Netanyahu, *The Marranos of Spain from the late XIV Century to the early XVI Century, according to the Contemporary Hebrew Sources* (New York: Academy for Jewish Research, 1966) and G. Cohen's critique in *Jewish Social Studies* (1967), XXIX, 178–184; B. Netanyahu, 'On the Historical Meaning of the Hebrew Sources', in *Hispania Judaica* (ed. Solà–Solé, J.M. Armistead, S. and Silverman, J.M. Barcelona: Puvill, 1980) 79–102; F. Márquez Villanueva, 'El problema de los conversos: cuatro puntos cardinales', in *Hispania Judaica* 51–75; N. Roth, 'Jewish Conversos in Medieval Spain; Some Misconceptions and New Information' in W. and C. Phillips (eds), *Marginated Groups in Spanish and Portuguese History* (Minneapolis: Society for Spanish and Portuguese Historical Studies, 1982), 23–53, and his book *Conversos, Inquisition and the Expulsion of the Jews from Spain*, cit.; E. Rivkin, 'The Utilization of Non-Jewish Sources for the Reconstruction of Jewish History', in *Jewish Quarterly Review* (October 1957), new Ser. no. XLVIII and the critique of this article by I. Révah, 'Les Marranes' in *Revue des Etudes Juives* (1959–1960), vol. CXVIII, 29–77; Y. H. Yerushalmi, *From Spanish Court to Italian Ghetto: Marranism and Judaism in the XVII Century* (New York: Columbia University Press,

1971); Henry Kamen, *The Spanish Inquisition* (London: Weidenfeld & Nicolson, 1965; Barcelona: Grijalbo, 1967); the same author's revised version *The Spanish Inquisition; a Historical Revision* (Weidenfeld, 1997); Netanyahu's most recent and massive work, reinforcing his opinion, is *The Origins of the Inquisition in Fifteenth Century Spain* (New York: Random House, 1995).

21 Netanyahu, *Origins of the Inquisition* . . . , 1084–1085.
22 H. Beinart, *Records of the Trials of the Inquisition in Ciudad Real*, 4 vols (Jerusalem: Israel Academy of Sciences and Humanities, 1974–1981); *Conversos on Trial* (translation of *Anussim be-din ha-Inqvizitsia* (Jerusalem: Magnes Press, Hebrew University, 1981); and *Trujillo: a Jewish Community in Extremadura on the Eve of the Expulsion from Spain* (Jerusalem: Magnes Press, Hebrew University, 1980).
23 A. Domínguez Ortiz, *Los judeoconversos en la España moderna* (Madrid: Mapfre, 1992) . . . , 43.
24 See the lengthy analysis by S. Assaf, 'Anussei Sefarad u-Portugal be-Sifrut ha-Teshuvot' ['The forced converts of Spain and Portugal in the Responsa literature'], in *Be-Oholei Ya'akov* (Jerusalem: Mossad Rav Kook, 1943) 145–180. (My thanks to Rabbis Mark Solomon and Louis Jacobs for their help with this source.) See also H.J. Zimmels, *Die Marranen in der Rabbinischen Literatur* (Berlin, 1932). For a more recent analysis see M. Orfali, *Los conversos españoles en la literatura rabínica: problemas jurídicos y opiniones legales durante los siglos XII–XVII* (Salamanca: Universidad Pontificia, 1982).
25 Rabbi Shimon Duran of Algiers, of a famous dynasty of rabbis who had to deal with this question, wrote between 1491 and 1495: 'There is a presumption that none of the *Anussim* marry Gentile women, and it is well-known to us that such is the case.' Quoted Assaf, 158.
26 Assaf, 'Anussei . . . ', 177.
27 See *Bevis Marks Records*, Part IV, 'The, Circumcision register of Isaac and Abraham Paiba (1715–1775)', transcribed, translated and edited by R. D. Barnett (London: Spanish and Portuguese Jews' Congregation and Jewish Historical Society of England, 1991), 5.
28 A. Mackay, 'Popular Movements and Pogroms . . . '.
29 *Memorias de los Reyes Católicos* (Madrid, 1962), ch. CXII, 256.
30 M. Ladero Quesada, 'Los judíos conversos en la Castilla del siglo XV', *Historia 16* (June 1992) no. 194, 39–52.
31 See also A.J. Saraiva, *Inquisição e Cristãos Novos* (Lisbon: Estampa, 1984).
32 The accounts of the *autos de fe* show that Judaizers frequently included poor, illiterate and humble people. See H. Méchoulan and G. Nahon, *Menasseh Ben Israel: The Hope of Israel* (Oxford: Oxford University Press, 1987) 7, note 13, which point out the deficits in the finances of the Inquisition caused by the poverty of so many Judaizers.

2   The Inquisition Begins Work

1 Cited by A. Domínguez Ortiz, *Los Judeoconversos en España y América* (Madrid: Istmo, 1988) 33.
2 Domínguez Ortiz calculates this sum as being equivalent to 1,240,000 million pesetas of 1992, or over £6.2 million (*Los judeoconversos en la España moderna*, 33).

3   H. Kamen, 'Confiscations in the economy of the Spanish Inquisition', in *Economic History Review*, 2nd ser. (1965) no. XVIII, 512–525.

4   Kamen, 'Confiscations . . . '.

5   On the finances of the Inquisition see the detailed study by J. Martínez Millán, *La hacienda de la Inquisición 1478–1700* (Madrid: CSIC, 1984).

6   See the introduction by H. Beinart to his *Records of the Trials . . .* , vol. 1, xiii–xiv.

7   Ibid., preface, vol. 1, xiii.

8   Blázquez Miguel, *Inquisición y Criptojudaísmo*, 105.

9   J.P. Dedieu, *L'Administration de la foi: l'Inquisition de Tolède (XVIe–XVIIIe siècles)* (Madrid: Casa de Velázquez, 1989) 31; see also his long article 'Les Causes de foi de l'Inquisition de Tolède (1483–1820); essai statistique', in *Mélanges de la Casa de Velázquez*, Madrid (1978) XIV, 144–171.

10 A. Domínguez Ortiz, *Los judeoconversos en España y América*, 34. Since many of the early Inquisition documents are missing, one cannot be sure if the various statements include burnings of effigies of fugitives or the dead.

11 S. Haliczer, *Inquisition and Society in the Kingdom of Valencia 1478–1834* (Berkeley and Los Angeles: University of California Press, 1990) 223.

12 Ladero Quesada, 'Los judíos conversos . . . '. This calculates the number of converts condemned, punished and rehabilitated between 1481 and 1512. The same figure of 50,000 was quoted in the *Memorial de Defensa del Estatuto de Limpieza de Sangre de la Catedral de Toledo* of 1547, cited by Caro Baroja, *Los judíos . . .* , I, 291, and Blázquez Miguel, *Inquisición y Criptojudaísmo*, 149, who thinks that the figure given by the authorities of the cathedral of Toledo must have included those converts who were reconciled during the periods of grace conceded for voluntary confession. The figure of 50,000 refers vaguely to 'the last fifty years', counting back presumably from 1547, so one cannot tell if the dating includes the earliest years of the Toledo Inquisition which witnessed violent attacks on the convert communities.

13 Blázquez Miguel, *Inquisición y Criptojudaísmo*, 281–315.

14 Domínguez Ortiz, *Los conversos . . .* , 23.

15 Cited from Diego de Saavedra Fajardo's *Idea de un príncipe cristiano representada en cien empresas* by H. Méchoulan, *Hispanidad y Judaísmo* (Salamanca: Universidad, 1987) 21.

16 Abarbanel gives the figure of 300,000 in the introduction to his commentary to the biblical book of *Kings*, transcribed by Solomon Ibn Verga in his *Sefer Shevet Yehudah* (Book of the Rod of Judah) (Adrianopolis, 1550). See the edition with introduction, translation and notes by M. José Cano (Barcelona: Riopiedras, 1991) 217. See also the various figures discussed by I. Loeb in 'Le nombre des Juifs de Castille et d' Espagne au Moyen Age', in *Revue des Études Juives* (1887) no. XIV, 161–183, who cannot reach a more precise figure than 60,000 to 100,000. However, his method is based on assuming that the existing populations of Jews of Hispanic descent in the late nineteenth century could be used to calculate how many had left Spain, discounting those who went to Navarre or Portugal or were lost. The method seems fraught with error.

17 *Los Judíos . . .* , I, 198–205.

18 90,000 according to Bernáldez (quoted by Caro Baroja, *Los judíos . . .*)

19 Motis Dolader, 'Población . . . '.

20 H. Kamen, 'The Mediterranean and the Expulsion of Spanish Jews in 1492', *Past and Present* (May 1988) no. 119, 30–55.
21 D. de Gois, *Crónica do Felicissimo rei D. Manoel*, (Coimbra, 1949–1955) I, 23 (quoted by Caro Baroja, *Los Judíos . . .*, I, 207), speaks of 20,000 Jewish households who went to Portugal at the time of the Expulsion, households 'in some of which there were ten or twelve people and others with more.'
22 H.P. Salomon, *Portrait of a New Christian: Fernão Alvares Melo (1569–1632)* (Paris: Fundação Calouste Gulbenkian and Centro Cultural Português, 1982), 14.
23 Caro Baroja, *Los judíos . . .*, I, 198.
24 This section is based mainly on the massive study by J. Amador de los Ríos, *Historia social, política y religiosa de los judíos de España y Portugal* (first published 1875–1876; Madrid: Aguilar, 1973) ch. IX.
25 M. Mitchell Serels, 'Two thousand missing Portuguese–Jewish children', in *Studies on the History of the Portuguese Jews* (Katz, I. and Serels, M., eds.) (New York: American Society of Sephardic Studies, 2000) pp. 193–201.
26 Amador de los Ríos, *Historia social . . .*, 785.
27 Caro Baroja, *Los judíos . . .*, I, 214–215, 223–225.
28 H. Livermore, *A History of Portugal* (Cambridge University Press, 1947) 242–245ff.
29 Lea, *A History . . .*, III, 259.
30 See the comments of J. Lúcio d' Azevedo, *Historia dos Christãos Novos portugueses* (Lisbon: Texeira, 1921), appx 25 and p. 338.
31 C. Amiel, 'Les Archives de l' Inquisition portugaise: regards et reflexions', in *Arquivos do Centro Cultural Português* (Paris: Fundação Calouste Gulbenkian, 1979) no. XIV, 421–443.
32 The Ferrara Bible was the first *printed* translation.
33 The Christian names of the signatories were Jerónimo de Vargas and Duarte Pinel.This translation, by Cecil Roth, understands the reference to birthplace and language as referring to Gracia Nasí rather than to the signatories. C. Roth, *Doña Gracia of the House of Nasi* (Philadelphia: Jewish Publication Society of America, 1948) 74 (1977 edition). I thank Professor H.P. Salamon for his help in clarifying these details.
34 See C. Roth, 'The Role of Spanish in the Marrano Diaspora', in *Studies in Books and Booklore: Essays in Jewish Bibliography and Allied Subjects* (Farnborough: Gregg, 1972) 111–120.
35 There is a novel about the family by Cathérine Clément, *La Senhora* (Paris: Calmann-Lévy, 1992).

3   Portuguese New Christians Move into Spain

1 Quoted in J. Mendes dos Remedios, *Os judeus em Portugal*, 2 vols (Coimbra: F. França Amado y Coimbra Editora, 1895 and 1928) II, 71ff.
2 Epistle to the Hebrews 12: 20 (New English Bible), referring to Exodus 19: 13.
3 Mendes dos Remedios, *Os judeus . . .*, II, 83–84.
4 A. Domínguez Ortiz, *Autos de la Inquisición de Sevilla (siglo XVII)* (Seville: Ayuntamiento, 1994) 78.
5 Y. Kaplan, *Judíos nuevos en Amsterdam: Estudio sobre la historia social e intelectual del judaísmo sefardí en el siglo XVII* (Barcelona: Gedisa, 1996) 14.

6   Lúcio D'Azevedo, *Historia* . . . , 158.

7   Domínguez Ortiz, *Los conversos* . . . , 87.

8   See document in Lea, *A History* . . . , III, 558–561.

9   See the edition with commentary by I. Révah of the *Alegación en que se funda la justicia y merced que algunos particulares del Reyno de Portugal, que estan dentro y fuera de los confines de España, piden y suplican a la Católica y Real Magestad del Rey don Felipe Tercero nuestro señor, se les haga y conceda, Dirigida al Ilustrissimo señor don fray Luys de Aliaga, Inquisidor General en los Reynos y señorios e su Magestad, su Confessor, y de su Consejo de estado. Por el Licenciado Martín de Cellorigo, juez de bienes confiscados de la Inquisición de Toledo (1619)*, in *Revue des Études Juives*, 4th ser. (July–December, 1963) II, no. CXXII, fascs 3, 4.

10 Quoted in Mendes dos Remedios, *Os Judeus* . . . , II, 107.

11 British Library, Egerton MS 344, folios 40ff. See Enrique Llamas, *Documentación Inquisitorial: manuscritos españoles del siglo XVI existentes en el Museo Británico* (Madrid: Fundación Universitaria Española, 1975).

12 A. Teixeira, *António Homem e a Inquisição* (Coimbra: Imprensa da Universidade, 1895–1902), 193.

13 British Library Egerton MS. 344, fos. 144–148 dated 27 June 1619.

14 For the history of inquisitional jurisdiction in Madrid, see J. Blázquez Miguel, *Madrid, Judíos, Herejes y Brujas: el Tribunal de Corte (1650–1820)* (Toledo: Arcano, 1990) 14–18.

15 Lúcio d'Azevedo, *Historia* . . . , 182.

16 See the documents preserved in the Egerton collection in the British Library, and those published by Elkan Adler in the *Revue des Études Juives*, XLVIII (1904) 1–28; XLIX (1904) 51–73; L (1905), 53–75; LI (1906), 251–264.

17 British Library, Egerton MS. 344, fos. 77ff.

18 Ibid., fo. 79.

19 Adler, document no.7.

20 J.H. Elliott, *The Count-Duke of Olivares: The Statesman in an Age of Decline* (New Haven–London: Yale University Press, 1986) 137.

21 J. Caro Baroja, *La sociedad criptojudía en la Corte de Felipe IV* (Madrid: Maestre, 1963) 33–35.

22 AHN, Inq., L. 5331/52.

23 Elliott *Olivares*, 68ff., gives budget figures, which reached 3.5 million ducats annually, added to a million ducats in naval estimates.

24 British Library, Egerton MS. 344, folios 1ff. 17–24.

25 A. Domínguez Ortiz, *Política y Hacienda de Felipe IV* (Madrid: Editorial de Derecho Financiero, 1960) 128–129.

26 See Elliott, *Olivares*, index under 'currency' and in particular 267–270.

27 British Library, Egerton MS. 344, fo. 7.

28 British Library, Egerton MS. 344, fos. 8–10.

29 British Library, Egerton MS. 344, fos. 34ff.

30 See M. Ebben, 'La corona española, el Santo Oficio y los banqueros portugueses', in *Hispania* (May–August 1993) no. LIII/2, 541–556.

31 Elliott, *Olivares*, 26.

32 Elliott, *Olivares*, 79; see also J. Israel, 'Manuel López Pereira of Amsterdam, Antwerp and Madrid: Jew, New Christian and Adviser to the Conde-Duque de Olivares', *Studia Rosenthaliana* (1985) no. XIX, 109–164.

4 Commerical Activities of the New Christians

1 See J.H. Elliott, *Imperial Spain 1469–1716* (first published 1963) (Harmondsworth: Penguin, 1973) ch. VIII.

2 See J. Israel, *European Jewry in the Age of Mercantilism 1550–1750* (Oxford: Clarendon Press, 1985) introduction. See also H.H. Ben-Sasson (ed.), *A History of the Jewish People* (Cambridge, Mass.: Harvard University Press, 1976) Ch. XXX, 'Jewish Settlement and Economic Activity in the Sixteenth and Seventeenth Centuries'.

3 Israel, *European Jewry . . .* , 43. The principal work on Hamburg Spanish and Portuguese Jews is H. Kellenbenz, *Sephardim an der unteren Elbe* (Wiesbaden, 1958). See also J. Edwards, *The Jews in Christian Europe 1400–1700* (London: Routledge, 1988) 111.

4 L. Wolf, 'Jews in Tudor England', in Roth, C. (ed.), *Essays in Jewish History* (London: Jewish Historical Society of England, 1934) 73–90.

5 Quoted by Révah in his edition of the *Alegación* of González de Cellorigo.

6 Ibid., 320.

7 See J. Boyajian, *Portuguese Bankers at the Court of Spain 1626–1650* (New Brunswick: Rutgers University Press, 1983) 2–13.

8 C. Roth, *A History of the Marranos*, New York: Meridian Books; Philadelphia: Jewish Publication Society of America 1959, 1st published 1932, 233.

9 For an explanation of the technical machinery of the *asientos*, see A. Castillo Pintado and J.I. Gutiérrez Nieto, 'La Hacienda Real', in R. Menéndez Pidal (ed.) *Historia de España*, 1979, XXV 1982, 217–232.

10 Boyajian, *Portuguese Bankers . . .* , 3–6.

11 Elliott, *Olivares*, 143–145, 159.

12 Elliott, *Olivares*, 105.

13 Domínguez Ortiz, *Los Judeoconversos en la España moderna*, 81.

14 Elliott, *Olivares*, 225.

15 Domínguez Ortiz, *Política y Hacienda . . .* , 129–130; see also Boyajian, *Portuguese Bankers . . .* , 24.

16 Quoted by Ebben, 'La corona española . . .'.

17 Adler, docs X–XV.

18 Adler, doc. XVII of 27 September 1630.

19 Quoted in Domínguez Ortiz, *Los judeoconversos en España y América*, 67.

20 P. Huerga Criado, *En la raya de Portugal: solidaridad y tensiones en la comunidad judeoconversa* (Salamanca: Ediciones Universidad, 1993) 137.

21 Lúcio d'Azevedo, *Historia . . .* , 196–197.

22 Ibid., 199.

23 Huerga Criado, *En la raya . . .* , 138–139.

24 Domínguez Ortiz, *Política y Hacienda . . .* , 131.

25 Lúcio d'Azevedo, *Historia . . .* , appx 9.

26 See J. Caro Baroja, *La sociedad criptojudía en la Corte de Felipe IV* (Madrid: Maestre, 1963) 54.

27 See M. Escamilla-Colin, *Crimes et châtiments dans l'Espagne inquisitoriale*, 2 vols (Paris: Berg International, 1992) I, 286.

28 Boyajian, *Portuguese Bankers . . .* , 58–59.

29 Kamen, *Inquisición española*, 290.

30 Mendes dos Remedios, *Os judeus . . .* , II, 100.

31   See M. Alpert, 'Did Spanish Jews Desecrate Christian Sacred Images and Why? The Case of the *Cristo de la Paciencia* (1629–1632), the *Romance* of 1717 and the Events of November 1714 in the Calle del Lobo', in L. Twomey (ed.) *Faith and Fanaticism: Religious Fervour in Early Modern Spain* (Aldershot: Ashgate, 1997). see also Y.H. Yerushalmi, *From Spanish Court to Italian Ghetto: Isaac Cardoso, a Study in Seventeenth-Century Marranism and Jewish Apologetics* (New York: Columbia University Press, 1971). For a contemporary description of the *auto de fe*, see *Relación del auto de fe del 4 de julio de 1632 celebrado en Madrid*, etc., British Library 593 h 17 (110). See also Caro Baroja, *Los judíos* . . . , II, 445–458.

32   See A. Domínguez Ortiz, 'El proceso inquisitorial de Juan Núñez Saravia, banquero de Felipe IV', *Hispania* (1955) XV, no. 51, 559–581; Caro Baroja, *Los judíos* . . . , II, 68–75.

33   See the wording of her appeal in Caro Baroja, *Los judíos* . . . , II, 74.

34   See J. Caro Baroja, 'El proceso de Bartolomé Febos or Febo', in *Homenaje a don Ramón Carande*, 2 vols (Madrid: Sociedad de Estudios y Publicaciones, 1963) 59–92.

5   Lives of Secret Jews in and outside Spain: Splits in the Rouen Community

1   On the beginning of the Marrano group in Rouen see I.S. Révah, 'Le Premier Etablissment des Marranes portugais à Rouen 1603–1607', *Revue de Philologie et d'Histoire Orientales et Slaves* (1953) XIII, 539–552.

2   See C. Roth, 'Les Marranes à Rouen: un chapitre ignoré de l'histoire des Juifs de France', *Revue des Études Juives* (1929), LXVIII, 113–155.

3   See I.S. Révah, 'Autobiographie d'un Marrane: édition partielle d'un manuscrit de João (Moseh) Pinto Delgado', *Revue d' Études Juives* (1961) II (CXIX), 41–130.

4   British Library, Egerton MS. 343, fos. 249–267.

5   Translation of *'Parece, que en la persecución contra la Iglesia pone el aprovechamiento mayor y perfección del judaísmo.'*

6   Morteira's document exists in manuscript form in the Etz Haim library of the Portuguese Jewish community of Amsterdam.

7   *Antídotos cristianos contra el veneno de las respuestas Judaicas que dieron a mis preguntas por escrito los Judíos de Amsterdam* [sic] *año 1631 por septiembre, estando yo en Ruán tratando de su conversión.*

8   Révah, 'Autobiographie . . . ', 67.

9   British Library, Egerton MS. 343, fos. 277 r. to 299 v.

10   Y. Kaplan, 'Wayward New Christians and Stubborn New Jews. The Shaping of Jewish Identity', *Jewish History* (1994) VIII, nos. 1–2, 27–41.

11   Révah, 'Autobiographie . . . '.

12   See the doctoral theses of my teacher, A.D. Fishlock, 'A Critical Study of the Poems of João Pinto Delgado, Published at Rouen in 1627' (University of London, 1952), and T. Oelman, 'Two Poems of Antonio Enríquez Gómez . . . ' (University of London, 1976).

13   *Romance al Divino Mártir, Judá Creyente, martirizado en Valladolid por la Inquisición.*

14 See T. Oelman, *Marrano Poets of the Seventeenth Century: An Anthology of the Poetry of João Pinto Delgado, Antonio Enríquez Gómez and Miguel de Barrios* (London: Associated Universities Presses, 1982) 176–218. On Lope de Vera, see R. Barnett, *Jewish Quarterly Review* (1924–1925) no. 15, 229–239.

15 Oelman's translation.

16 On these two Marranos see C. Roth, *A History of the Marranos*, 258–259, and L. Wolf, 'Cromwell's Jewish Intelligencers', in his *Essays on Jewish History*, 93–114.

17 AHN, Inq., L. 177, C. 11. Rodríguez Cardoso was burnt in effigy.

18 English translation from J.H. Hertz, *The Authorised Daily Prayer Book with Commentary* (London, 1942) 19.

19 Deuteronomy 6: 'Hear, O Israel, the Lord is our God, the Lord is one.' As the court secretary noted, the three parts of the verse indicate the Trinity, though the Jews did not believe this. This account is taken from J. Caro Baroja, *Los judíos* . . . iii, 377–9. Other details have been taken from AHN, Inq., L. 177, C. 11.

20 See H. Beinart, 'Moshe and Ya'akov Gomes, Natives of Peyrehorade (near Bordeaux), Before the Inquisition Court', *Jewish History* (1992) VI, 1–2 (Frank Talmage Memorial Volume), 13–24 (Hebrew Section).

21 AHN, Inq. L. 174. C. 7.

22 AHN, Inq., L. 134, C. 18.

23 He was denounced in Lisbon by Héctor Mendes Bravo, who had been brought up as a Jew in Venice and Amsterdam but had become convinced of the truth of Christianity. Mendes Bravo knew that San Antonio had broken with the Jewish community in Amsterdam and had been baptised in Antwerp. See C. Roth, 'The Strange Case of Héctor Mendes Bravo', *Hebrew Union College Annual* (1944) XVIII, 221–245.

24 On Mondays and Thursdays the morning prayers are supplemented by a reading of part of the biblical text which is to be read the next Sabbath. Evidently the Marranos recognized these days as more important than the other weekdays.

25 On this trial, see H. Beinart, 'Travels of Jews from Morocco to Spain in the XVIIth Century' (in Hebrew), in *Salo W. Baron Memorial Volume* (Jerusalem: American Academy for Jewish Research, 1974) III, 15–39.

26 J. Barrionuevo de Peralta, *Avisos de don Jerónimo Barrionuevo de Peralta*, 4 vols (Madrid: Colección de Escritores, 1892) II, 383.

27 See illustration no. 18 in Elliott, *Olivares* . . . The frontispiece of the edition shows the Count-Duke slaying a dragon.

28 Haliczer, *Inquisition and Society* . . . , 242–243.

29 Y.H. Yerushalmi, 'Professing Jews in Post-Expulsion Spain and Portugal', in *Salo W. Baron Jubilee Volume*, II, 1023–1028.

6 The Decline of Spain and the New Christians

1 Elliott, *Olivares*, 548.

2 Boyajian, *Portuguese Bankers* . . . , 138–139.

3 See the interesting analysis by A. Lazo, 'Un antisemitismo sin judíos', *La Aventura de la Historia* (March 1999) no. 5, 16–20.

4   Hostility against New Christians because of the war against the Dutch is discussed in D.M. Swetschinski, 'Kinship and Commerce: the Foundations of Portuguese Jewish Life in Seventeenth Century Holland', *Studia Rosenthaliana* (1981) XV, 52–74. It was true also that Amsterdam was considered by the Marranos to be their champion against the Spanish monarch, seen as the Egyptian Pharaoh of modern times. See J. Contreras, 'La versión judía: leyendo negra y leyenda rosa', *Historia 16* (May 1992) no. 193, 65–78.
5   British Library, Egerton MS. 343, fo. 165 v. (My translation.)
6   Ibid., fo. 170.
7   For an analysis of the relative values of Catholicism, Protestantism and Judaism as they affected Christian attitudes towards Jews, see H. Maccoby, *A Pariah People: the Anthropology of Antisemitism* (London: Constable, 1996), 33–36.
8   AHN, *Sección de Consejos*, Legajo 7256, quoted in Domínguez Ortiz, *Política y Hacienda . . .* , 133.
9   Domínguez Ortiz, *Los judeoconversos en la España moderna*, 91.
10   J. Caro Baroja, *Inquisición, criptojudaísmo y brujería* (Barcelona: Ariel, 1970) 80–82.
11   Boyajian, *Portuguese Bankers . . .* , 133ff.
12   Barrionuevo, *Avisos . . .* , I, 23.
13   Ibid., III, 80.
14   Ibid, II, 443 and 468 (19 July 1656). In his utopian work *Oceania*, of 1656, James Harrington argued that Ireland should be opened to the Jews who would make it prosper (D. Katz, *The Jews in the History of England 1485–1850* (Oxford: University Press, 1994) 138. Is this the origin of the rumour?
15   Barrionuevo, *Avisos . . .* , IV, 318–319.
16   Barrionuevo, *Avisos . . .* , IV, 475 and 498.
17   J.P. Dedieu, 'The Archives of the Holy Office of Toledo as a Source for Anthropology', in G. Henningsen and J. Tedeschi, *The Inquisition in Early Modern Europe: Studies in Sources and Methods* (De Kalb: Northern Illinois University Press, 1984) 181.
18   A. Domínguez Ortiz, *Autos de la Inquisición de Sevilla (Siglo XVII)* (Seville: Ayuntamiento, 2nd edn, 1994), 91–108: also Mario Méndez Bejarano, *Historia de la judería de Sevilla* (Madrid, 1922; new edn, Seville: Castillejo, 1993) 138–139.
19   Willemse, *Un 'Portugués . . .'* , preface, xviii; N. Griffiths, 'Popular religious scepticism in post-Tridentine Cuenca', in Twomey, *Faith and Fanaticism . . .* , 95–126.
20   Escamilla-Colin, *Crimes et châtiments . . .* , I, 259.
21   I.S. Révah, 'Le procès inquisitoriale contre Rodrigo Méndez Silva, historiographe du roi Philippe IV', *Bulletin Hispanique* (1965) 67, 225–252.
22   Caro Baroja, *Los judíos . . .* , publishes one of the manuscripts of the *Tizón* in vol. III, appx 8.
23   Yerushalmi, *From Spanish Court . . .* , 180–181.
24   Blázquez Miguel, *Inquisición y Criptojudaísmo*, 219.
25   Caro Baroja, *Los judíos . . .* , II, 107–113.
26   Quoted in Pérez Villanueva and Escandell Bonet, *Historia de la Inquisición . . .* , I, 1045–1046.
27   Yerushalmi, *From Spanish Court . . .* , 206.

28 A. de Prado Moura, *Las hogueras de la intolerancia: la actividad represora del Tribunal Inquisitorial de Valladolid (1700–1834)* (Valladolid: Junta de Castilla y León, 1996) 117.

29 *Relación del auto de fe celebrado en Valladolid el 18 de mayo de 1727* (Biblioteca Nacional, Madrid, R. 2725).

30 AHN, Inq. L. 1808. C. 12. Relaciones de causas de Zaragoza, fos. 47ff.

31 *Relación del auto celebrado en Cuenca el 22 de noviembre de 1722* (British Library 4071 i 3).

32 See R. de Lera García, 'La última gran persecución inquisitorial contra el criptojudaísmo: el tribunal de Cuenca 1718–1725', *Sefarad* (1987) XLVII, fasc. 1, 87–113.

33 *'Así por falta de dinero como por el embarazo de cuatro hijos que tenía'*. AHN, Inq., L. 157, C. 11. Trial of Manuela Hurtado de Mendoza Pimentel, evidence of Agustina Pimentel.

34 R. Barnett, 'Diplomatic Aspects of the Sephardic Influx from Portugal in the Early 18th Century', *Transactions of the Jewish Historical Society of England* (1977) XXV, 210–221.

35 All information on Gonzalo Báez de Paiba comes from the Introduction to Willemse, *Un 'portugués'* . . . , I, Introduction and Transcription; II, Facsimile (Paris: Fundação Calouste Gulbenkian, 1974).

36 Escamilla-Colin, *Crimes et châtiments* . . . , I, 372.

37 Willemse, I, *Un 'Portugués'* . . . , cxxi.

38 *Relación del auto celebrado en Valladolid el 13 de junio de 1745* (British Library 4071 i 3). See also de Prado Moura, *Las hogueras* . . . , 108, who notes that Luis de la Vega, whom the *Relación* lists as having been burnt at the stake, was sentenced instead to flogging and galleys, and the galley sentence was lifted. Could the others sentenced to the galleys also have been excused this punishment, a death sentence at their ages?

39 These are the *Relaciones de auto de fe* published by the Madrid printer, publisher and bookseller Serrete, sets of which are to be found in the British Library and the Biblioteca Nacional, Madrid.

40 *Relación del auto celebrado en Granada el 30 de noviembre de 1721* (British Library 4071 bb 3).

41 *Relación del auto de fe celebrado en Sevilla el 14 de diciembre de 1721* (British Library 4071 i 4.)

7 Under the Rod of the Holy Office

1 On this family and other similar ones see Caro Baroja, *Los judíos* . . . , II, 115ff.

2 AHN, Inq., L. 132, C. 16; trial of Mencia de Almeida.

3 AHN, Inq., L. 160, C. 11; trial of Diego López de Castro.

4 Beinart, *Conversos on Trial* . . . , 282.

5 Quoted by Caro Baroja, *Los judíos* . . . , III, 121, n. 55.

6 AHN, Inq., L. 148, C. 5

7 The trial details are in AHN, Inq., L. 132, C. 15

8 The Cuenca trial documents often include these inventories of clothes and possessions, and offer an interesting picture of what a person of given

standing might own. Gabriel de Córdoba, for example, who was in charge of collecting various rents, was arrested on 25 February, 1714. The officers of the court removed three shirts, two pairs of underpants, two mattresses, a bedspread, two pillows, two woollen pillowcases, three coarse linen sheets, four pairs of socks and a pair of black stockings, a pair of serge stockings, a handkerchief, two table napkins and two combs, a sleeveless doublet, four pairs of shoes and a hand towel. On that winter day in a city high up in the mountains, Gabriel wore a cape with a silk cord, a hat of fine cloth, a jacket, also of good quality, breeches, a baize waistcoat and shoes with silver buckles (ADC, Inq., 568/7033, fos. 34–35).

Ventura Luis entered gaol on 1 June 1716. With her she took a woollen apron, 2 wool skirts, another of white baize, an embroidered linen petticoat, linen chemises with lace at the neck and on the sleeves, a white cotton bodice, a black wool coat with a false belt, a white baize mantilla with a black ribbon on the edge, an image of Our Lady in gilded silver, a silver toothpick, a necklace of small seed pearls and jet with a gilded silver cross, a pair of Cordovan goatskin shoes with tin buckles, red serge stockings, blue garters, a taffeta hair snood, seed pearl earrings, blue glass bracelets and a diamond to test false stones. In her skirt pockets she carried a jet rosary, a tobacco box of gilded silver and an ivory toothpick case. From her house the officers took a wooden bed, two mattresses, three sheets, a blanket, a white coverlet, two pillows, two napkins, two hand towels, a chemise and petticoat, waistcoats, a serge skirt, a frying pan, a lamp, a pine stool, a straw-bottomed chair, a picture of Jesus, four plates, two cups, a bowl and a saucer.

9 The Inquisition building in Cuenca still exists, though much altered throughout the centuries. See Solías. S., Huétamo, J.M. and Coll, J., *El edificio de la Inquisición de Cuenca: evolución de un programa arquitectónico 1573–1975* (Cuenca: Diputación Provincial, 1986) 99ff.

10 Nicolás Eymerich (inquisitor-general of Aragón), *Manual de Inquisidores para uso de las Inquisiciones de España y de Portugal* (Montpellier, 1821. First published Avignon, 1376.)

11 Willemse, *Un 'portugués . . .* , introduction, I, xxix.

12 Ibid., lxxvii.

13 Escamilla-Colin, *Crimes et châtiments . . .* , I, 593.

14 Ibid., 598–599.

15 AHN, Inq. L. 174, C. 8

16 The last few words on this sheet (fo. 140) cannot be read but the intention is clear.

8 The Inquisition and the Crisis of the Second Half of the Seventeenth Century

1 See John Lynch, *Spain under the Habsburgs*, vol. 2, 'Spain and America 1598–1700' (Oxford: Blackwell, 1969) and Henry Kamen's revisionist view, *Spain in the Latter Seventeenth Century 1665–1700* (London: Longman, 1980).

2 Blázquez Miguel, *Inquisición y Criptojudaísmo*, 285–315.

3 Dedieu, 'Les causes de foi . . . '.

4   J. Blázquez Miguel, *Madrid: judíos, herejes y brujas* (Toledo: Arcano, 1990) 77.

5   See the study by María Isabel Pérez de Colosia Rodríguez, *Auto Inquisitorial de 1672: el criptojudaísmo en Málaga* (Málaga: Diputación Provincial, 1984).

6   Francisco Garau, SJ, *La Fee Triunfante en Quatro Autos* (Palma, 1691).

7   On the repression of secret Judaism on Majorca and the Chueta question, see A. Selke, *The Conversos of Majorca: Life and Death in a Crypto–Jewish Community in XVII Century Spain* (Jerusalem: Magnes Press, Hebrew University, 1986).

8   There was a written account by José del Olmo, the *Relación Histórica del auto general de fe que se celebró en Madrid en el año 1680 con asistencia del Rey don Carlos II* (Madrid, 1680). On this auto see J.M. Vegazo Palacios, *El auto general de fe de 1680* (Málaga: Algazara, 1995).

9   Escamilla-Colin, *Crimes et Châtiments . . .* , I, 93.

10 R. Gracia Boix, *Autos de fe y causas de la Inquisición de Córdoba* (Córdoba: Diputación Provincial, 1983) 579.

11 Diogo da Anunciação Justiniano Alvares, *Sermam do auto da fe* etc. (Lisbon, 1705); [David Nieto] *Respuesta al Sermón* etc. (Villafranca [London ?], no date, 1710 ?); see also E. Glaser, 'Invitation to Intolerance; a Study of the Portuguese Sermons Preached at Autos da Fe', *Hebrew Union College Annual* (1956) no. 27, 327–385, and J. Mendes dos Remedios, 'Sermões en Autos da fe', *Biblos* (1927) III, 6–17.

12 Escamilla-Colin, *Crimes et châtiments . . .* , I, 75. On 15 July 1680 the Toledo court told the *Suprema* that many of the penitents in the *auto* of 30 June did not clearly hear the penances and punishments imposed on them.

13 Isaac Cardoso, *Las Excelencias de los Hebreos*, (Amsterdam, 1679) 323, cit.; Yerushalmi, *From Spanish Court . . .* , 395–396; S.B. Liebman, *Réquiem por los olvidados: los judíos españoles en América 1493–1825* (Madrid: Altalena, 1984) 60–61 (transl. from *New World Jewry 1493–1825: Requiem for the Forgotten* (New York: Ktav, 1982)). Maldonado da Silva is the hero of Marcos Aguinis's novel, *La gesta del marrano* (Buenos Aires: Planeta Argentina, 1991).

14 H. Thomas, *The Slave Trade: the History of the Atlantic Slave Trade 1440–1870* (London: Macmillan, 1998; paperback) 179–180.

15 Liebman, 60.

16 For these examples of heroic refusal to abandon Judaism, see Fernando de Montesinos, *Auto de fe celebrado en Lima a 23 de enero de 1639* preface and p. 21 (Madrid: 1640).

17 See G. Matute y Luquín, *Colección de los autos generales y particulares de fe, celebrados en el tribunal de la Inquisición de Córdoba* (Córdoba, 1825); British Library, Egerton MS. 2058; see also Cecil Roth, 'Abraham Núñez Bernal et autres martyrs contemporains de l'Inquisition', *Revue des Études Juives* (1936) vol. C, 38–51.

18 *'Judío tan pertinaz que, asistido toda la noche en la Inquisición y todo el dia en el cadalso de religiosos graves y santos, cuya predicación derritiera bronces y ablandara escollos . . . cansados de su protervia, se retiraban confusos.'* Quoted in Domínguez Ortiz, *Los judeoconversos en la España Moderna*, 97.

19 Gracia Boix, *Autos de fe . . .* , 593.

20 Roth, 'Abraham Núñez Bernal . . .'.

21 *Relación del auto celebrado en Murcia del 30 de noviembre de 1724* (British Library 4071 i 3).

22   Escamilla-Colin, *Crimes et châtiments . . .* , II, 689 and 745, suggests that an illness may have played an important part in Diego's outburst and change of attitude.

23   See M.V. González de Caldas, 'Nuevas Imágenes del Santo Oficio de Sevilla: el Auto de fe', in Angél Alcalá y otros (*et al*) *Inquisición española . . .* , 237–265. There is an interesting analysis of the case in M. Escamilla-Colin, 'Heroïsme, désespoir ou folie? Le cas de Diego López Duro', in Busse, W. and Varol-Borgnes, M.C. (eds), *Hommage à Haïm Vidal Sephiha* (Berne: Lang, 1996) 425–433.

24   AHN, Inq., L. 157, C. 11. Trial of Manuela Hurtado de Mendoza y Pimentel. Information about one prisoner often came up in testimony reported in the trial of another.

25   Escamilla-Colin, *Crimes et châtiments*, I, 746.

26   AHN, Inq. Libro 668; Blázquez Miguel, *Madrid, judíos . . .* , 78; Escamilla-Colin, *Crimes et châtiments*, I, 79–80.

27   See J.J. Le Blanc, 'Nouveaux Chrétiens accusés de judaïsme par le Saint Office de Séville, au XVIIIe siècle', *Revue d' Études Juives* (1980) CXXXI (1–3), 205–206.

28   De Lera García, 'La última gran persecución . . .', 87–137.

29   AHN, Inq. Legajo 3155.

30   Ibid.

31   Ibid.

32   Kamen, 'Confiscations . . .'. A regulation of 1654 allowed the Holy Office to take only the personal property of the guilty. The firms often survived in other hands.

33   R. de Lantéry, *Memorias de R . . . de L . . . , mercader de Indias en Cádiz 1673–1700* (Cádiz: Alvaro Picardo, 1949) 19.

34   Ibid., 184. '*Quizás se alegrara de que le tratasen de lo que era dentro de su corazón porque los que son tocados de eso hacen gala de que los llamen judíos*'.

35   See J. Israel, 'Duarte Nunes da Costa (Jacob Curiel) of Hamburg. Sephardi Nobleman and Communal Leader (1585–1664)', *Studia Rosenthaliana* (1987) XXI, 14–34; also E. Samuel, 'The Curiel Family in 16th Century Portugal', in *Transactions of the Jewish Historical Society of England* (1989–1990) XXXI, 111–136.

36   See C. Rubens, 'Joseph Cortissos and the War of Spanish Succession', in *Transactions of the Jewish Historical Society of England* (1970–1973) XXIV, 114–133, based on Cortissos's papers deposited in the University of Southampton. See also D.S. Katz, *The Jews in the History of England . . .* , 157ff.

37   On Belmonte see Caro Baroja, *Los judíos . . .* , II, 165. On the subject of Jewish diplomatic agents in general see Israel, *European Jewry . . .* , 136–137.

38   There are original documents about this company in the British Library (Add. MS. 20951).

39   Mendes dos Remedios, II, 362. On the Companhia do Brasil see C.R. Boxer, 'Padre Antonio Vieira, SJ, and the Institution of the Brazil Company in 1649', *Hispanic American Historical Review* (1949) XXIX, 474–497.

40   An interesting description of the effect of the Inquisition on the Portuguese economy can be found in L.M.E. Shaw, 'The Inquisition and the Portuguese Economy', *Journal of European Economic History* (1989) XVIII, 415–431.

41   C.A. Hanson, *Economy and Society in Baroque Portugal 1668–1703* (London: Macmillan, 1981) ch. IV.

42 Ibid., 97.
43 Mendes dos Remedios, *Os judeus*, II, 392; Shaw, 'The Inquisition . . . ', claims
    that 1329 New Christians were tried between 1681 and 1692.

9 'A great deal of Judaism is to be found in Spain'

1 *'Muchísimo judaísmo se encierra en España.'* F. Moya Torres, *Memorial al Rey
   Felipe V, acerca del mal universal de España y modo de remediarlo* (no place, no
   date, circa 1727) para. 283.
2 Ibid., para. 283–284.
3 Ibid., para. 290.
4 H. Méchoulan, *Le sang de l'autre ou l'honneur de Dieu: Indiens, Juifs, Morisques
   au siècle d'Or* (Paris: Fayard, 1976) 119.
5 De Lera García, *La Ultima*....
6 Huerga Criado, *En la raya* ...,
7 J. Israel, 'The Economic Contribution of Dutch Sephardi Jewry to
   Holland's Golden Age 1595-1713,' *in Empires and Entrepots: the Dutch, the
   Spanish Monarchy and the Jews, 1585–1713* (London: Hambledon Press,
   1990) 417–447.
8 Lea, *A History*..., I, 336.
9 Ibid.; see also the great nineteenth-century historian M. Menéndez y Pelayo's *Historia de los heterodoxos* (Madrid: Biblioteca de Autores Cristianos,
   1956) II, 407.
10 On Macanaz see C. Martín Gaite, *Macanaz, otro paciente de la Inquisición*
    (Madrid: Taurus, 1970); original title: *El proceso de Macanaz: historia de un
    empapelamiento* (Madrid: Moneda y Crédito, 1969).
11 See A. Alvarez de Morales, *Inquisición e Ilustracion 1700–1834* (Madrid:
    Fundación Universitaria Española, 1982). For details of Macanaz's proposals
    to defend royal privileges in ecclesiastical matters, see J.C. Galende Díaz 'El
    Santo Oficio y los primeros borbones', *Hispania* (1988) XLVIII, no. 169,
    553–598.
12 Martin Gaite, *Macanaz*..., 305.
13 See A. Martínez Albiach, *Religiosidad hispana y sociedad borbónica* (Burgos:
    Facultad Teológica del Norte de España, 1969) 446.
14 Martín Gaite, *Macanaz, ...*, 320.
15 *Defensa Crítica de la Inquisición* (Madrid, 1788). British Library Egerton MS.
    342 contains this work in a handwritten version probably prepared for the
    printer. See Llamas, *Documentación Inquisitorial*...
16 Pérez Villanueva and Escandell Bonet, *Historia de la Inquisición*..., I, 233.
17 AHN, Inq., Libro 1324, fo. 312, quoted by Martínez Millán, 'La Persecucíon
    inquisitorial contra los cripto-judíos al principio del siglo XVIII: el tribunal de
    Murcia 1715–1725', *Sefarad* (1989), XLIX, fasc. 2, 307–363.
18 AHN, Inq., L. 160, C. 11. The evidence of Antonio Rodríguez Carrasco and
    that of Maria de Tudela are sewn into other bound trial documents where
    their testimony is used.
19 Escamilla-Colin, *Crimes et châtiments . . .* , I, 47. These 441 victims include
    those punished for crimes other than Judaizing, though it may be assumed
    that the latter was the principal offence.

20   Martínez Millán, 'La persecución inquisitorial . . .' For the contrast between
     Valladolid and other courts see de Prado Moura, *Las hogueras* . . . , 81ff. and
     100–111. See also Blázquez Miguel's commentary in his *Inquisición y
     Criptojudaísmo*, 246; Escamilla–Colin, *Crimes et châtiments* . . . , I, 760–761,
     921.
21   Dedieu, 'Les causes de foi . . .', table 1.
22   See J.C. Galende Díaz's doctoral thesis, 'La crisis del siglo XVIII y la Inqui-
     sición española: el caso de la Inquisición toledana (1700–1820) (Madrid:
     Universidad Complutense, 1988).
23   Escamilla–Colin, *Crimes et Châtiments* . . . , I, 47.
24   Haliczer, *Inquisition and Society* . . . , 333.
25   F. García Ivars, *La represión en el tribunal inquisitorial de Granada 1550–1819*
     (Madrid: Akal, 1991) 91–92: R. de Lera García, 'La gran ofensiva antijudía de
     la Inquisición de Granada (1715–1727) in *Comunicações apresentadas ao
     Primer Congreso Internacional sobre Inquisição* (Lisbon: Universitaria Editora,
     1987) 1087–1109.
26   See the comments of J. Israel in his *European Jewry* . . . , 244–247.
27   AHN, Inq., L.186, C.3. Evidence of Isabel de Ribera at trial of her husband
     Francisco de Torres.
28   See A. Herzberg, *The French Enlightenment and the Jews* (New York: Columbia
     University Press, 1968, 1990) 49–50.
29   AHN, Inq. Alegaciones Fiscales 3722/178.
30   AHN, Inq., L.186, C.3. Testimony of Torres's cousin, Leonor de Martos.
31   AHN, Inq., Libro 1170, fo.19. De Lera García (1987), 'La última gran
     ofensiva . . .'.
32   AHN, Inq., L.160, C.11. Trial of Diego López de Castro.
33   Escamilla-Colin, *Crimes et Châtiments* . . . , II, 273.
34   AHN. Inq., L.186, C.3.
35   See the family tree (Figure 4).
36   AHN, Inq., L.157, C.12.
37   The family history of María Feliciana and her sister Manuela is told in great
     detail by Caro Baroja in *Los judíos* . . . , III, 71.
38   Galende Díaz, *La crisis del siglo XVIII*, 228.
39   AHN, Inq., Libro 1170, fo.19, quoted in Lera García, '*La última gran
     persecución* . . .', 93.
40   AHN, Inq., Libro 714, letters from the *Suprema* to the Toledo court. The
     book contains letters in which the Toledo inquisitors report the arrests of
     various families.
41   AHN, Inq., L.160, C.11.
42   The sources for the *autos* held between 1700 and 1756 are: *Relaciones*
     published by Serrete (Biblioteca Nacional R. 8560 and R. 2725, and British
     Library 4071 i 3 and 4); Matute y Luquín, *Colección* . . . ; Gracia Boix, *Autos de
     fe* . . . ; AHN, Inq., L.1, C.1 (a chronological list of *autos* held in Toledo); J.
     Blázquez Miguel, *El tribunal de la Inquisición en Murcia* (Murcia: Academia
     Alfonso X el Sabio, 1986) and his *La Inquisición en Cataluña: el tribunal del
     Santo Oficio en Barcelona 1487–1820* (Toledo: Arcano, 1990); de Lera García,
     'La ultima gran persecución . . .' and 'La gran ofensiva' . . . , Galende Díaz,
     'La crisis del siglo XVIII and 'La Inquisición toledana desde la llegada de los
     borbones', *Anales Toledanos* (1988), XXV, 245–284; F. Fita, 'La Inquisición de

Logroño y un judaizante quemado en 1719', *Boletín de la Real Academia de la Historia* (1904) XLV, cuaderno V, 451–460; García Ivars, *La represión* ...; de Prado Moura, *Las hogueras* ...

43   The lists given by de Prado Moura (p. 81ff.) do not detail the victims of each *auto*. In some there may not have been any Judaizers, although 341 people of the 368 punished altogether were Judaizers. My lists have produced a total of 204, so 137 victims would have to be added to those I have identified in this Castilian town.

44   10 of these, exceptionally, were declared innocent at the *auto de fe* of 14 December 1704 and should be deducted from the total (Escamilla-Colin, *Crimes et Châtiments* ..., I, 920).

45   Some *autos de fe* are listed in various sources but without numbers of victims.

46   At this *auto de fe* and a number of others at Valladolid and Granada, listed by de Prado Moura and García Ivars, no details of persons punished at the *auto* are given.

47   One was reconciled in effigy.

48   One person was declared innocent of the accusation.

49   Menéndez y Pelayo, *Historia de los heterodoxos*, II, 453, quoting J.A. Llorente, *Historia Crítica de la Inquisición en España*, 4 vols (1st edn Paris 1812; 1st Spanish edn Barcelona 1818; republished Madrid: Hiperión, 1980) IV, 52. Llorente presents figures that he had 'in front of him' ('*a la vista*'). These are 79 relaxed to the stake in person, 63 in effigy and 829 others, which Llorente totals incorrectly as 981 rather than 971.

50   F. Pérez y Prado, *Compendio de las tres Leyes: natural, escrita y evangélica. De la gracia en Adán y Eva y su reparación en IHS y MA* (Jesucristo y María Auxiliadora) (Seville 1726).

51   Ibid., 66.

52   Ibid., 130. 'Basques', the oldest people in the peninsula, was a code word for Jews among the Judaizers.

53   Ibid., 131.

54   AHN, Inq., L. 167, C.11, fo.26.

55   Archivo Diocesano de Cuenca (henceforth ADC, Inq.) L.571/7056 trial of Antonio Rodríguez ('Pie de Gorrino'), fo.63 v.

56   A. Hyamson, *The Sephardim of England* (London: Methuen, 1951; republished Spanish and Portuguese Jews' Congregation, 1991) 16.

57   Pérez de Prado, *Compendio* ..., 155.

58   ADC, Inq., L. 571/7057–8.

59   Hyamson, *The Sephardim* ..., 110.

60   D. Reher, *Town and Country in pre-Industrial Spain: Cuenca 1550–1870* (Cambridge University Press, 1990) 16–19.

61   AHN, Inq., L.174, C. 8.

62   ADC, Inq., L.571/7056.

63   Ibid.

64   Ibid.

65   AHN, Inq., L.167, C. 11.

66   Ibid.

67   AHN, Inq., L.186, C. 3; trial of Francisco de Torres.

68   ADC, Inq., L.572/7060; trial of María Luis.

69   AHN, Inq., L.157, C. 11.
70   ADC, Inq., L.572/7063.

10   'Which he did in obedience to the Law of Moses'

1   J. Blázquez Miguel, *La Inquisición en Castilla – La Mancha* (Córdoba: Servicio de Publicaciones de la Universidad, 1986) 82.
2   David M. Gitlitz's massive study, *The Religion of the Crypto-Jews* (Philadelphia: Jewish Publication Society, 1996) brings examples from the late fifteenth and early sixteenth centuries in Spain, and later from South America. His evidence parallels what has been found in seventeenth- and eighteenth-century Inquisition sources in Spain.
3   AHN, Inq., L.174, C.10.
4   AHN, Inq., L.174, C.1.
5   AHN, Inq., L.186, C.3.
6   AHN, Inq., L.186, C.3, fo.358 v.; evidence of Francisco de Torres.
7   C-H. Frèches, *António José da Silva et l'Inquisition* (Paris: Fundação Calouste Gulbenkian et Centro Cultural Português, 1982) 52–53.
8   Ibid.
9   Frèches, 33.
10   ADC, L.571/7056, fo.5.
11   Leviticus 22: 34–43. See H. Beinart, *Conversos on Trial: the Inquisition in Ciudad Real* (Jerusalem: Magnes Press, Hebrew University, 1981) 271, n.148.
12   AHN, Inq., L.174, C.8, fo.6 verso.
13   M. Ben Israel, *Thesouro dos Dinim*, 2 vols (Amsterdam: printed by Eliahu Aboab, 1645–1647. 2nd edn., 1710) ch.V.
14   AHN, Inq., L.174, C.8, fo.7.
15   AHN, Inq., L.174, C.1.
16   Quoted in Caro Baroja, *Los judíos . . .* , appx LVII.
17   See on this Passover, M. Alpert, 'A Marrano Pesach', in *Proceedings of the Tenth British Conference of Judeo–Spanish Studies, Queen Mary and Westfield College, July 1997* (London: Queen Mary and Westfield College, 1999) 103–109.
18   AHN, Inq., L.160, C.11.
19   AHN, Inq., L.174, C.16. María Pereira (23 September 1658).
20   ADC, Inq., L.572/7060.
21   AHN, Inq., L.186, C.3.
22   Ibid.; the witness was Isabel de Ribera, wife of Francisco de Torres.
23   *Relación del auto de fe celebrado en Madrid el día 22 de febrero de 1722* (Biblioteca Nacional, Madrid. R.8560).
24   Quoted by E. Lipiner, *Santa Inquisição: terror e linguagem* (Rio de Janeiro: Editora Documentária, 1977) 23.
25   AHN, Inq., L.157, C.11.
26   ADC, Inq., L.572/7063.
27   AHN, Inq., L.186, C.3.
28   AHN, Inq., L.167, C.11.
29   See G. Scholem, *Major Trends in Jewish Mysticism* (1942) (New York: Schocken, 1961) 309.

30 See Kaplan, *Judíos Nuevos* . . . , 108ff.
31 AHN, Inq., L.186, C.6.
32 AHN, Inq., L.157, C.12.
33 ADC, Inq., L.571/5078.
34 ADC, Inq., L.572/7063.
35 ADC, Inq., L.568/7033.
36 ADC, Inq., L.572/7063. Another Antonio Rodríguez, who managed the salt-petre monopoly in Tembleque, had deposited several thousand pesos with 'Pig's Foot'.
37 ADC, Inq., L.572/7063.
38 AHN, Inq., L.167, C.11.
39 AHN, Inq., L.167, C.1.
40 Jaime Contreras, *El Santo Oficio de la Inquisición en Galicia 1560–1700; poder, sociedad y cultura* (Madrid: Akal, 1982) 605.
41 ADC, Inq., L.572/7063.
42 Ibid.
43 AHN, Inq., L/160, C.11; L.157, C.12; L.186, C.3.
44 AHN, Inq., L.160, C.11.
45 AHN, Inq., L.157, C.11.
46 Ibid.
47 AHN, Inq., L.186, C.3.
48 De Lera García, 'La última gran persecución . . .'.
49 *Relación del auto de fe de Zaragoza del 18 de octubre de 1722* (British Library 4071 bb 43).
50 Yerushalmi, *From Spanish Court* . . . , 289, discusses the potential reading of a Spanish Judaizer.
51 AHN, Inq., L.175, C.4.
52 The translation is that of the New English Bible (1970), Apocrypha 72.
53 AHN, Inq., L.157, C.11. The italicized words were underlined by the Inquisition secretary.
54 *Las veynte libros de F. Josepho de las antigüedades Judaycas, y su vida por el mismo escripta, con otro libro del imperio de la razon en el cual trató del martirio de los Macabeos* (Antwerp, 1554); *Respuesta de Josepho contra Apión Alexandrino, traducido por el capitan Joseph Semah Arias* (evidently an ex-*Marrano*) (Amsterdam, 1687) and *De Bello Judaico* (Seville, 1536 and 1557).
55 Maximiano Oliveira Lemos, *Ribeiro Sanches; a sua vida e a sua obra* (Oporto: Editorial Tavares, 1911) 11.
56 Selke, *The Conversos* . . . , 32–33.
57 Y.H. Yerushalmi, '*Anusim ha-ḥozrim le-yahadut be me'ah ha-17: hascaltam ha-yehudit ve-hakhsharatam ha-nafshit* ('Forced Converts Returning to Judaism in the XVIIth Century: Their Jewish Education and Their Personal Preparation'), *Proceedings of the Vth World Congress of Jewish Studies*, III (Jerusalem; World Union of Jewish Studies, 1972) 201–209 (English summary on p. 247).
58 De Lera García, 'La última gran persecución . . .'.
59 *Bevis Marks Records*, part IV, 'The Circumcision Register of Isaac and Abraham de Paiva' (ed. R. Barnett) (London: Spanish and Portuguese Jews' Congregation and Jewish Historical Society of England) 25–27.
60 Escamilla–Colin, *Crimes et châtiments* . . . , II, 401.

61   AHN, Inq., L.157, C.11.
62   ADC, Inq., L.568/7033.
63   AHN, Inq., L.186, C.3.
64   AHN, Inq., L.160, C.11.
65   AHN, Inq., L.2020/27.
66   Beinart, *Conversos on Trial*, 282.
67   AHN, Inq., L.186, C.3; Blázquez Miguel, *El tribunal* . . . , 140.
68   AHN, Inq., L.160, C.11.
69   Ibid.
70   AHN, Inq., L.157, C.11.
71   ADC, Inq., L.572/7060.
72   AHN, Inq., L.160, C.11.
73   AHN, Inq., L.2020/27.
74   AHN, Inq., L.174, C.10.
75   AHN, Inq., L.174, C.10.
76   AHN, Inq., L.160, C.11.
77   Willemse, *Un 'portugués'* . . . , 29.
78   AHN, Inq., L.160, C.11.
79   ADC, Inq., L.568/7033.
80   Ex-Marranos in Amsterdam would gather to recite lamentations on the
     three Sabbaths preceding the Ninth of Ab, anniversary of the destruction of
     the temple in Jerusalem. (M. Bodian, *Hebrews of the Portuguese Nation:
     Conversos and Community in Early Modern Amsterdam* (Bloomington: Indiana
     University Press, 1997) 46.) This day falls normally in July or August, which
     perhaps inclined Rodrigo de la Peña to confuse it with the date of Taberna-
     cles.

Conclusion

1   J.P. Dedieu, 'Responsabilité de l'Inquisition dans le retard économique de
    l'Espagne. Eléments de réponse', in *Origines du retard économique d l'Espagne,
    XVIe–XIXe siècles* (Paris: CNRS, 1983) 143–153.
2   J.A. Van Praag, 'Almas en litigio', *Clavileño* (1950) no. I, 14–26.

The Hunt for the Hidden Jew: Crypto-Judaism after the Inquisition

1   Mario Méndez Bejarano, *Histoire de la juiverie de Séville* (Madrid: Editorial Ibero-
    Africano-Americano, 1922), 227.
2   Aronsfeld, C., *The Ghosts of 1492: Jewish Aspects of the Struggle for Religious
    Freedom in Spain 1848-1976* (New York: Columbia University Press for *Jewish
    Social Studies*, 1979), 2.
3   Henri Méchoulan, 'La cédule de 1802 ou le dernier sobresaut de l'antiju-
    daïsme espagnol d'Etat'. *Revue des Etudes Juives* (1984), No. 143.
4   Jean-Jacques Rousseau, in his *Confessions* (Penguin Classics translation,
    Harmondsworth, 1954, pp.65-66), mentions the phenomenon of Moroccan
    Jews seeking baptism for unworthy ends, though he claims that the people

who did so only pretended to be Jews.
5   See J.J. Lichtenstein, 'The Reaction of Western European Jewry to the Re-estab-
    lishment of a Jewish Community in Spain in the Nineteenth Century'
    (unpublished doctoral thesis, Yeshiva University, 1962), 63.
6   See the Everyman edition (1906), 110.
7   Aronsfeld, 4-6.
8   Quoted by Lichtenstein, 236-237.
9   See David Littman, 'Mission to Morocco' in (S. and V. Lipman eds.) *The
    Century of Moses Montefiore* (OUP for Littman Library, 1985), 26.
10 Niall Ferguson, *The House of Rothschild*, 2 vols, Penguin, 1998, 83-88.
11 J. Lisbona, *Retorno a Sefarad: la política de España hacia sus judíos en el siglo XX*
    (Barcelona, Riopiedras, 1993), 19.
12 A. Pulido Fernández, *Españoles sin patria y la raza sefardí* (Madrid 1905.
    Reprinted University of Granada. 1993). See also M. Alpert, 'Dr. Angel Pulido
    and philo-Sephardism in Spain' *Jewish Historical Studies* (2005), vol. 40, 105-
    119.
13 On this subject there has been a lot of recent research. See, for instance,
    Marquina, A. and Gloria Ospina, *España y los judíos en el siglo XX* (Madrid:
    Espasa, *1987*), Lisbona, J.A., *Retorno a Sefarad* (Barcelona: Riopiedras, 1993),
    and González, Isidro, *El retorno de los judíos* (Madrid: Nerea, 1991). In English,
    see Aronsfeld, cit. 47-51.
14 The author spent *Yom Kippur* of 1971 in the Madrid synagogue sitting
    between recent arrivals from Argentina and Cuba.
15 So far (2007) I have found only hearsay evidence for this. Three people in
    question did not reply when I asked them if they could demonstrate Jewish
    ancestry.
16 The word *Chueta* may mean 'pork chop' in a sort of mirror reference to the
    Jewish prohibition of pork, or be the diminutive of the Majorcan Catalan
    word for 'Jew'.
17 The names are: Aguiló, Bonnín, Cortés, Forteza, Fuster, Martí, Miró, Picó,
    Piña, Pomar, Segura, Taronji, Valenti, Valleriola and Valls. See Selke, A. cit.
    and Moore, Kenneth *Those of the Street: the Catholic-Jews of Mallorca*
    (University of Notre Dame Press), 1976, 13-14. Isaacs, A. Lionel, *The Jews of
    Majorca* (London: Methuen), 1936, gives a picture of the Chuetas before the
    tourist development of the island.
18 In Spain women retain their single names and people use a patronymic and
    a matronymic.
19 Nissim Ben-Avraham published *Els Anussim, el problema dels xuetons segons la
    legislació rabínica* ('The Chueta problem according to rabbinic legislation'
    (Palma de Mallorca: Font, 1992).
20 Moore, 174. Most of the exogamous marriages have been, however, with non-
    Majorcan Spaniards.
21 See Trudy Alexey, *The Mezuzah in the Madonna's Foot* (New York: Simon and
    Schuster, 1993), Chapter 21; S. Ward, 'Converso descendants in the American
    Southwest: a Report on Research, Resources and the Changing Search for
    Identity' *Proceedings of the 1998 Conference of the European Association for Jewish
    Studies* (ed. A. Sáenz-Badillos), Leiden: Brill, 1999, 677-686.
22 Roth, C, *A History of the Marranos*, (Philadelphia: Jewish Publications Society,
    1932: reprint. Harper Torchbooks, New York, 1966), 351.

23   See Michael Studemund-Halévy, 'Les Juifs au Portugal aujourd'hui', *Los Muestros*, December 2000, No.41, 27-33.

24   See the memoir of Israel Solomon, quoted by Solomon Schechter in 'An unfamiliar aspect of Anglo-Jewish History'. *Publications of the American Jewish Historical Society*, Vol. 25, 72-73, quoted by Roth, 357-358.

25   Julio Caro Baroja, cit., iii, 246 ff. quotes some Portuguese sources which show that Crypto-Judaism was no secret.

26   S. Schwarz, 'Os cristãos-novos em Portugal no século XX'(Lisbon; Livraria Universal Armando J. Tavares, 1925).

27   Schwarz's statements should perhaps be taken with a pinch of salt. Not all the secret Jews were ignorant. Indeed, there were professional men among them.

28   See Edgar Samuel, 'Jewish missionary activity in Portugal between the Wars', *Jewish Historical Studies* (2007), Volume 41, 173-181. Correspondence of 25 June and 12 August 1924 with the Chief Rabbi in appendices.

29   See his *Essays in Jewish History* (ed. C. Roth), (London: Jewish Historical Society of England, 1934), 363-383.

30   Barros Basto always referred to himself with the Hebrew name Bar-Rosh, because of its phonetic similarity to Barros. All references to his life and events among the *marranos* are taken from Mea Elvira de Azevedo and Ignacio Steinhardt, *Ben Rosh*, (Oporto: Afrontamento,1977), except where other sources are mentioned.

31   Mea and Stenhardt, 89.

32   Ibid. 107 and ff.

33   Barros Bastos was Jewish on his father's side only.

34   Published on 30 October 1931 in the London *Jewish Chronicle*.

35   Endelman, Todd, *The Jews of Georgian England* (Ann Arbour: University of Michigan Press, 1999, Chapter 8.

36   Archives of the Spanish and Portuguese Jews' Congregation London, MS. 1789.

37   D. Friedenberg 'The Jewish catacombs of Portugal', *Midstream* (1960 Spring), 2-4 and 105-107.

38   See Anita Novinsky, 'The Last Marranos', *Commentary* 43, no.5, 1967, 76-81.

Bibliography

1. Primary sources, bibliographies and catalogues

Madrid

Archivo Histórico Nacional, Inquisition Section (AHN, Inq.).

Blázquez Miguel, J. 'Catálogo de procesos inquisitoriales del Tribunal de Corte', *Revista de la Inquisición*, 3 (1994), 205–257.

Catálogo de las causas contra la fe seguidas ante el Tribunal del Santo Oficio de Toledo (Madrid: AHN, 1903).

Cuenca

Archivo Diocesano de Cuenca, Sección de Inquisición (ADC, Inq.).

Pérez Rodríguez, D. *Catálogo del Archivo de la Inquisición de Cuenca* (Cuenca, 1982).

London

Bevis Marks Records, Part IV: The Circumcision Register of Isaac and Abraham de Paiba 1715–1775 (transcribed, translated and presented by Barnett, R. and continued by Rodrigues Pereira, M.) (London: Spanish and Portuguese Jews' Community and Jewish Historical Society of England, 1991.)

Llamas, E. *Documentación Inquisitorial: manuscritos españoles del siglo XVI existentes en el Museo Británico* (Madrid: FUE, 1975).

British Library, MSS. Egerton 343, 344, 1834, 1887, 2058. MSS. Add. 20915, 21447, 28462, 29868.

Adler, E. 'Documents sur les marranes d'Espagne et de Portugal sous Philippe IV' (*Revue des Etudes Juives*, XLVIII (1904) 1–28; XLIX (1904) 51–73; L (1905), 53–75; LI (1906) 251–264.

Contemporary accounts

Relación del auto general de la fee que se celebró en la ciudad de Córdoba a 21 del mes de diciembre de 1627 (Seville, 1627).

Relación verdadera en la cual se da cuenta y declara el auto de fe que se celebró en la Villa de Madrid en quatro días del mes de julio . . . etc. (Granada, 1632).

Auto de la Fe celebrado en Lima a 23 de enero de 1639. Al Tribunal del Santo Oficio de la Inquisición de los Reynos del Perú, Chile, Paraguay y Tucumán, por el Licenciado Don Fernando de Montesinos, presbítero, natural de Osuna (Madrid, 1640).

Auto público de Fe celebrado en la ciudad de Sevilla a domingo 29 de marzo (Seville, 1648).

Romance nuevo del portentoso caso que ha sucedido en la Corte de Madrid . . . etc. (Madrid: Juan Sanz, no date, probably 1632).

Olmo, J. del *Relación histórica del auto general de fe que se celebró en Madrid este año de 1680* (Madrid, 1680).

Series of *Relaciones* of autos de fe catalogued in Biblioteca Nacional (Madrid) and British Library (London).

Van der Vekene, E. *Bibliotheca Bibliographica Historiae Sanctae Inquisitionis*, 3 vols (Vaduz: Topos, 1982).

2. Secondary sources

Actas de las Jornadas de estudios sefardíes 1980 (Cáceres: Universidad de Extremadura, 1981).

Aguinis, M. *La gesta del marrano* (Buenos Aires: Planeta argentina, 1993).

Alejandre, J.A. *El veneno del Dios: la Inquisición de Sevilla ante el delito de solicitación en confesión* (Madrid: Siglo XXI, 1994).

Alonso, B. *Los judíos en Orense: siglos XV al XVII* (Orense: Imp. Otero, 1904).

Alpert, M. 'Did Spanish Crypto-Jews Desecrate Christian Sacred Images and Why? The Case of the *Cristo de la Paciencia* (1629–32), the *Romance* of 1717 and the events of November 1714 in the *Calle del Lobo*', in L. Twomey (ed.), *Faith and Fanaticism: Religious Fervour in Early Modern Spain* (Aldershot: Ashgate, 1997).

Alpert, M. 'Ante la Inquisición: el caso de Manuel San Vicente Portilla y la Inquisición de Toledo, 1721', *Historia 16* (June 1997), no. 254, 60–63.

Alpert, M. 'The Secret Jews of 18th Century Madrid', *Revue d'Études Juives* (January–June 1997) 156, fascs 1–2, 135–171.

Alpert, M., 'Dr. Angel Pulido and philo-Sephardism in Spain', *Jewish Historical Studies* (2005), Vol. 40, 105-119.

Alpert, M. 'A Marrano Celebration of the Jewish Passover' (London: Queen Mary and Westfield College, *Proceedings of the 1997 Conference on Judeo-Spanish Studies*, 1999), pp. 103–109.

Alvarez de Morales, A. *Inquisición e ilustración 1700–1834* (Madrid: FUE, 1982).

Amador de los Ríos, J. *Historia social política y religiosa de los judíos de España y Portugal* (1875–1876; republished Madrid: Aguilar, 1960).

Amiel, C. 'Les archives de l'Inquisition portugaise', *Arquivos do Centro Cultural Português* (Paris: Fundação Calouste Gulbenkian, 1979), XIV, 421–443.

Amiel, C.'La mort juive au regard des Inquisitions ibériques', *Revue de l'histoire des religions* (1990) vol. CCVII/4, 389–412.

Amiel, C. 'Crypto-Judaïsme et Inquisition: la matière juive dans les édits de la foi des Inquisitions ibériques', *Revue de l'histoire des religions* (1993) vol. CCX/2, 145–168.

Amzalak (Bensabat), M. *David Nieto, noticia bibliográfica* (Lisbon, 1923).

Arbós, C. ' Los cancioneros castellanos del siglo XV como fuente para la historia de los judíos españoles', in Kaplan, J. (ed.), *Jews and Conversos: Studies in Society and the Inquisition* (Jerusalem: World Union of Jewish Studies, Magnes Press, Hebrew University, 1985) 74–83.

Asensio y Toledo, J.M. *Un cervantista portugués del siglo XVIII (Antonio José da Silva) quemado por el Santo Oficio de la Inquisición: apuntes biográficos* (Seville, 1888).

Asaf, S. 'Anussei Sefarad u-Portugal be-sifrut ha-teshuvot' in *Be' Oholei Ya'akov* (Jerusalem: Mossad Rav Kook, 1943) 145–180.

Assis, Y. 'Sexual Behaviour in Medieval Hispano–Jewish Society' in *Jewish History: Essays in Honour of Chimen Abramsky* (eds Rapoport Albert, A. and Zipperstein, S.) (London: Peter Halban, 1985) 25–59.

Lúcio d'Azevedo, J. *História de António Vieira*, 2 vols (Lisbon: Texeira, 1918–1920).
Lúcio d'Azevedo, J. *História dos Christãos Novos portugueses* (Lisbon: Texeira, 1921).
Baer, Y. *A History of the Jews in Christian Spain*, 2 vols (Philadelphia: Jewish Publication Society of America, 1978).
Baião, A. *Episódios dramaticos da Inquisição portuguesa*, vol.1, *Homens de Letras e de Ciencia por ela condenados* (Lisbon: Seara Nova, 1972).
Barnett, R. 'Dr. Samuel Núñez Ribeiro and the Settlement of Georgia', in *Migration and Settlement: Proceedings of the Anglo-American Jewish Historical Conference 1970* (London: Jewish Historical Society of England, 1971), 63–100.
Barnett, R. 'Diplomatic aspects of the Sephardic influx from Portugal in the early eighteenth century', *Transactions of the Jewish Historical Society of England* (1977) xxv, 210–221.
Barrionuevo, Jerónimo de. *Avisos 1654–1658*, 4 vols (Madrid: Colección de Escritores Castellanos, 1892).
Barrios, M. *El tribunal de la Inquisición en Andalucía* (Seville: Rodríguez Castillejo, 1991).
Beinart, H. 'Ha-Inqvisitzia ha-sefardit ha-leumit be-feulatah mi-ḥutz la-gevulot sefarad' ('The work of the Spanish Inquisition outside the frontiers of Spain'), in *Proceedings of the Fifth World Congress of Jewish Studies*, 1969 (Jerusalem: World Union of Jewish Studies, 1972), 55–71 (English summary on p. 210).
Beinart, H. 'The Records of the Inquisition: A Source of Jewish and Converso History', in *Proceedings of the Israel Academy of Sciences and Humanities* (Jerusalem, 1968), ii 211–227.
Beinart, H. 'Hispano-Jewish Society', in Ben-Sasson, H. and Ettinger, S. (eds), *Jewish Society through the Ages* (London: Vallentine, Mitchell, 1971), 220–238.
Beinart, H. 'The Converso Community in 15th Century Spain', and 'The Converso Community in 16th and 17th Century Spain', in Beinart, H. (ed.) *The Sephardi Heritage* (London: Vallentine, Mitchell, 1971) 1, 425–478
Beinart, H. 'Halikhatam shel yehudim mi-maroqo l'sefarad be-reshit ha-me'ah ha-17' ('Travels of Jews from Morocco to Spain at the Beginning of the XVIIth Century'), in Lieberman, S. (ed.) *Salo Wittmayer Baron Jubilee Volume*, Hebrew section (Jerusalem: American Academy of Jewish Research, 1974) iii, 15–39.
Beinart, H. *Trujillo: A Jewish Community in Extremadura on the Eve of the Expulsion from Spain* (Jerusalem: Magnes Press, Hebrew University, 1980).
Beinart, H. *Records of the Trials of the Inquisition in Ciudad Real*, 4 vols (Jerusalem: Israel Academy of Sciences and Humanities, 1974–1981).
Beinart, H. *Conversos on Trial: the Inquisition in Ciudad Real* (Jerusalem: Magnes Press, the Hebrew University, 1981).
Beinart, H. 'Moshe ve-Ya'akov Gomes, yelidei Penhorade (le-yad Bordeaux), nidunei ha-Inqvisitzia' ('Moshe and Ya'akov Gómez, Natives of Peyehorade, near Bordeaux, Tried by the Inquisition'), in *Jewish History, Frank Talmage Memorial Volume* (1997), vol. vi, 1–2.
Beinart, H. 'The Conversos and Their Fate', in *Spain and the Jews* (ed. Kedourie, E.) (London: Thames & Hudson, 1992), pp. 92–123.
Beinart, H. *Los judíos en España* (Madrid: Mapfre, 1992).
Bel Bravo, M.A. *El auto de fe de 1593: los conversos granadinos de origen judío* (Granada: Universidad de Granada, 1988).
Ben-Avraham, N. *Els Anussim: el problema dels xuetons seguns la legislació rabínica* (Palma de Mallorca: Miquel Font, 1992).

Bennassar, B. *L'Homme Espagnol: attitudes et mentalités du XVIe au XIXe siècles* (Paris: Hachette, 1975).

Bennassar, B. *Inquisición española: poder político y control social* (Paris, 1979; Spanish translation Barcelona: Crítica Grijalbo, 1981).

Ben-Sasson, H. (ed.), *A History of the Jewish People* (Cambridge Mass.: Harvard University Press, 1976).

Bermant, H. *The Cousinhood: The Anglo-Jewish Gentry* (London: Eyre & Spottiswoode, 1971).

Blázquez Miguel, J. *El tribunal de la Inquisición en Murcia* (Murcia: Academia Alfonso X el Sabio, 1986).

Blázquez Miguel, J. *La Inquisición en Castilla – La Mancha* (Córdoba: Servicio de Publicaciones de la Universidad, 1986).

Blázquez Miguel, J. 'Catálogo de los procesos inquisitoriales del tribunal del Santo Oficio de Murcia', *Murgitana* (1987), no. 74.

Blázquez Miguel, J. *Inquisición y Criptojudaísmo* (Madrid: Kaydeda, 1988).

Blázquez Miguel, J. *Herejía y ortodoxia en Talavera y su antigua tierra; procesos de la Inquisición 1478–1820* (Talavera: Hierba, 1989).

Blázquez Miguel, J. *La Inquisición en Cataluña: el tribunal del Santo Oficio en Barcelona 1487–1820* (Toledo: Arcano, 1990).

Bloom, H. *The Economic Activities of the Jews of Amsterdam in the Seventeenth and Eighteenth centuries* (Williamsport: Bayard Press, 1937).

Bodian, M. '"Men of the Nation": The Shaping of Converso Identity in Early Modern Europe', *Past and Present* (1994), no. 143, pp. 48–76.

Boxer, C.R. 'Padre Antonio Vieira S.J. and the institution of the Brazil Company in 1649', *Hispanic American Historical Review* (1949) XXIX, pp. 474–497.

Boyajian, J.C. *Portuguese Bankers at the Court of Spain 1626–1650* (New Brunswick: Rutgers University Press, 1983).

Braga, T. *O Martyr da Inquisição portuguesa António José da Silva-o Judeu* (Lisbon: Associação do Registo Civil, 1904).

Caballero Gómez, M.V. 'El Auto de fe de 1680: un lienzo para Francisco Rizi', *Revista de la Inquisición* (1994) no. 3, 69–140.

Antonio Cabezas, J. *Madrid y sus judíos* (Madrid: El Avapiés, 1987).

Cardaillac, L. 'Vision simplificatrice des groupes marginaux par le groupe dominant dans l'Espagne des XVIe et XVIIe siècles', in *Actes du Colloque International: les problèmes de l'exclusion en Espagne au XVe et XVIe siècles* (Paris: Publications de la Sorbonne, 1983) 11–23.

Caro Baroja, J. *La sociedad criptojudía en la corte de Felipe IV* (Madrid: Maestre, 1963).

Caro Baroja, J. 'El proceso de Bartolomé Febos o Febo', in *Homenaje a Don Ramón Carande* (Madrid: Sociedad de Estudios y Publicaciones, 1963) 59–79,

Caro Baroja, J. *Inquisición, brujería y criptojudaísmo* (Barcelona: Ariel, 1970).

Caro Baroja, J. *Los judíos en la España moderna y contemporánea*, 3 vols (Madrid: Istmo, 1978).

Caro Baroja, J. *Las formas complejas de la vida religiosa: religión, sociedad y carácter en la España de los siglos XVI y XVII* (Madrid: Akal, 1978).

Cohen, M.A. 'Towards a New Comprehension of the Marranos', *Hispania Judaica* I: *History*, pp. 23–35.

Cohen, M.A. 'The Sephardic Phenomenon: A Reappraisal', *American Jewish Archives* (Cincinnati, Spring–Summer 1992) 1–81.

Contreras, J. *El Santo Oficio de la Inquisición en Galicia 1560–1700: poder, sociedad y cultura* (Madrid: Akal, 1982).

Contreras, J. 'Family and Patronage: The Judeo-Converso Minority in Spain', in Perry, M. and Cruz, A. (eds.), *Cultural Encounters: the Impact of the Inquisition in Spain and the New World* (Berkeley: University of California Press, 1991) 127–145.

Corral, J. del, *El Madrid de los Austrias* (Madrid: El Avapiés, 1983).

Corral, J. del, *El Madrid de los Borbones* (Madrid: El Avapiés, 1985).

Dedieu, J.P. 'Les Causes de foi de l'Inquisition de Tolède (1483–1820): essai statistique', in *Mélanges de la Casa de Velázquez* (1978) XIV, 144–171.

Dedieu, J.P. *L'Administration de la foi: l'Inquisition de Tolède (XVIe–XVIIIe siècles)* (Madrid: Casa de Velázquez, 1989).

Domínguez Ortiz, A. 'El proceso inquisitorial de Juan Núñez Saravia, banquero de Felipe IV', *Hispania* (1955) LXI, 559–581.

Domínguez Ortiz, A. *Política y Hacienda de Felipe IV* (Madrid: Editorial de Derecho Financiero, 1960).

Domínguez Ortiz, A. *Sociedad y Estado en el siglo XVII español* (Barcelona: Ariel, 1976).

Domínguez Ortiz, A. *Autos de la Inquisición de Sevilla* (Seville: Ayuntamiento, 1992).

Domínguez Ortiz, A.'Los conversos de origen judío después de la Expulsión', in *La clase social de los conversos en Castilla en la edad moderna* (Madrid: CSIC, 1955), republished with introductory essay by F. Márquez Villanueva (Granada: Universidad de Granada, 1991).

Domínguez Ortiz, A. *Los judeoconversos en la España moderna* (Madrid: Mapfre, 1992).

Domínguez Ortiz, A. *Los judeoconversos en España y América* (Madrid: Istmo, 1988).

Ebben, M. 'Un triángulo imposible: la Corona española, el Santo Oficio y los banqueros portugueses 1627–1655', *Hispania* (mayo-agosto 1993) LIII, no. 184, 541–556.

Edwards, J. 'Religious Belief and Social Conformity: The "Converso" Problem in Late-Medieval Córdoba', *Transactions of the Royal Historical Society* (1981) XXXI, 115–128.

Edwards, J. 'The Conversos: A Theological Approach', *Bulletin of Hispanic Studies* (1985) LXII, 39–49.

Edwards, J. 'Religious Faith and Doubt in Late Medieval Spain: Soria circa 1450–1500', *Past and Present* (1988), no. 120, 3–25. See debate on the question in *Ibid.* no.128 (1990) 152–161.

Elliott, J. *The Count-Duke of Olivares: The Statesman in an Age of Decline* (New Haven: Yale University Press, 1986).

Elliott, J. *Spain and Its World 1500–1700: Selected Essays* (New Haven: Yale University Press, 1989).

Endelman, T. *Radical Assimilation in English Jewish History 1656–1945* (Bloomington and Indianapolis: Indiana University Press, 1990), ch. 1.

Epstein, I. *The Responsa of Rabbi Solomon ben Adreth of Barcelona (1235–1310) as a source of the History of Spain* (London: Kegan Paul, 1925).

Epstein, I. *The Responsa of Rabbi Simon ben Zemah Duran* (Oxford University Press, 1930).

Escamilla-Colin, M. *Crimes et châtiments dans l'Espagne inquisitoriale*, 2 vols (Paris: Berg International, 1992).

Escamilla-Colin, M. 'Les Juifs et l'Inquisition au XVIIe siècle', *XVII Siècle* (April–June 1994), no. 183, pp. 221–245.

Escamilla-Colin, M. 'Héroïsme, désespoir ou folie? Le cas de Diego López Duro', in Busse, W. and Varol-Bornes, M.C. (eds), *Hommage à Haïm Vidal Sephiha* (Berne: Peter Lang, 1996) 415–433.

Espadas Burgos, M. *Niveles materiales de vida en el Madrid del Siglo XVIII* (Madrid: Ayuntamiento, 1979).

Fita, F. 'La Inquisición de Logroño y un judaizante quemado en 1719', *Boletín de la Real Academia de la Historia* (1904) XLV, 451–160.

Frèches, C. *António José da Silva et l'Inquisition* (Paris: Fundação Calouste Gulbenkian, Centro Cultural Português, 1982).

Galende Díaz, J.C. 'La Inquisición toledana desde la llegada de los Borbones', *Anales Toledanos* (1988) XXV, 245–284.

Galende Díaz, J.C. *La crisis del siglo XVIII y la Inquisición española: el caso de la Inquisición toledana (1700–1820)* (Madrid: Universidad Complutense, 1988).

Galende Díaz, J.C. 'El Santo Oficio y los primeros borbones', *Hispania* (1988) XLVIII, no. 169, 553–598.

Galende Díaz, J.C. 'Recorridos inquisitoriales en el Madrid borbónico', *Hispania Sacra* (1993) XLV, no. 91, 16–25.

Garau, F. *La fee triunfante/en quatro autos celebrados en Mallorca...* (Palma de Mallorca, 1691).

García Cárcel, R. *Orígenes de la Inquisición española: el tribunal de Valencia 1478–1530* (Barcelona: Península, 1976).

García Ivars, F. *La represión en el tribunal inquisitorial de Granada 1550–1819* (Madrid: Akal, 1991).

Geddes, M. 'An Account of the Inquisition of Portugal, with a List of the Prisoners Who Came out of the Inquisition of Lisbon, in an Act of Faith Celebrated anno 1682, and Another in 1707', in *Miscellaneous Tracts*, vol. 1, no. V (London: 2nd edn, 1709); 'A Narrative of the Proceedings of the Inquisition in Lisbon, with a Person now Living in London, During his Imprisonment There', ibid., no. VI.

Gini de Barnatán, M. 'Notas sobre documentos inéditos de criptojudíos en el Siglo XVIII', *Maguen-Escudo* (Caracas) (1991) no. 79, 26–32.

Gitlitz, David, M. *Secrecy and Deceit: The Religion of the Crypto-Jews* (Philadelphia: Jewish Publication Society of America, 1966).

Glaser, E. 'Invitation to Intolerance: A Study of the Portuguese Sermons Preached at Autos de Fe', in *Hebrew Union College Annual* (1956) no. 27, 327–385.

Goldish, M. 'Jews, Christians and Conversos: Rabbi Solomon Aailion's Struggles in the Portuguese community of London', *Journal of Jewish Studies* (1994) XLV, 227–257.

Gracia Boix, R. *Colección de documentos para la historia de la Inquisición de Córdoba* (Córdoba: Monte de Piedad y Caja de Ahorros, 1982).

Gracia Boix, R. *Autos de fe y causas de la Inquisición de Córdoba* (Córdoba: Diputación Provincial, 1983).

Haliczer, S. *Inquisition and Society in the Kingdom of Valencia 1478–1834* (Berkeley and Los Angeles: University of California Press, 1990).

Hanson, C. *Economy and Society in Baroque Portugal (1668–1703)* (London: Macmillan, 1981).

Henningsen, G. and Contreras, J. 'El "Banco de Datos" del Santo Oficio. Las Relaciones de Causas de la Inquisición', *Boletín de la Real Academia de la Historia* (1977) CLXXIX, 547–570.

Henningsen, G. and Tedeschi, J. (eds), *The Inquisition in Early Modern Europe* (De Kalb: North Illinois University Press, 1986).

Huerga Criado, P. 'Una familia judeoconversa: la quiebra de la solidaridad', *Sefarad* (1989) XLIX, fasc. 1, 97–121.

Huerga Criado, P. *En la raya de Portugal: solidaridad y tensiones en la comunidad judeoconversa* (Salamanca: Ediciones Universidad, 1994).

Pérez Villanueva, J. (ed.), *La Inquisición española: Nueva visión, nuevos horizontes* (Madrid: Siglo XXI, 1980).

Pérez Villanueva, J. and Escandell Bonet, B. (eds) *Historia de la Inquisición en España y Améica*, 2 vols (Madrid: Biblioteca de Autores Cristianos, 1984).

Israel, J. 'Spain and the Dutch Sephardim 1609–1660', *Studia Rosenthaliana* (1978) XII 1–61.

Israel, J. 'The Economic Contribution of Dutch Sephardi Jewry to Holland's Golden Age 1595–1713', *Tijdschrift voor Geschiednis* (1983), no. 96, 505–535.

Israel, J. *European Jewry in the Age of Mercantilism 1550–1750* (Oxford: Clarendon Press, 1985).

Israel, J. 'Manuel López Pereira of Amsterdam, Antwerp and Madrid: Jew, New Christian and Adviser to the Conde–Duque de Olivares',*Studia Rosenthaliana* (1985) XIX, 109–164.

Israel, J. 'Duarte Nunes da Costa (Jacob Curiel) of Hamburg, Sephardi nobleman and communal leader 1585–1664', *Studia Rosenthaliana* (1987) XXIII, 14–34.

Israel, J. 'Sephardic Immigration into the Dutch Republic 1595–1672', *Studia Rosenthaliana* (1989) XXIII, 45–53.

Jiménez Monteserín, M. *Introducción a la Inquisición española: documentos básicos para el estudio del Santo Oficio* (Madrid; Editora Nacional, 1980).

Kamen, H. 'Confiscations in the Economy of the Spanish Inquisition', *Economic History Review*, 2nd ser. (1965) XVIII, 512–525.

Kamen, H. *The Spanish Inquisition* (London: Weidenfeld & Nicolson, 1965).

Kamen, H. *Spain in the Later Seventeenth Century 1665–1700* (London: Longman, 1980).

Kamen, H. 'Una crisis de conciencia en la España del Siglo de oro: la Inquisición contra la Limpieza de Sangre', *Bulletin Hispanique* (1986) 88, nos. 3–4, 321–356.

Kamen, H. *The Spanish Inquisition: A Historical Revision* (London: Weidenfeld & Nicolson, 1997).

Kany, C. *Life and Manners in Madrid 1750–1800* (Berkeley: University of California Press, 1932).

Kaplan, Y. *Jews and Conversos: Studies in Society and the Inquisition* (Jerusalem: Magnes Press, Hebrew University, 1985).

Kaplan, Y. *From Christianity to Judaism: The Story of Isaac Orobio de Castro* (transl. R. Loewe) (Oxford University Press, 1989).

Kaplan, Y. 'The Jewish Profile of the Spanish and Portuguese Community of London during the Seventeenth Century', *Judaism* (1992) 41, no. 3, 229–240.

Kaplan, Y. 'Wayward New Christians and Stubborn New Jews', *Jewish History* (1994) VIII, nos. 1–2, 27–41.

Kaplan, Y. *Judíos nuevos en Amsterdam: Estudio sobre la historia social e intelectual del judaísmo sefardí en el siglo XVII* (Barcelona: Gedisa, 1996).

Kenig, E. 'Branca Dias et Diogo Fernandes, des Nouveaux–Chrétiens au Brésil', in *Arquivos do centro Cultural Português* (Paris, Fundação Calouste Gulbenkian, 1979), XIV, 203–224.

Kramer–Hellinx, N. *Antonio Enríquez Gómez: literatura y sociedad en El siglo pitagórico y Vida de don Gregorio Guadaña* (New York: Peter Lang, 1992).

Kriegel, M. *Les Juifs à la fin du Moyen Age dans l'Europe Méditérranéenne* (Paris: Hachette, 1979).

Ladero Quesada, M.A. 'Los judíos conversos en la Castilla del Siglo XV', *Historia 16* (1992) XVI, no. 194, 39–52.

Le Blanc, J. 'Nouveaux Chrétiens accusés de judaïsme, par le Saint Office de Séville, au XVIIIe siècle', *Revue d'Etudes Juives* (1980) CXXXIX, nos 1–3, 205–206.

Lea, H. *A History of the Inquisition of Spain*, 4 vols (New York: Macmillan, 1906–1907).

Lemos, M. Oliveira, *Ribeiro Santos, a sua vida e a sua obra* (Oporto: Tavares Martins, 1911).

Lera García, R. de, 'La última gran persecución inquisitorial contra el cripto-judaísmo: el tribunal de Cuenca 1718–1725', *Sefarad* (1987) XLVII, fasc. 1, 87–137.

Lera García, R. de, 'Gran ofensiva antijudía de la Inquisición de Granada 1715–1727', in *Comunicações apresentadas ao Congreso Internacional sobre Inquisição, Lisboa 1987* (Lisbon: Universitária Editora, 1987), 1087–1109.

Lipiner, E, *Santa Inquisicão: terror e linguagem* (Rio de Janeiro: Editora Documentária, 1977).

Lipman, V. 'Sephardi and other Jewish Immigrants in England in the Eighteenth Century', in *Migration and Settlement: Proceedings of the Anglo-American Jewish Historical Conference* (London: Jewish Historical Society of England, 1970), 37–63.

Llorente, J. *Historia crítica de la Inquisición española*, 8 vols (Barcelona, 1818), new edn, 4 vols (Madrid: Hiperión, 1980).

Loeb, I. 'La correspondance des Juifs d'Espagne avec ceux de Constantinople', *Revue d'Études Juives* (1887), 262–276.

Lorence, B. 'The Inquisition and the New Christians in the Iberian Peninsula. Main Historiographic Issues and Controversies', in Ben-Ami, I (ed.) *The Sepharadi and Oriental Jewish Heritage* (Jerusalem: Magnes Press, Hebrew University, 1982), 3–72.

Iehuda Machabeo *(sic). Orden de oraciones del mes con los ayunos del solo y congregación y Pascuas, nuevamente enmendado, por dispensa de Eliau y David Uziel* (Amsterdam, 1656).

Mackay, A. 'Popular Movements and Pogroms in Fifteenth Century Castile', *Past and Present* (1972) no. 55, 33–67.

Mackay, A. 'The Hispanic–Converso Predicament', *Transactions of the Royal Historical Society*, vol. 35 (1985) 159–179.

Manasseh ben Israel, *Thesouro dos Dinim que o povo de Israel he obrigado saber, e observar*, 2 parts (Amsterdam, 1645–1647; 2nd edn 1710).

Manasseh ben Israel, *The Hope of Israel* (eds H. Méchoulan and G. Nahon) (Oxford: University Press, 1987).

Maqueda Abreu, C. *El auto de fe* (Madrid: Istmo, 1992).

Márquez Villanueva, F. 'El problema de los conversos: cuatro puntos cardinales', in *Hispania Judaica*, Vol. I, Solà-Solé, J.M., Armistead, S. and Silverman. J.H. (eds) (Barcelona: Puvill, 1980), 51–75.

Martín Gaite, C. *Macanaz, otro paciente de la Inquisición* (Madrid: Taurus, 1975). Original title: *El proceso de Macanaz: historia de un empapelamiento* (Madrid: Moneda y Crédito, 1969).

Martínez Albiad, A. *Religiosidad hispana y sociedad borbónica* (Burgos: Facultad teológica del Norte de España, 1969).

Martínez Millán, J. *La Hacienda de la Inquisición: 1478–1700* (Madrid: CSIC, 1984).

Martínez Millán, J. 'Estructuras de la Hacienda Inquisitorial', in Alcala, A. *et al.* *Inquisición española y mentalidad inquisitorial* (Barcelona: Ariel, 1984) 147–173.

Martínez Millán, J. 'La persecución inquisitorial contra los cripto-judíos a principio del siglo XVIII: el tribunal de Murcia 1715–1725', *Sefarad* (1989) XLIX, fasc. 2, 307–363.

Matute y Luquín, G. *Colección de los autos generales y particulares de Fé celebrados por el tribunal de la Inquisición de Córdoba* (Córdoba, 1825).

Méchoulan, H. *Le sang de l'autre ou l'honneur de Dieu: Indiens, Juifs, Morisques au Siècle d'Or* (Paris: Fayard, 1979).

Méchoulan, H. 'Catholicisme et Judaïsme dans *La Certeza del Camino*', *Revue d'Etudes Juives* (1984) CXLIII, nos 3–4, 461–473.

Méchoulan, H. *Hispanidad y judaísmo en tiempos de Espinoza. Edición de 'La certeza del camino' de Abraham Pereyra (Amsterdam, 1666)*, (Salamanca: Universidad de Salamanca, 1987).

Méchoulan, H. 'Du racisme religieux de Torrejoncillo à l'antijudaïsme "éclairée" de Feijoo', *Revue d'Etudes Juives*, (July–December 1995) XLIV, nos. 3–4, 363–385.

Mendes dos Remedios, J. *Os Judeus em Portugal*, 2 vols (Coimbra, F. França Amado, 1895; Coimbra Editora, 1928).

Mendes dos Remedios, J. 'Sermões en autos da fe', *Biblos* (Coimbra), (1927) III, 6–17.

Mendes dos Remedios, J. 'Costumes judaicos descritos por un converso', *ibid*, 18–29.

Meyuhas Ginio, A. 'The Conversos and the Magic Arts in Alonso de Espina's *Fortalitium Fidei*', in *Mediterranean History Review*, (1990) no. 5, 169–182.

Menéndez y Pelayo, M. *Historia de los heterodoxos*, 2 vols, (Madrid: Biblioteca de Autores Cristianos, 1967).

Motis Dolader, M.A. 'Población, urbanismo y estructura política de las aljamas judías de Aragón en el Siglo XV', *Hispania* (1996) LVI/3, no. 194, 885–944.

Moya Torres, F. *Memorial al Rey Felipe V acerca del mal universal de España y modo de remediarlo* (no place, no date; 1727?).

Nahon, G. 'Les Sephardim, les Marranes et leurs archives dans les travaux récents de I.S. Révah', *Revue d'Etudes Juives* (1973) CXXXII, nos. 1–2, 5–48.

Nahon, G. 'Les marranes espagnols et portugais et les communautés juives issues du marranisme, dans l'historiographie récente (1960–1975)', *Revue d'Etudes Juives* (1977), CXXXVI, nos. 3–4, 297–367.

Netanyahu, B. *The Marranos of Spain from the late XIVth Century to the early XVIth Century, according to contemporary Hebrew sources* (New York: American Academy for Jewish Research, 1966).

Netanyahu, B. 'On the Historical Meaning of the Hebrew Sources', in *Hispania Judaica*, Vol. I, Solà–Solé, J.M., Armistead, S. and Silverman, J.H. (eds) (Barcelona: Puvill, 1980), 79–102.

Netanyahu, B. *The Origins of the Inquisition in Fifteenth Century Spain* (New York: Random House, 1995).

Neuman, A. *The Jews in Spain: Their Social, Political and Cultural Life During the Middle Ages* (Philadelphia: Jewish Publication Society of America, 1944).

Novinski, A. 'Some Theoretical considerations About the New Christian Problem', in Ben-Ami, I. (ed.), *The Sepharadi and Oriental Jewish Heritage* (Jerusalem: Magnes Press, Hebrew University, 1982) 3–13.

Nunes Ribeiro Sanches, A. *Christãos novos e Christãos velhos em Portugal* (ed. Rego, R.) (Lisbon: Livrária Paisagem, 1956).

Orden de los Cinco Ayunos que son Tahanith de nueve de Ab, el de Tebeth, el de Ester, el de Thamuz y el de Guedaliah, por estilo seguido, y corriente, conforme se usa en este Kahal Kados (Amsterdam: David Tartas, 1684).

Orfali, M. *Los conversos españoles en la literatura rabínica: problemas jurídicas y opiniones legales durante los siglos XII–XVI* (Salamanca: Universidad Pontificia, 1982).

Orfali, M. 'Contexto teológico y social de la Biblia de Ferrara', in Hassan, I. (Ed.), *Introducción a la Biblia de Ferrara*, (Madrid: Sociedad Estatal Quinto Centenario, 1994), 229–251.

Pérez de Colosia Rodríguez, M. *Auto inquisitorial de 1672: el criptojudaísmo en Málaga* (Málaga: Diputación Provincial, 1984).

Pérez de Prado y Cuesta, F. *Compendio de las tres leyes, Natural, Escrita y Evangélica. Pérdida de la Gracia en Adán y Eva y su reparación en IHS y MA* (Seville: no date, probably 1726).

Peters, E. *Inquisition* (Berkeley: University of California Press, 1989).

Prado Moura, A. de *Las hogueras de la intolerancia: la actividad represora del Tribunal Inquisitorial de Valladolid (1700–1834)* (Valladolid: Junta de Educación, Consejería de Educación y Cultura, 1996).

Pullen, B. *The Jews of Europe and the Inquisition of Venice (1550–1670)* (London–New York: I.B. Tauris, 1993 and 1997).

Reher, D. *Town and Country in pre–industrial Spain: Cuenca 1550–1870* (Cambridge University Press, 1990).

Révah, I. 'Le premier établissment des Marranes portugais à Rouen (1603–1607)', *Annuaire de l'Institut de Philologie et d'Histoire Orientales et Slaves* (Brussels) (1953) no. XIII, 539–552.

Révah, I. 'Les Marranes' in *Revue d'Etudes Juives* (1959–1960) CXVIII, 29–77.

Révah, I. 'Autobiographie d'un marrane. Edition partielle d'un manuscrit de João (Moseh) Pinto Delgado', *Revue d'Etudes Juives* (January–June 1961) CXIX, no.2, 41–130.

Révah, I. 'Un pamphlet contre l'Inquisition d'Antonio Enríquez Gómez', *Revue d'Etudes Juives*, (January–June 1962) CXXI, no. 1, fascs 1, 2, 81–168.

Révah, I. 'Le plaidoyer en faveur des "Nouveaux-Chrétiens" portugais du licencié Martín González de Cellorigo', *Revue d'Etudes Juives* (July–December 1963) CXXII, no. 2. fascs 3, 4, 281–398.

Révah, I. 'Le procès inquisitorial contre Rodrigo Méndez Silva, historiographe du roi Philippe IV', *Bulletin Hispanique* (1965) no. 67, 225–252.

Riandière la Roche, J. 'Du discours de l'exclusion des Juifs: antijudaïsme ou antisémitisme?', in *Les problèmes de l'exclusion en Espagne au XVIe et XVIIe siècles. Actes du colloque* (Paris: Publications de la Sorbonne, 1983) 51–75.

Rivkin, E. 'The Utilization of Non-Jewish Sources for the Reconstruction of Jewish History', *Jewish Quarterly Review*, new ser. (1957), XLVIII, 192–3.

Ribeiro Sanches, *see* Nunes Ribeiro Sanches.

Roth, C. 'Les Marranes à Rouen', *Revue d'Etudes Juives* (1929) LXXXVIII, 113–155.

Roth, C. 'Quatre Lettres d'Elie de Montalto: contribution à l'histoire des Marranes', *Revue d'Etudes Juives* (1929) LXXXVII, 137–168.

Roth, C. *A History of the Marranos* (Philadelphia: Jewish Publication Society of America, 1932; new edn, New York: Meridian Books, 1959).

Roth, C. 'The Religion of the Marranos', *Jewish Quarterly Review* (1931–32) new ser. XXII, no. 1, 1–35.

Roth, C. 'The Strange Case of Hector Mendes Bravo', *Hebrew Union College Annual* (1944) XVIII, 221–245.

Roth, C. *History of the Jews in Italy* (Philadelphia: Jewish Publication Society of America, 1946).

Roth, C. 'The Role of Spanish in the Marrano Diaspora', in *Hispanic Studies in Honour of Ignacio González Llubera* (ed. Pierce, F.) (Oxford: Dolphin, 1959) 299–309.

Roth, N. 'Jewish Conversos in Medieval Spain: some misconceptions and new information', in Phillips, W. and Phillips, C. (eds), *Marginated Groups in Spanish and Portuguese History* (Minneapolis: Society for Spanish and Portuguese Historical Studies, 1989) 23–53.

Roth, N. *Conversos, Inquisition and the Expulsion of Jews from Spain* (Madison: University of Wisconsin, 1995).

Rubens, C. 'Joseph Cortissos and the War of the Spanish Succession', *Transactions of the Jewish Historical Society of England* (1970–1973) XXIV, 114–133.

Salamon, H. *Portrait of a New Christian: Fernão Alvares Melo (1569–1632)* (Paris: Fundação Calouste Gulbenkian e Centro Cultural Português, 1982).

Saraiva, A. *Inquisição e Cristãos Novos* (Lisbon: Estampa, 1985).

Selke, A. *The Conversos of Majorca: Life and Death in a Crypto-Jewish Community in XVII Spain* (Jerusalem: Magnes Press, Hebrew University, 1986).

Shaw, L. 'The Inquisition and the Portuguese Economy', *Journal of European Economic History* (1989) no. XVIII, 415–431.

Sicroff, A. *Los estatutos de limpieza de sangre: controversia entre los siglos XV y XVII* (Madrid: Taurus, 1985: transl. from the French edition, Paris: Didier, 1979).

Studies on the History of the Portuguese Jews (Katz, I. and Serels, M. eds.) (New York: Sepher-Herman for the American Society of Sephardic Studies, 2000).

Swetschinski, D. 'Kinship and Commerce: The Foundations of Portuguese Jewish Life in XVIIth Century Holland', *Studia Rosenthaliana* (1981) no. 15, 52–74.

Teixeira, A. *António Homem e a Inquisição* (Coimbra: Imprenta da Universidade, 1895–1902).

Van Praag, J. 'Almas en litigio', *Clavileño* (1950) no. 1, 14–26.

Vegazo Palacios, J. *El auto general de fe de 1680* (Málaga: Algazara, 1995).

Vieira, A. *Do modo de proceder a Inquisição de Portugal com os seus presos: informação que ao Pontifice Clemente X deo o P. António Vieira etc.* (Lisbon: Imprenta Nacional, 1821).

Vieira, A. *Noticias recónditas y postumas del procedimiento de las Inquisiciones de España y Portugal en sus presos* ('Villafranca' [London], 1722).

Voltes Bou, P. 'Documentos para la historia del tribunal de la Inquisición de Barcelona durante la Guerra de Sucesión', *Analecta Sacra Tarraconensia*, (1953) XXVI, 245–275.

Vosters, S. 'Los sefardíes de Amsterdam', *Historia 16* (1989) no. 111, 109–120.

Willemse, D. *Un 'Portugués' entre los castellanos. El primer proceso inquisitorial contra Gonzalo Báez de Paiba 1654–57*, 2 vols (Paris: Fundação Calouste Gulbenkian, 1974).

Wolff, P. 'The 1391 Pogrom in Spain: Social Crisis or Not?', *Past and Present* (February 1971) no. 50, 4–18. **

Yerushalmi, Y. *From Spanish Court to Italian Ghetto. Isaac Cardoso; a Study in Seventeenth Century Marranism and Jewish Apologetics* (New York: Columbia University Press, 1971 and 1980).

Yerushalmi, Y. 'Anussim ha-ḥozrim le-yahadut be me'ah ha-17: haskaltam ha-yehudit ve-hakhsharatam ha-nafshit' ('forced converts returning to Judaism in the XVIIth century: their Jewish education and their psychological preparation'), in *Proceedings of the Vth World Congress of Jewish Studies*, vol. II (Jerusalem: World Union of Jewish Studies, 1972) 201–209 (English summary on p. 247).

Yerushalmi, Y. 'Professing Jews in Post-Expulsion Spain and Portugal', in Lieberman, S. (ed.), *Salo Wittmayor Baron Jubilee Volume*, 3 vols (Jerusalem: American Academy for Jewish Research, 1974) II, 1023–1058.

Yerushalmi, Y. 'L'Antisémitisme racial est-il apparu au XXe siècle? De la *limpieza de sangre* espagnole au nazisme: continuités et ruptures', *Esprit* (1993) 3–4, 5–36.

Zimmels, H. *Die Marranen in der Rabbinischen Literatur* (Berlin, 1932).

The Hunt for the Hidden Jew: Crypto-Judaism after the Inquisition

Alexey, Trudy *The Mezuzah in the Madonna's Foot* (New York: Simon and Schuster, 1993).

Alpert, M, 'Dr. Angel Pulido and philo-Sephardism in Spain' *Jewish Historical Studies* (2005), vol. 40, 105-119.

Aronsfeld, C., *The Ghosts of 1492: Jewish Aspects of the Struggle for Religious Freedom in Spain 1848-1976* (New York: Columbia University Press for *Jewish Social Studies*, 197.

Azevedo, Mea Elvira de, and Steinhardt, Ignacio, *Ben Rosh*, (Oporto: Afrontamento, 1977).

Borrow, George, *The Bible in Spain*, Everyman edition (London, 1906).

Cardoso de Bethencourt, M. 1903, 'The Jews in Portugal', *Jewish Quarterly Review*, Volume 15, 2nd part, 260 and ff.

Endelman, Todd, *The Jews of Georgian England* (Ann Arbour: University of Michigan Press, 1999.

Ferguson, Niall, *The House of Rothschild*, 2 vols, Penguin, 1998.

Friedenberg, D. 'The Jewish catacombs of Portugal', *Midstream* (1960 Spring), 2-4 and 105-107.

Isaacs, A. Lionel, *The Jews of Majorca* (London: Methuen, 1936).

Lichtenstein, J.J., 'The Reaction of Western European Jewry to the Reestablishment of a Jewish Community in Spain in the Nineteenth Century' (unpublished doctoral thesis, Yeshiva University, 1962).

Lipman S. and V.(eds.) *The Century of Moses Montefiore* (OUP for Littman Library 1985).

Lisbona, J, *Retorno a Sefarad: la política de España hacia sus judíos en el siglo XX* (Barcelona, Riopiedras, 1993).

Marquina, A. and Gloria Ospina, *España y los judíos en el siglo XX* (Madrid: Espasa, 1987).

Méchoulan, H. 'La cédule de 1802 ou le dernier sobresant de l'antijudaïsme espagnol d'Etat'. *Revue d'Etudes Juives* (1984), No. 143.

Méndez Bejarano, M *Histoire de la juiverie de Séville* (Madrid: Editorial Ibero-Africano-Americana, 1922).

Moore, K, *Those of the Street: the Catholic-Jews of Mallorca* (University of Notre Dame Press), 1976.

Novinsky, A, 'The Last Marranos', *Commentary* 43, no.5, 1967, 76-81.

Pulido Fernández, A, *Españoles sin patria y la raza sefardí* (Madrid 1905. Reprinted University of Granada 1993).

Samuel, Edgar, 'Jewish missionary activity in Portugal between the Wars', *Jewish Historical Studies* (2007), Volume 41, 173-181.

Schechter, S, 'An unfamiliar aspect of Anglo-Jewish History', *Publications of the American Jewish Historical Society*, Vol. 25, 72-73.

Schwarz, S, 'Os cristaõs-novos *em Portugal no século XX*' (Lisbon;Livraria Universal Armando J. Tavares, 1925).

Studemund-Halévy, M, 'Les Juifs au Portugal aujourd'hui', *Los Muestros*, December 2000, No.41, 27-33.

Ward, S., 'Converso descendants in the American Southwest: a Report on Research- Resources and the Changing Search for Identity', *Proceedings of the 1998 Conference of the European Association for Jewish Studies* (ed. A. Sáenz-Badillos), Leiden: Brill, 1999, 677-686.

Wolf, L, *Essays in Jewish History* (ed. Roth), (Jewish Historical Society of England, 1934), 363-383.

Index

Notes: Spanish names are indexed by the first surname, Portuguese by the second; names beginning with da, d' or de are listed under the initial letter of the name, not under letter 'd'.